THE FILMS OF
DUSTIN HOFFMAN

The Films of

D. TERWILLIGER

DUSTIN HOFFMAN

by Douglas Brode

CITADEL PRESS   SECAUCUS, N.J.

for my son
SHANE
with hopes you grow as
straight and strong
as your namesake

Acknowledgments

With grateful thanks to all those people and institutions who put great time, energy, and effort into this project and made its completion possible: Drorit Szafran-Heitner, Bill DeLapp, Judy and Charles Bernard Bornstein, Myrna Masoff, Al Shea, Barbara Nellis, Don Walls, Lou Cedrone, Lou Gaul, Dale Schneck, Charles H. Sanders, Richard Pack, Nat Segaloff, Jack Clark, Jack Jordan, Bernie Carragher, Sharon Johnson, Carmie Amata; and the people of the Library Facilities at the Academy of Motion Picture Arts and Sciences, and the people of the Library Facilities at Lincoln Center, New York; also,

all the people at Columbia Pictures, Embassy Pictures, Joseph E. Levine Productions, United Artists Pictures, Jerome Hellman Productions, American International Pictures, Sidney Pink Productions, 20th Century-Fox, National General Pictures, Cinema Center Films, Cinerama Releasing, A.B.C. Pictures, Allied Artists, Corona/General Productions, Paramount Pictures, Rizzoli Films/Francoriz Productions, Warner Bros., Wildwood Enterprises, First Artists, Nevart Apikian, James MacKillop, and Debra Terwilliger.

First edition
Copyright © 1983 by Douglas Brode
All rights reserved
Published by Citadel Press
A division of Lyle Stuart Inc.
120 Enterprise Ave., Secaucus, N.J. 07094
In Canada: Musson Book Company
A division of General Publishing Co. Limited
Don Mills, Ontario
Manufactured in the United States of America
Designed by A. Christopher Simon

LIBRARY OF CONGRESS CATALOGING IN PUBLICATION DATA

Brode, Douglas, 1943-
   The films of Dustin Hoffman.

   1. Hoffman, Dustin, 1937-   . 2. Moving-picture
actors and actresses—United States—Biography.
I. Title.
PN2287.H56B76   1983   791.43′028′0924   [B]   83-14314
ISBN 0-8065-0869-8

Contents

Dusty: The Many Faces of Dustin
   Hoffman   7

THE FILMS   63

The Tiger Makes Out   55
The Graduate   61
Midnight Cowboy   79
Madigan's Millions   91
John and Mary   97
Little Big Man   105
Who Is Harry Kellerman and Why Is
   He Saying Those Terrible Things
   About Me?   117

Straw Dogs   127
Papillon   137
Alfredo, Alfredo   147
Lenny   157
All the President's Men   167
Marathon Man   177
Straight Time   185
Agatha   195
Kramer vs. Kramer   203
Tootsie   211
Epilogue: The Oscar and After   219
Afterword: Our Last Interview   223

Dusty: The Many Faces
of Dustin Hoffman

The story of Dustin Hoffman's sudden and unexpected ascension from virtual obscurity to international superstardom via the success of a single film—*The Graduate*—has long since become apocryphal: partly fact and partly fiction, it now stands as the greatest Hollywood fantasy of "overnight success" since Lana Turner was purportedly discovered sipping a soda at Schwab's Drugstore several decades earlier.

In 1966, *enfant terrible* Mike Nichols—having conquered Broadway with his direction of Neil Simon's clever comedies, then gone on to a dazzling film directorial debut with his controversial milestone movie, *Who's Afraid of Virginia Woolf?*—was searching for a new face to play the lead in his next venture, *The Graduate*. Having tested dozens of handsome young hopefuls, all of whom looked like living embodiments of the blond, Waspish hero of Charles Webb's novel, his mind began to wander to a critically acclaimed character actor whose work he had admired in New York; Nichols had seen Dustin Hoffman in his Obie award-winning *Journey of the Fifth Horse*, heard wonderful things about his performance in *Eh?*, and had once tested the young actor himself for a part in the Broadway musical *The Apple Tree*, though that role had eventually gone to Alan Alda. So Hoffman was contacted, and arrangements were made for him to fly to Hollywood for the screen test. But first Hoffman read the book this new film was to be based on and, having finished it, placed the volume down on a table beside a copy of the current *Time* Magazine, which featured the Man of the Year on its cover. In the first onslaught of the new youth consciousness, they had picked Tomorrow's Youth, and the face they chose as youth's representation was extremely Aryan, athletic, even preppieish.

That's what Nichols needs, the short, awkward Jewish actor decided. The part calls for a young Robert Redford. So why did he call *me*? Hoffman was certainly not Benjamin Braddock—at least he was not the Benjamin of the book. What he could not possibly know then was that Nichols planned to expand the minor novel into a major film concept, using the book as nothing more than a starting point.

By the time Dustin reached Los Angeles, he was suffering not only from jet lag, but also exhaustion from the taxing stage role he had been playing, not to mention incredibly nervous about a major movie test. He was also apprehensive about being back in the town of perfect tans he had grown up in and which had, in his boyhood days, so intimidated him. All the confidence he had hoped to exude disintegrated. When he walked in to shoot the test, he took one look at Katharine Ross and sensed she was precisely the kind of debutante/princess who had never noticed him in high school. Katharine, meanwhile, looked up at him and, slightly shocked, tried to adjust to the fact that this short, big-nosed character actor was going to test for the role of the tall, irresistible boy she was supposed to fall in love with. "He looked about three feet tall," she later recalled, "deadly serious—even totally humorless—and completely unkempt. All I could think was, 'This is going to be a disaster!' "

When Dustin began playing his scene with Katharine, he was unprepared and flubbed his lines. Nichols shut down the test for a while and let Dustin go out to study them more carefully. When he returned, he flubbed more of them than he had before. "I can't figure it," the director sighed. "You study the lines, and then you are *worse*!" When the screen test was finally finished, Dustin apologetically approached Nichols.

"Well, you've seen me at my worst," he said. "God, I *hope* so!" Nichols retorted.

Understandably, Dustin was suitably depressed. He grabbed for his coat and headed for the door. As he did, a New York subway token fell out of his pocket. A crew member picked it up, ran after him, and handed it to the young actor, explaining: "Here, kid. You're gonna *need* this!"

Six days later, Nichols called New York and offered Dustin the part. One explanation of the reason why has Nichols and producer Larry Turman so exasperated after dozens of tests that they finally took the last three and determined to pick one of them. According to this version, Turman desperately said, "I'd be happy with *that* one," and it was Dustin. More likely, though, is the story that insists Nichols wanted to cast *against* type, and that he responded to the "confused panic" of Dustin's test: that was precisely how Nichols conceived of Benjamin Braddock. For this was not going to be Charles Webb's story as dramatized by Mike Nichols, but rather Nichols' *reinterpretation* of that story—and of the character. But when Nichols told Dustin he had the part, the performer tried to talk the director out of it. "Benjamin Braddock is just not Jewish," Hoffman insisted. "Ah," Nichols retorted, "but he's Jewish on the *inside*." And in saying that, Nichols supplied Dustin with the "key" he needed to bring Benjamin to life onscreen.

At any rate, the next step was to get movie mogul Joseph E. Levine's okay. Nichols brought Dusty into the man's imposing office—or, rather, Dustin tagged in behind Nichols. Levine looked up from his desk, acknowledged Mike, and asked if Dustin were the window washer he had sent out for. Dustin, always the clown, said he was, and set to work cleaning. Nichols, meanwhile, explained to the dumbfounded Levine that this was the actor he had picked for their upcoming film project. Levine laughed, enjoying the joke. Then he realized Nichols was serious.

"*Him*?" he shrieked, pointing directly at Dusty. "You picked *him*?" Then he studied Dustin closely—*very* closely. "I'm beginning to see it," he muttered. Then, the examination complete, he announced: "Yeah, I see why you picked him!"

Getting the role of Benjamin would, you might think, make Dustin and his girlfriend (and later wife) Anne Byrne—who were very often nearly broke—wildly happy. The opposite happened. When he told her the news, they were immediately depressed. The couple looked around their small Greenwich Village apartment and knew their life would never be as simple again, that their world, their relationship, and they themselves would be forever changed by Hollywood's intervention. All at once, they were nostalgic for what they had been working for years to escape from. And several months later, when Dustin returned to New York with the shooting of *The Graduate* behind him, he sensed that if the film were successful at the box office, it would probably make him an important star.

What he had no way of foreseeing was that it would turn him into that, and something more: a generational hero, a spokesman for a "new youth" he had next to nothing in common with. On the eve of *The Graduate's* premiere, Leonard Lyons happened to mention in his widely read column that newcomer Dustin Hoffman had had to rent a tuxedo to wear to the gala opening. The story spread, and grew out of all proportion: what was meant as nothing more than a colorful bit of information was widely interpreted by the alienated young—the then-emerging youth culture of the late sixties—as the essence of Hoffman's nonconformity, of his flaunting of Hollywood tradition, of his distaste for the irrelevant old-fashioned star behavior.

This marked the accidental beginning of a legend—a legend constructed more around Hoffman than from him. No matter that Dustin didn't own a tux because, *numero uno*, he had never been able to afford one before and, secondly, he had never had sufficient use for such an item to warrant investing in it. While that may have been the simple truth of the situation, it was not the way the situation was popularly understood. Dustin Hoffman was immediately on his way to being railroaded into the first significant youth cult personality since James Dean emerged as one following the release of *Rebel Without a Cause* more than a decade earlier.

There is an irony in the fact that, just as American youth was adopting "Don't Trust Anyone Over 30!" as its motto, their first countercultural hero was himself 31. Like the other significant youth hero of 1967-8, the gray haired, middle-aged maverick Democrat Eugene McCarthy—whom Hoffman admired and campaigned for—Dustin conveyed a sense of integrity in a world grown corrupt. "Both the politician and the movie star," Daniel Chapman observed at the time, "convey honesty to a generation fed up with chameleon blowhards in the political world and perfectly chiseled blowhards in the celluloid world." Benjamin Braddock's contempt for the shams of the upper-middle-class lifestyle was interpreted as the most damning indictment of that affluent culture since

Rebel, and, naturally, the young man who starred in this new picture automatically became the logical successor to Dean; onscreen, Dustin was, for American youth, a romantic reflection of their self-image. Hoffman had gone into *The Graduate* an actor, playing a particular role, but he emerged from it as a cultural icon.

Politically, he agreed with the young people, but he recoiled in horror from playing the role they designated for him. Hoffman was in touch with himself enough to know that he was not Benjamin Braddock and, unlike James Dean—who relished his cultdom—Dustin desperately wanted to escape from his image. "Girls used to stop me on the street and ask if I was 'the graduate,'" he later recalled. "I wanted to say, 'No, but I *am* Dustin Hoffman, and I'm the *actor* who *played* him.' They thought I was an innocent who walked around with 'The Sounds of Silence' always playing in the background wherever I went. What happened to James Dean is very dangerous. Once you *become* the myth, turn into a public thing, you must get to feel omnipotent—that you can never die." "Do you represent today's youth?" an interviewer asked him in 1968. "I'm just an actor," Dustin replied. "I don't feel I represent *anybody*." And yet, sounding very much like the spokesman for youth he claimed not to be, Dustin said in 1969: "The youth outburst in this country is a good thing. The kids are angry because the American leaders made mistakes and refused to admit it."

During the early days of the Gene McCarthy campaign, Hoffman had been warned against actively campaigning by studio experts and Hollywood image makers, who tried to force him into the mold of the oldtime movie stars—oblivious to the fact that he was instead the forerunner of a new breed. "I was advised not to get involved because it might hurt my box office," he announced at the time. "People who didn't like McCarthy might stop coming to my movies. I didn't believe it. Besides, I didn't care. When I think of the future, who can worry about box office?" Shortly, there was a turnaround in popular thinking, and before long any actor who *wasn't* involved in the McCarthy campaign was out of the limelight, causing Hoffman to grow somewhat cynical about his own involvement. "I

don't think it's particularly courageous for an actor to speak out politically," he said toward the campaign's conclusion. "It's fashionable to be involved now."

Hoffman, significantly, was among the first to get involved *before* it became fashionable. Apparently, the campaign interested him less after it became so chic; probably, he liked it better when he was putting himself—and his "box office image," whatever that is—on the line. "One can be political in my line of work, and yet be honest," he explained years later. "Do what you believe in, but at the same time know that self-promotion is a part of it." In that statement is a "key" to understanding Hoffman: he is not necessarily opposed to doing things that could be interpreted as self glorifying, but he is opposed to being hypocritical about them, or pretending to himself his motives are pure and simple and unselfish.

If his attitudes came in like a breath of fresh air, so too did his looks. As Mel Gussow put it, "In a new entertainment age that considers awkwardness an asset and physical beauty excess baggage, Dustin is now fashionable. He has given new hope to hordes of homely men." Interestingly enough, Hoffman's identification with the currents of change that were already affecting society goes back even to *before* his movie stardom. In his 1965 *Commonweal* review of *Eh?*, critic Wilfrid Sheed had compared Hoffman to a Beatle, finding in his performance not just an impressive range of acting ability but also an undercurrent of style—an attitude, an unarticulated philosophy—that would very shortly make itself felt in the popular and later in the performing arts. Hoffman's talent would have made him a successful actor (though, conceivably, an anonymous one) in any era he might have been born into; what made him a star—*the* star of his time, in fact—was a case of timing he had nothing to do with and could not have controlled had he wanted to. Bob Dylan had warned us, in his music, that "the times they were a-changin'," and as they changed, a situation was created in which people who had previously been thought of as star material and accepted as sex symbols—Tony Curtis, Rock Hudson, Robert Wagner and the like—would

have increasing difficulty finding work, while people who, a mere five years earlier, would have themselves chuckled had anyone suggested they might be movie star sex symbols (Hoffman, Gene Wilder, Alan Arkin, Elliott Gould) were about to form a new wave of movieland "anti-stars."

Hoffman himself acknowledged the impact of The Beatles—particularly Ringo Starr—as being connected with his success. "They sort of Euro-peanized us," he said. "Before them, our society hadn't been The Great Society as much as it had been the Revlon Society. Now, there's a desire to cut through that greasy kid stuff. Suddenly, our tastes have become so anti-American image—anti-*Saturday Evening Post* Norman Rockwell cover." In fact, a notion of how significant a role timing played in Hoffman's success can be seen by the seemingly unconnected fact that, when he began acting in movies, young men began wearing their hair long. Had this detail not been the case, it's altogether possible Hoffman would not have clicked quite the way he did. For, as old friend Sally Kempson observed on the set of one of Dustin's early films: "Dustin's credibility as a sex symbol depends to an amazing degree on the way he wears his *hair*. With his hair short, or combed back from his forehead, he is odd-looking, unhandsome. With his hair long, he looks charming—even beautiful."

At any rate, *The Graduate* made Hoffman the young man of the moment, even though he knew this was a bizarre trick played on him by the fates. "I've always thought of myself as being *behind* the times. I'm just not attracted to whatever is going on 'right now.' The mass media spends so much time glorifying and exploiting the whole 'youth' thing that I just get sick of it. There seem to be only two words at the moment—'Beautiful!' and 'Groovy!'—and I hate both of them."

But his fabled "overnight success" should not eclipse the fact that Dustin Hoffman was a respected and acclaimed actor long before a trick of timing turned him into a popular star. "I plummeted to stardom" was the way he laughingly described his own success, as he had worked for more than ten years (when, indeed, he could find work) to establish himself in the New York Theatre World.

Acting has almost always been a part of his life, though originally it was for pretty odd reasons. Dustin tried out for his first role—Tiny Tim in his Los Angeles grade school's Christmas show—not because he had any strong desire to act, but because he viewed it as a means of getting out of some of those classes that bored him to desperation. His grades were usually mediocre, occasionally awful. He was what educators today would call an "unmotivated child." In fact, his first real artistic notoriety was not for acting, but music. His mother—motivated by a personal desire to, whenever possible, introduce her children to things cultural—saw to it that he had classical training for piano. And if the lessons began as little more than a whim, Dustin proved such a natural at the keyboard that everyone soon assumed he would become a professional musician, an inclination to which he himself leaned at the time.

Soon, he was a regular feature at school assemblies, often subbing for scheduled events that failed to show. But movies had begun to shape his mind even at that early age, for he had clearly seen a number of those films in which gifted young pianists were picked out, by beautiful but emotionally deep women, for their attentions. "At parties," Dustin later admitted to an interviewer from *McCall's*, "the first thing I did was find the piano. I would sit on the end of the bench and leave room for That Girl to sit down and say, 'Boy, do you have sensitive hands.' She never did." And even today, he objects to pretentious reasons for going into the arts: "If someone says he wants to act so he can meet pretty girls, there's more of a chance he'll become a great actor than if he says he can't live without acting."

When he entered college, he did so as a music major, and assumed some day he would be a classical pianist; gradually, his interest shifted to the more loosely structured styles of jazz. But there is a certain irony in the fact that the generational hero of the sixties enrolled in Santa Monica City College the same month that the generational hero of the fifties, James Dean, was killed in an automobile accident. He spent only an abortive year at school, and the only good thing that happened there was picking up, as an elective, a course in dramatics, which would in turn lead to his serious ambitions as an actor.

At first, though, he was neither serious nor ambitious. "I didn't want to act for any positive reasons," he admitted in retrospect, "but as a sheer negative reaction to the necessity of studying. I thought if I could become an actor, I could get away from all those responsibilities, and that's what appealed to me." He gave up the dream of being a pianist at eighteen when he began to believe he wasn't good enough.

But there is another aspect to his switch from music to acting: fear of being alone. To practice piano properly, he would have to isolate himself for hours at a time. With acting, he could spend an equal number of hours working at his art, but do so in the company of an ensemble. "The thing I liked about acting," he later admitted, "was that you could be creative with other people around." Also, the urge to act grew out of an insecurity within himself. "When I first went into acting," Dustin recalled years later, "I didn't like myself very much. I didn't really know who I was. And I would feel something I didn't get in real life when I was working on a stage."

At a Passover dinner, his Aunt Pearl leaned across the table and asked what he was going to be. "An actor," he announced, admitting it even to himself for the first time. Everyone at the table laughed, and Aunt Pearl led a lengthy explanation of why he could not be that, because he was not good-looking enough. Despite that warning, he pursued his new interest by attending the famed Pasadena Playhouse. Surprisingly, the experience didn't prove much better than college. The theatre was full of tall, tanned types, with perfect features and exquisite diction. "Walking surfboards," Hoffman contemptuously—and, perhaps, a bit enviously—called them. Dustin felt so different that he became obsessive about it, purposefully heightening his "different" qualities as if, by becoming self-conscious about them, he would turn a deficit into a plus. So he began to dress the part of the nonconformist; one actor who was there at the time recalls Dustin as wearing "a funny fur vest, no shirt, and ripped—almost shredded—jeans."

At first, Dustin did fantasize about becoming a movie star, and he still believes anyone who doesn't admit that is their reason for going into acting is an outright liar. But looking around at his colleagues had the effect of making him scrutinize himself more closely. Almost every boy there resembled a young Rock Hudson or a new Tab Hunter. He had better knock the ridiculous fantasies out of his head, he told himself. And so for Dustin, the Playhouse's motto— "Work with the stars, *become* a star!"—soon became oppressive. He sensed that if he made it, it would be as a character actor, not as a star.

And he began to believe he was in the wrong place: "I dreamed only of Broadway." Yet many of his ideas about art were derived from a book given to him at that time by his favorite teacher and director at Pasadena, Barney Brown. It was Brewster Ghiselin's *The Creative Process*, a collection of some thirty-five essays by various men of genius. The one that most affected the impressionable young Dustin was a piece by Mozart, in which the great composer explained that very often the world-famous melodies came to him seemingly from out of nowhere, appearing in his head as though placed there by an outside force, without his having to consciously work at creating them. It was an idea Dustin would never forget, and one which would influence his performance style in years to come.

Shortly thereafter, Dustin's first break at the Pasadena Playhouse happened when Brown cast him in Arthur Miller's *A View From the Bridge*, and confided to Hoffman that he knew the boy possessed "something special." He also guessed Dustin would have to nurture his talent a long time until it would be accepted. "You'll probably be thirty before it happens for you," he told him. Meanwhile, Dustin applied for and got a scholarship to a summer dance camp in Colorado that mostly catered to rich kids. There, he chanced to meet two struggling New York based dancers— Daniel Nagrin and Helen Tamiris—who were passing the summer on the camp's faculty. After listening to their talk about the Manhattan scene, Dustin was seized with the ambition to move there himself. Helen and Daniel insisted that, if he made the move, he should look them up. Before very long, he would do just that.

It was in 1958 that he hit the Big Apple, and he was twenty-one at the time. Pasadena Playhouse colleague Gene Hackman, who had made the move some time earlier, had not yet found any acting roles but was working regularly as a furniture mover to support his family in a one-and-a-half room apartment, and Dustin, desperately alone, moved in. Sleeping next to the ancient refrigerator, Dustin was awakened every night at two and at four, when the machine went into sudden but regular convulsions. After a while, the noise died down and he went back to sleep. In fact, the New York Theatre Scene outside the safety of the small apartment looked so intimidating that he became a sleepaholic as a means of avoiding it. Sometimes, he would sleep around the clock in order to avoid going outside and begin the long period of failure and rejection he sensed was waiting for him.

Despite that, Dustin didn't feel a stranger in a strange land but rather as though he had "come home." "A spiritual New Yorker," he was like the fabled ugly duckling who is ugly only because he is mistakenly living with ducks, only to discover in time he is actually a swan. "I wouldn't have been such a misfit if I had grown up here," he growled. "What a wasted childhood!" For even as a boy growing up in L. A., he had sensed he belonged in New York: he would watch The Dead End Kids on Saturday afternoons and dream of swimming with them in the polluted East River. Even today, he exhibits a Woody Allenish chauvinism about The Big Apple: "I love New York; I consider it my home, I love being able to walk to museums, theatres, restaurants. Every time I go out of the city and fly back, and take a cab in from the airport, I get the same thrill out of being here. The only thing I'd change in my life, if I could, is that: I'd have myself born in New York." His opinion of his own birthplace?: "If you stay in Beverly Hills too long, you turn into a Mercedes."

As an aspiring actor, Dustin quickly learned the rules of the Manhattan theatre game: unable to get an agent without first having a track record and unable to acquire a track record without an agent to represent him, he joined the hundreds of other hopefuls who took on an assortment of oddball jobs to pay the rent and food bills as they wandered from one audition to the next. Dustin had an apparent advantage over most of his colleagues and competitors, for he could type over eighty words a minute, and hence office jobs were a possibility. The problem was, he found them psychologically oppressive, and most lasted half a day at best—because during lunch break he would disappear. "After a while," he claims, "I began to bring my own lunch to work, just to stop myself."

But some of the jobs allowed him the chance to fine tune his acting skills, at least in the broadest sense, as when he found employment several Christmases at Macy's Toy Department, dressed in a heavy sweatshirt and faking a French Canadian accent in order to facilitate the sale of hockey games. Another time, he found work as a hospital attendant in a psychiatric ward, where contact with patients actually increased his insecurity as an actor—and, perhaps, in some bizarre way influenced his style of performance. Watching one madman literally "become things"—an electric razor, for instance— Hoffman wondered why he, a supposed professional actor, wasn't able to achieve such a oneness with his characters, and observed the patient with hopes of learning his secret. What he couldn't handle was holding the patients down while the electric shock treatments were administered.

His sympathy was further aroused by a former doctor, now a patient, who no longer functioned properly owing to a stroke. His still stylish wife would come by regularly, and the man could not recognize her. Then one day as she entered, it was obvious he knew, for at least a second or two, precisely who she was. He ran to her, screaming, "I can't help it—I'm trying!" Then, before everyone's eyes, he turned into a vegetable again. Years later, Dustin would break into tears when relating that moment to people. "They wanted to commit me," he says, half kiddingly, "so I quit."

But the notion of *becoming* rather than *acting* was now implanted in his brain. While selling orange drinks during intermissions at the Long-acre Theatre when Zero Mostel was doing *Rhinoceros* there, Dustin marvelled at the man's proficiency at not just "evoking" a rhinoceros onstage but appearing to turn into one every night, and Hoffman sensed if he was ever to make it, he too would have to learn to perform such miracles. Eventually, he did, for it was that ability to achieve such a oneness with his roles that would establish the sense of conviction his best performances are noted for. One day shortly thereafter, he happened to pass the huffing, puffing Zero on the street, and—without quite knowing what he was doing or why, but desperately desiring to make contact, one actor to another—Dustin shouted out, "Lewis Gilbert says to give you his best." "And give it right back to him," Zero bellowed, waving a fist in the air as he continued on his way. Dustin was speechless for some hours afterward.

In addition to attending endless auditions and constantly changing part-time jobs, being a New York actor calls for taking lessons from one of the respected established actors. In one of Lonnie Chapman's classes, Dustin floored all the other students, and his teacher as well, by improvising a wild, energetic, freewheeling interpretation of the word "Life" by darting around the room, crashing into the walls, and surprising even himself with each and every move. Like his unknown friend at the psychiatric ward and Mr. Mostel, Dustin had learned that sometimes it is best to not think a performance out, but to learn to fly with it—to do, in acting, what Mozart had done with music.

The only part of the normal New York theatre-scene lifestyle Dustin avoided was making the rounds of agents' offices. The constant rejection was too difficult, for they were looking for "photogenic faces." Instead of hearing that he was "unhandsome," Dustin slipped his pictures under their office doors and ran away. "I worked and I studied and I cried and I slept a lot," he later said in summarizing that period of his life. Mainly, he worked: he took a job as a counterman at Rudley's Restaurant, where they paid him a mere pittance but allowed him to eat as much as he liked for lunch. One day, when the boss was conveniently out, he downed six of the paper thin steaks the place was famous for. Upon the boss's return, he was summarily fired. While working behind the counter of a store, he would break the monotony by insulting women shoppers, then when they grew outraged and threatened to report him, he would convince them they were on *Candid Camera*, insisting it was all just a stunt, and send them home to watch TV in hopes of seeing themselves; they never did.

During the New York newspaper strike, the Modell's Army and Navy store paid him fifteen dollars to dress up in an old Paul Revere costume and walk up and down Times Square, reading the news; he used the money to buy himself some army surplus clothes at the store.

He would spend the day typing for the Yellow Pages, then work as a waiter in a restaurant that night. And it was never hard to turn a crummy job into an acting lesson. As a waiter, Dustin would affect a French accent to see if he could pull if off with the customers. Sometimes he would get caught, as when a customer began speaking back to him in French, but most often his ruse succeeded. One job he found was washing dishes at the popular Greenwich Village improvisational club, The Premise, where one day he found the courage to audition for Joan Darling. She and the other members were fascinated by his flair, taken aback by the vulgarity of his material, and afraid he couldn't be trusted in front of an audience. He went back to washing dishes. In time, he worked as: a stringer of Hawaiian leis in the flower district; a fundraiser for muscular dystrophy; an organizer in the morgue department at *Time* Magazine. For a period of ten years, he earned less than $2,000 a year. His amazingly supportive parents never lost faith in him, and for years sent him the $200 a month they could afford to spare; without it, Hoffman readily admits, he would not have been able to survive.

But survive he did. He studied with Lee Strasberg for a while, though there were several memorable shouting matches between them. Still, no Broadway—or even off-Broadway—roles came his way. Auditions, lessons, and part-time jobs came and went, but he acted only in regional theatre and summer stock, and thanked heavens that at least those roles were coming through. One particularly difficult winter, he began to obsessively count the days left until June, seriously wondering if he would mentally and emotionally survive until the stock season opened and he could get back on a legitimate stage once again. When, in 1963, Ulu Grosbard was directing a Broadway revival of Miller's *A View from the Bridge*, with both Jon Voight and Robert Duvall in the cast, Hoffman was so frustrated at his inability to land roles that he considered himself lucky when Grosbard hired him as his assistant. He lived by sleeping on the floor of newfound friends' apartments, then approached Daniel Nagrin and Helen Tamiris at their dance studio. They let him sleep in a small back room after closing for the night, and he in turn worked as their custodian, playing piano during their classes. They also agreed to allow him to hold some acting classes there when they weren't using the premisis, and Dustin had kids coming in from such places as East Harlem and the Lower East Side Boys' Club. The latter also hired him to direct, and he was happy enough for a while, working creatively in the theatre. He actually considered giving up acting entirely in favor of directing, a job he performed—and, from all reports, performed well—for an entire season at a regional theatre in North Dakota. In time, though, he found the teaching part of it to be a frustrating experience. The good teacher of acting, in his opinion, had to be able to focus on the performers and not be concerned with the play itself. He, on the other hand, always wanted to make the actors subservient to the play's overall vision.

His out-of-town work continued, and in places like Fargo, he survived the constant blizzards and made a reputation for himself as being the perfect person to play hunchbacks and cripples. But even during this difficult period, something of the magnetism that would later help metamorphose this awkward, unsure boy into not only a star but a sex symbol, occasionally made itself felt. People who caught this unheralded character actor as a petty gangster in a small regional theatre production of *Three Men and a Horse* found themselves reacting with volatility to the unknown's exciting presence. He may not have been conventionally attractive, by any means, and the part wasn't big enough to in itself allow him to establish his acting credentials. But there was an undeniable magic to him: he possessed that intangible quality that made you sit up and take notice.

Then came his first theatrical job in the New York area, a role in a Gertrude Stein play, *Yes Is for a Very Young Man*, performed at Sarah Lawrence College in Bronxville, New York—which might be described as off-off-off-off Broadway.

The budget was so small that he had to pay his own train fare to get there. Dustin was paid thirty dollars for his work and, after subtracting the travel expense, found that he had made three dollars. Shortly thereafter, he landed a role in a revival of Sidney Kingsley's *Dead End* that ran for a week at the 41st St. Theatre. Also in it were two other struggling talents, Bill Macy (who would later star in TV's *Maude)* and Gerry Ragni (who would go on to write *Hair*). Significantly, an agent saw Dustin and took him on, allowing him to stop worrying about his inability to make the rounds of their offices; he was a *professional* now.

Shortly thereafter came "the breakthrough"— an honest-to-goodness role in a Broadway play. Only it didn't turn out quite as Dustin had expected. The role was a walk-on, and the show—*A Cook for Mrs. General*—quickly closed to bad notices. As a misfit G.I., Dustin counted himself lucky to get even a single line of dialogue: during group roll call, he was to say, "Yes, sir!" On opening night he choked up and instead it came out, "Caw, caw!" Reviewers didn't see fit to mention his name, but one did describe in detail the weird sound that escaped from one actor's mouth. Dusty cut out the review, underlined that passage, and stuck it in his scrapbook. Far more satisfying was a subsequent job with Boston's Theatre Company, which took him out of the Manhattan scene for a season, but provided the opportunity to prove his mettle as an actor.

As part of a repertoire group, he performed strong character parts in plays by the widest imagineable assortment of significant writers: Eugene Ionesco, Harold Pinter, Bertolt Brecht, Jean-Paul Sartre, and the like. He worked there for a long nine-month season, at the subhuman wage of $65 a week, but the experience was one most actors would pay for, if they could only afford it: a crash course in how to perform the contemporary classics. It even featured a nice side benefit: when *Waiting for Godot* was transported to New York for a one-evening stand at the Circle in the Square, Dustin—playing the scene-stealing role of Pozzo—at last had his opportunity to play off-Broadway for one glorious night.

But his greatest personal accomplishment in

Boston came when he played an overweight old Irishman in Brendan Behan's *The Quare Fellow*, and a woman came back stage afterwards asking Dusty—who had by this time removed his heavy make-up—if she could meet the big blustery fellow who had reminded her of W. C. Fields. He told her that she had, that *he* was the man. She laughed and said that, seriously, she really *would* like to meet that man. He again insisted it was he, and she became impatient with the young man's impudence and left.

At that moment, Dustin Hoffman knew that, in his own eyes at least, he had finally arrived. All around him were other actors—most better-looking, many who had enjoyed more success than he—who were dropping out of the theatre scene. But Hoffman, his friend Gene Hackman, and sometime roommate Robert Duvall stuck in there, year after year, in the face of constant failure. "I believe the three of us made it because we didn't give up," Dustin insists. "I feel if you have talent and are not too self-destructive, and hang in there long enough, it happens. I know a dozen good actors who just gave up too soon."

He continued to pursue the strong roles, even though he was amassing a reputation as being less than easy to work with. Many actors who are as gentle as lambs with their director/shepherds early in their careers turn out to be far more frisky after achieving stardom; Dustin was different, for his fellow performers remember him as "being difficult" even when he was a nobody. "The ideal director," he once claimed, is "someone who guides you without your even knowing it, without imposing himself." The comment reflects on his numerous problems with directors he has worked with.

Hoffman had favorably impressed the people who were mounting a production of *Sgt. Musgrave's Dance* at the Theatre de Lys with his virtuoso audition, then disappointed them terribly. During the sixth day of rehearsal, Dustin's director looked at him cockeyed and said, "Why don't you take the day off?" As Hoffman quietly started to leave, the director called after him: "Why don't you take the next few *days* off?" The director didn't need to take it any further: Dustin understood he was out of the show. And that threatened to become not just a singular unhappy situation but a recurring syndrome: he

tried out for the part of the hunchbacked homosexual in Ron Ribman's *Harry, Noon and Night* at the American Place Theatre, and director George Morrison later declared that "it was the most brilliant audition I've ever seen." But during rehearsals, Morrison found Dustin's character dissolving rather than being defined. "One day," he recalls, "he disappeared before my eyes."

Dustin was cast in *Journey of the Fifth Horse*, once again on the basis of a strong audition, then lost the spark during preparation. He sensed his director wanted him to solidify his character too early in rehearsal, and argued: "I haven't given eight years of my life waiting for this role to give a summer stock performance in it." "But where," the director demanded, "is the character?" "There is no character," Dustin explained, "because I haven't *found* him yet."

Dustin thought through his role of a pathetic Russian clerk again and again, and each intellectual assault on the character only took him a step further away from it. On opening night, he walked onstage feeling a failure even before he began, but then—operating purely on instinct—he said his first line in a high pitched, nasal voice. He had, out of utter despondency, "let himself go"—and was able, on a less cerebral level than he had been working, to find the character immediately. Without knowing it, he had reached back to the advice of Mozart. "The *key* to the character" is how he described that voice which had surprised even him—for once he had desperately lighted on it, every other aspect of the character fell into place, creating a classic role which won him an Obie award. As *Esquire* aptly put it, "he was an inner directed actor who had to find his character when it came to him, and directors who tried to force his performance to coalesce before he was ready sent him into a sort of catatonic trance, from which he would emerge shortly in rage and frustration."

Hoffman himself never knows where or how he will discover that "key"—or even if he will. Years later, while filming *Little Big Man*, things did not really get rolling for him as "Jack Crabb" until he shot a scene in which a drunken, down-and-out Jack is panhandling from some pioneers. Dustin decided to do it as a song 'n' dance come-

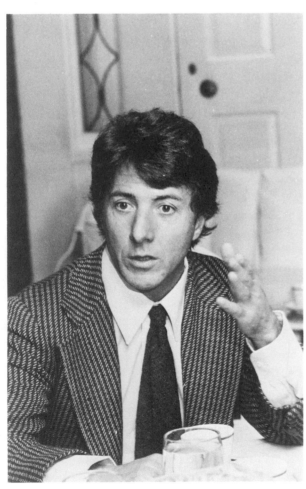

on, ending with the passing of a tin cup. But uncertain as to what would be an appropriate song of that era, he approached co-star Jeff Corey, who told him the authentic old-time cowboys always sang "Green Grow the Lilacs." From the moment Dustin added a few bars of that song to what his character said, something quasi-mystical happened to him: for by musically getting on the same wavelength as those old-time westerners, he all at once felt one of them, and was no longer Dustin Hoffman, movie actor, pretending to be Jack Crabb, but Jack Crabb— muleskinner, gunfighter, and scout to General Custer. The song was the key that unlocked the character, and Dustin wondered for years how inferior his performance in the film might have been had he not lighted on it.

Ron Ribman, who wrote two of Dustin's early New York successes—*Harry, Noon and Night* and *Journey of the Fifth Horse*—put it this way: "Dustin has the ability to annihilate his own ego and *become* the character." And Jon Voight, who worked with Hoffman in *Midnight Cowboy* when each was developing his own unique style of film performance, noticed that "the things Dusty picks up on are very *specific, textural* things." He noticed during one day's shooting that a bit of business Dustin executed—biting off an ugly hangnail with a swift, downward movement of the arm—was something they had both observed an actual derelict doing the day before. "He cements his character with little specifics," Voight told a *Redbook* reporter, "like a particular gait he sees on the street, an item of clothing, the way somebody scratches. He is very aware of the *physical* presence—for instance, for this role he had them shave his hair so he'd have bald spots in funny places."

At any rate, after *Harry* and *Journey*, Hoffman was becoming a *somebody*—in New York at least—and now, when the "difficulties" arose, there was a different turn of events. When the problems started with *Eh?* it was the first two directors, rather than Dustin, who were fired. When Alan Arkin was brought in as the ultimate replacement, he asserted his authority by calling Dustin down in front of the entire cast. Hoffman knew the director had been right, acquiesced, and they got along famously from that point on,

providing yet another choice characterization in the process. In dealing with Hoffman's "difficultness," Arkin makes a significant distinction: "There are two kinds of difficult people in the theatre—those who are passionate about their work, and those who are passionate about themselves. Dustin and I coalesced because he is of the former."

"The purpose of an audition," Dustin explains, "is to get the job. You grab hold of everything you know, anything that stimulates you. Then you get the job and the director thinks you'll start by pulling out all the stops, but that's when I go down to the basement, and start to explore. And I'm *so* low they don't think I'm doing anything. That's when most directors start to say, 'You gotta get the character locked in!' but the last thing I want to do is put the old locks in it. There's a period in rehearsal where you want to be a child and pour a glass of water on the rug to see what it's going to look like. Some directors panic. They think the rug's going to look like that on opening night. The director's job should be to open the actor up and, for God's sake, leave him *alone!* There are an awful lot of good actors around, and not even a handful of good directors."

Three weeks after Dustin won the Obie award as best off-Broadway actor for *Journey*, the show closed and he was out of work. But there were nice moments, even in the difficult days—the kind of nice moments that can perhaps happen *only* in the difficult days. One night, when Dustin was understudying *The Subject Was Roses*, Dustin's parents were planning on being in town for the evening and the actor Dustin was understudying, realizing just how much it would mean to the Hoffmans to see their son in a Broadway show, instructed Dustin to have his parents pick up tickets for that evening's performance, then called in sick. It was the only evening Dustin ever got to go on—but in that case, at least, once was enough.

While wandering down Eleventh St. in the Village, Hoffman frequently passed Mel Brooks, a neighbor he did not know but whose work he very much admired. One day, Dustin summed up the courage to stop Brooks and tell him so. A friendship was sparked, and when Brooks began putting together *The Producers*, he offered Dustin the role of the crazed Nazi playwright. Hoffman was delighted, and was all set to do the picture until *The Graduate* came his way. "At least you'll meet my wife," Brooks joked. "She's going to seduce you in it."

The rest, as they say, is history. Dustin was in short time acknowledged as the foremost of a new breed of performer, the offbeat anti-star of the emerging "New Hollywood" of the late sixties. "The character actor as superstar," *Playboy* said of him. Speaking about acting, Dustin told interviewer Ingrid Groller: "I've been acting since I was seventeen, and I can still say I don't know how. All I know are certain things that I've learned. The biggest thing is that when it doesn't *feel* right, there's a reason for it. So you go until it *does* feel right—and no one makes you feel what's right more than your own *gut*." By "no one," he probably means the director; by "gut," he refers to the importance of *instinct* over *intellect*. Even his insistence that he "doesn't know how" is important, and probably works for the best, for becoming too self-conscious of one's own technique can often harm it.

Thus, one cannot fairly analyze Dustin's "philosophy" of acting, since that word would imply an awareness about his craft which he appears to avoid. One can analyze his *approach*, though—the way in which he consistently encounters the highly varied parts he has played. What he does, essentially, is to combine his talent at observing human nature—creating a storehouse of "information" in his memory to rely on—with his equally successful ability to allow a role to overtake him, rather than the other way around: to let his talent free to pick from the storehouse of character traits and so form the personality he will play. But the cardinal rule of acting is, he understands, "not to let the technique show." He likes to quote Brando as having once said, "Don't do anything on film you can't do thirty times over again in real life." That notion of art—that the best art is always the art that *conceals* art—dates back to the Renaissance, and a concept the Italian painters called "sprezzatura." More recently, it was the basis for much of Hemingway's attitude toward both bullfighters and writers: if the viewer or reader is in any way *aware* of the artist's technique—even aware of how *good* the technique is—then that technique is not valid. It must appear to be artless, as if the performer is not working hard at all and that anyone could do what he does, although of course he is working incredibly hard and is also uniquely talented, so talented in fact that he can conceal even his effort from us.

Coupled with this there is, for Hoffman, the sexual aspect of performance. When he and Robert Duvall were performing off-Broadway, they would each night peek through the curtain before the performance started and pick a particularly pretty girl to play to. They noticed that if they couldn't spot one, then their performances wouldn't be as strong that evening. Once, during Dusty's off-Broadway career, he "entertained" a girlfriend in the dressing room minutes before the performance was to start. He later regretted it: "Afterwards, there was no need to make love to the audience." *Making love to the audience*—a key concept in understanding Hoffman as a performer. "All I know," he has said, "is I try to be as *personal* as I can in my work—by being personal, to be able to bring to it a truth in what I observe and what I feel. A perception." And this "personal" quality is at the source of all his work. For no matter what the medium of expression may be, any serious artist will invariably dredge up experiences from his own life as a source of creative expression, and Hoffman's approach has often taken this route.

When, as Benjamin in *The Graduate*, he had to convey his awkwardness in relating to Mrs. Robinson (Anne Bancroft) for the first time, he allowed his mind to drift back to an incident from junior high school days, when he and a girl were called on to provide the entertainment at an assembly. While sitting below the stage, waiting for the teachers and the rest of the students to file in, Hoffman grew so self-conscious about being there along with her that, almost without being aware of his own actions, he placed his hand on her breast—not to fondle or stimulate it but only to destroy the oppressive·nothingness that was passing between them. When someone called their names from the corridor, the girl, terrified, ran away, and Hoffman banged his head against the wall in utter embarrassment.

On the set of *The Graduate,* while shooting his first big scene with Bancroft, he forced himself to emotionally relive the experience as the cameras were rolling, and that is what gives the moment on celluloid its strong sense of conviction.

Thereafter, Nichols would insist Dustin draw on his own past experiences in order to make the character come to life onscreen. In the scene in which Dustin registers at the hotel with Bancroft for the first time, Nichols took Dustin aside and asked him to concentrate on something sexual from his past that was as frightening for him as checking into a hotel with his mother's best friend is for Benjamin. Immediately, Dustin seized on the time he went into a drugstore to order prophylactics and encountered a female druggist. It was while keeping this experience sharply in focus in his mind that Dustin approached the hotel clerk—Buck Henry—who said, "I'll get the bellboy for you, Mr. Gladstone," and hit the bell. That much was in the script; what was not was Dustin's reaction, for working on impulse that grew out of his correct emotional frame of mind owing to his use of a parallel experience, Dustin quickly put his hand on top of Henry's so that he could not ring the bell again—and the moment became a classic gem in and of itself.

Nichols knew he needed special little touches like these to make the film something more than just another pleasant sex farce, and allowed Dustin to contribute various qualities of his own. For the hotel bar scene, Nichols wanted the feeling of a kid behaving uncomfortably with older people, and told Dustin to play Benjamin as though he were, to alleviate his insecurity, imitating someone older. Dusty immediately decided to imitate his older brother Ronald, because when they were children, Dustin used to answer Ronald's phone calls and pretend he was him. Upon learning this, Nichols instructed Dustin to imitate Ronald when Ronald was upset about something, and Dustin recalled Ronald used to hold his breath even as he talked, then suddenly let it out in a gasp. That's the way the scene was played, and the famous "Eh—" noise Dustin makes, which was so crucial to the scene working as comically as it does, was born.

Thirteen years later, the fact that the situation in *Kramer vs. Kramer*—a husband and wife splitting and trying to deal with the child involved—had parallels to his own situation at the time was not lost on him either. "I had not done a film where my life circumstance paralleled what I was doing professionally," he admitted, "and I enjoyed it. That's perverse, I know, but I enjoyed it because it's what I always wanted to do—it's what *any* actor wants to do." In *The Graduate,* he had played his big love scene with Anne Bancroft by psychologically locking into a comparable real life scene from his own past; in *Kramer,* he played the separation by psychologically locking into his life's situation at about the time the movie was being made. But when asked, on the eve of *Kramer's* release, if the film were "autobiographical," he insisted it was not: he had not, after all, lost a wife and son but a wife and two daughters. For a while, he had actually toyed with the notion of having his own daughter play the child's role, but his instincts told him not to do that. For that would indeed have made it an autobiographical film, and he might be too close to the material to keep it from becoming sentimentalized. Instead, it was executed as a personal film—and while he could draw freely from his own experience to give it conviction and impact, it would not depict a situation that was precisely the same as what he had gone through.

But whether it is Benjamin Braddock or Ted Kramer, each character he has played represents one facet of the many-faceted Hoffman, a part of himself—or at the very least an expression of a potential he knows exists within him—that he comes to understand better by portraying or, in a sense, exorcising it by objectifying it as a screen "character": "Somehow," he says, "I'm always fighting to break through, so what you're getting onstage is what's going on *in me.* I'm trying to show you that part of me that wants to love, that wants to kill, that wants to find my way out, that feels there is no way out." And while he is too good an actor to ever "play himself," he does assume roles that allow him to isolate certain single elements of his complex self and come to understand those sides of his own psyche better by delineating them onscreen: "Ratso," he has admitted, "represents that part of myself that feels inadequate, fraudulent; and Lenny is that part of myself that feels important, unique." In addition to giving us a wide variety of fascinating screen performances, Dustin has created a canon of work that might be termed "theatrical self-psychoanalysis," and if we are to understand the films he has made on the level of self-expression, then it is first necessary to understand his basic personality traits, for only then can we see how they are isolated in the successive pictures.

Perhaps his theatrical application of analysis grows from regular exposure to the real thing: at various times in his life, Dusty has visited the shrink of his choice as many as five times a week. "I always felt the basic premise of analysis," he once told interviewer Fred Richards, "the desire to learn about one's self, is one of the prime motivating forces of higher forms of life. It also taught me that to be neurotic is to be human.

We're all imperfect by design. I think analysis is most beneficial to a person like myself, who isn't too crazy—just an average neurotic." Actually, Dustin is anything but average. Interviewing the star just before the release of *Kramer*, Aimee Lee Ball perceptively noted "a curious dichotomy of the near morose and the playful . . . a latticework of contradictions somehow existing in harmony."

In truth, he is a man of constant oppositions: hit him on the right day (or the right moment) and he is the intellectual eager to discuss Nietzsche; an hour later, he is the low brow vulgarian, relating the most offensive dirty jokes with a redneck relish. He has absolutely no interest in smoking, drinking, or gambling, but has always been addicted to beautiful women, celery flavored soda, anything that is avocado green, and most notably, foul language—his

On the set of *Kramer vs. Kramer,* Dustin confers with producer Stanley Jaffe while writer-director Robert Benton looks on.

swearing could make the most hardened sailor blush. But Hoffman's bizarre, seemingly contradictory actions may be only his extreme way of expressing his mood of the moment in a style that seems slightly schizophrenic to strangers simply because it is a far more honest representation of his current state of mind than most of us would ever allow people to see. "If you go out with him," best friend Murray Schisgal explains, "and he's feeling terrible, he *tells* you 'I feel terrible.' and he *looks* and *sounds* terrible. There is no façade. It's comfortable being with Dusty, because he is what he is—at *all* times."

"What he is" began long before he was even born: with his family. Dustin's people came to America when his grandfather, feeling ever more oppressed in his native Rumania, brought his small tribe to the New World and settled in Chicago. Though he had been a Talmudic scholar in the old country, he could find work only as a barber here, and the experience so crushed his spirit that he eventually had to be committed to a mental hospital. At that point, Dustin's grandmother assumed responsibility for holding the family together, and became the breadwinner by taking on her husband's job. Noting at once that baseball was the foremost topic of conversation among customers, she calculatedly cultivated a knowledge of the sport, which soon turned her into the most popular barber in the neighborhood—and one easily able to support her family.

Seven years later, and searching for greener pastures, the Hoffmans—now with Harry, Dustin's father-to-be, as titular head of the family—piled into a Model A Ford and, with about fifty dollars between them, headed for California. On reaching Los Angeles, Harry's first job during those difficult days of the Depression was working as a ditchdigger, helping to create one of the intricate Hollywood freeways. Before long, though, he wrangled himself a job in the motion picture business, serving as a prop man and, occasionally, a set designer. But Harry Hoffman was too creative and too ambitious to set his sights on props or sets as anything but a temporary stopgap. He was already dreaming of becoming an assistant director, and he already knew the man he wanted to work with: Frank Capra. Working with such an enormous talent would prepare him for what he would, in time, move on to: directing. Then one day, a superior took him aside and said directly, "Harry, you will *never* be a director. You will never even be an *assistant* director."

"Why not?" Harry Hoffman asked, bewildered.

The man walked to his desk, and out of the drawer he pulled a list. On it were the names of friends and relatives of important people in the company who were in line for an assistant directorship. Before Harry Hoffman could get such a position, every one on that list would have to have his "favor" first. Harry studied the size of the list, shook his head with understanding, and left. Shortly thereafter, he was employed in the furniture business, sometimes as a designer and sometimes as a salesman.

His wife, however—the former Lillian Gold—continued to idolize movie stars. "A closet flapper," in her famous son's words, she named her first boy after Ronald Colman, her second after Dustin Farnum. Then, as Harry Hoffman's fortunes went up and down owing to the crazy economy, the family moved back and forth, from the high digs of Beverly Hills to the low spots of Los Angeles. One year, they might reside in a pleasant, even stylish neighborhood, where the impressionable young Dustin tried to forge an identity for himself; suddenly, the boy would find himself living in a rough, downtown area, and had to adjust his self-image to fit it. But when the adjustment was complete, they would move back to Beverly Hills again.

Interestingly enough, Dustin recalls feeling more comfortable in the rougher neighborhoods, where there were no pretenses and no phoniness: one's status was not measured by the size of the family car. Here, he hung out with a Mexican and a black, and the three were part of a gang that entered into a running feud with a rival faction called "pachuchos." For safety, Dustin kept a knife taped to his leg, but he confesses to being more of an observer than a participant in the gang fights that ensued—his lifelong tendency to observe dating as far back as that.

His first exposure to serious drama came when his brother Ron gave him a copy of *Death of a Salesman*. It was a traumatic reading experience, and one which convinced Dustin at an early age that drama can be most effective when it articulates in universal terms your own specific situation. Reading about the two very different sons and their tenuous relationship to the troubled, well intentioned, but failed Willy Loman, Dustin recalled later that "it seemed to me that it was the story of our own lives at that time." Dustin's father acknowledges a similarity to Willy Loman, too. "I was too busy trying to make a living," he admitted in reflection, acknowledging that he did not spend as much time with Ronald and Dustin as he wishes he had.

But when Dustin was struggling to make it in New York, both parents kept faith in him and sent what money they could; so the Hoffmans were understandably thrilled when he achieved success in Hollywood, for "Our Son, the Movie Star" fulfilled not only his own fantasies of making it big in tinsel town, but theirs as well. Mike Nichols recalls the day they visited the *Graduate* set. Dustin became terribly self-conscious, repeatedly running off to the bathroom whenever he could, fearing they would probably announce they were his parents. They did just that, and then the onetime frustrated director took Nichols aside for some friendly advice. "You know, it was nice the way you shot that scene," Harry confided, "but I think on the next one, you really ought to . . ."

Their delight in Dustin's popularity after the film's release knew no bounds. At once, they purchased subscriptions to papers like the *Hollywood Reporter* and *Variety* to keep tabs on the box office returns. Dustin's father would call his son at all hours to tell him how much the picture had grossed in various cities, while Dustin's mom would call nearby theatres to check if there were still long lines, unable to sleep soundly without having *The Graduate*'s continued success confirmed regularly. And a dozen years later, accompanying Dustin to the premiere party for *Kramer*, Dustin's father recognized the interviewer who approached him, with TV cameras rolling, as David Sheehan, who had once given Dustin a negative review. As Sheehan attempted a charming interview with the star, Dustin's father decided to kiddingly "almost" punch Sheehan for revenge, but he missed (or,

rather, *didn't* miss) and the punch connected, leaving a shocked and visibly shaken Sheehan searching for the proper words on national television, and a red-faced Dustin beaming at his father with a combined look of embarrassment and love.

The loving model of his parents must have made the break-up of his own marriage to Anne Byrne that much harder to deal with. "Dustin has always been a homebody," his mother Lillian explained at the time. "He very much wants to find domestic happiness. He loves family life." Though his family was Jewish, they did not bring him up in an' orthodox home. One of their favorite holidays was Christmas, celebrated by them as an American ritual rather than a religious ceremony. To assuage any possible guilt feelings over having a Christmas tree, the Hoffmans allowed Dustin to decorate it with bagels. Despite this, Dustin managed to develop a classic Jewish guilt complex that has haunted him all his life.

When friend Robert Duvall picked up a leading role in a 1965 episode of *The Naked City* TV series, he was able to persuade the casting director into giving Dustin a supporting role as a petty crook. Dustin was paid $500 for it, the first decent money he saw as an actor. A friend convinced him a wise way to spend a portion of that would be to invest in one of those handsome Burberry overcoats sold at the British American House; then, when he made the rounds, he would look more like a successful working actor, and it might have a psychological effect on casting people, thus netting him more jobs. Dustin nervously wondered if he ought to use the money to eat for the next three months, but eventually was convinced his friend's idea was a good one.

Late one afternoon, he went into the store and, though it was a cool November day, felt himself dripping with sweat, so guilt ridden was he over spending his first real earnings on such a luxury. As he tried on coats and then paid for one, a warning system inside him kept screaming that he was making a terrible mistake, that he would be found starved to death inside that beautiful coat, but it was now too late to back out and not look a fool in front of the clerks. With the coat under his arm in a cardboard box, he wandered out onto the street, literally growing dizzy with anxiety. The moment he stepped foot on the pavement, though, the early evening street scene around him began to go black. To Dustin, it was as though the powers that rule the universe were striking New York City dead because of the self-indulgent purchase he had made. "Oh, my God," he thought, *"What have I done?"* He wanted to run inside and give the coat back, screaming that he didn't deserve it, but it was too late: he had caused the world to come to an end. He almost passed out. Only later did he learn it was the famous New York City blackout, but a part of him never entirely accepted that it wasn't all his fault.

Combined with this Jewish guilt complex is a massive sense of insecurity that dates back to his childhood—and even to his name. "From the earliest time I can remember, people kept turning around and laughing at me," he once recalled. "Nobody else had my name. I was always being compared to a Dustbin." Years later, Katharine Ross's character was supposed to fall wildly in love with him during *The Graduate's* story, but Katharine herself was considerably cooler. Once, between scenes, Dustin found himself sitting beside her, waiting for the camera to be filled with film and the lighting arranged. His infamous insecurity got the better of him and, as he had done to his junior high school musical co-star years earlier, he leaned over and grabbed her in an embarrassing place. "Don't *ever* do that again!" Katharine screamed. Dustin sheepishly apologized, then told her frankly: "I was insecure. I just wanted to grab onto *something.*"

After the film's release, Hoffman—when asked by newspaper interviewers about his relationship with his pretty co-star—casually told them she was the sort of girl who had always snubbed him in high school. The statement is revealing for more than its self-effacing quality. Hoffman is, in many respects, the living embodiment of a notion put forth in a popular book, *Is There Life After High School?* The authors interviewed a wide range of people who had achieved celebrity status—movie stars, important politicians, social activists, etc.—and they revealed their impetus

to achieve fame and fortune grew from the fact that in high school (which each cited as the single most formative experience of his or her life) they had been treated as the class nebishes, those skinny, pimply, unrecognized types who anonymously wander the halls. Very often, their classmates who had been honor students, or voted "Most Popular" or "Most Likely To Succeed," had done little with their lives, and yet were satisfied enough with the way their lives had turned out. Essentially, such people had succeeded the first time out—in high school—and felt no strong psychological need to prove themselves again, no compulsion to "show everyone" how they had been underrated by doing great things with their lives.

F. Scott Fitzgerald typified such a person with his creation of Tom Buchanan in *The Great Gatsby*, whose whole life is a slow letdown after the incomparable popularity he experienced as a high school and college athlete: "One of those men who reach such an acute limited excellence at twenty-one that everything afterwards savors of anticlimax." Hoffman, on the other hand, resembled Gatsby, who "sprang from a platonic conception of himself," whose frustrated early ambitions caused him to achieve later in life beyond anyone's wildest expectations, to show everyone how they had missed the potential he had offered them, to make up for being ignored by pretty girls by becoming, despite his physical limitations, one of the world's great sex symbols through the sheer power of his will to do so. "I'll show you all!" And that's precisely what he did.

According to a 1968 *McCall's* article that attempted to come to grips with his offbeat appeal, Dustin was described as having "what appears to be a hastily arranged face—a beak nose, beady eyes, a thick thatch of black hair—a face that is boyishly appealing, but not handsome in any traditional movie star way." *Time* waxed eloquent in describing his unique countenance: "The hair is from a thatched roof in Cambodia, the nose and chin from a 1948 Chevrolet, the hooded eyes from a stuffed hawk. Even the voice seems assembled, an oboe with a post-nasal drip." Tony Galluzzo of the *Motion Picture Herald* put it this way: "He has the kind of face which, upon first impression, instills compassion or even downright sympathy. One is compelled to go over to him, pat him on the shoulder and offer condolences without ever wondering why." In an interview published shortly after his first public notoriety, Lisa Reynolds described him thusly: "a long, serious face, ideally shaped for brooding. Even when he's not brooding about something, he looks as though he might be." Michael Williams observed that he "looks like the original Thurber model for the male animal." A few years later, *Playboy* tagged him as an "unprepossessing, almost runty fellow with the mournful hound-dog eyes and oversized nose." Bob Lardine said, "He is rather plain-looking, resembling both Sonny *and* Cher." Owing to his "prominent" nose, friend Robert Duvall once labelled Dustin "Barbara Streisand in drag." Critic David Zeitlin put it this way: "With a schnoz that looks like a directional signal, skittish black-beady eyes and a raggedy hair-cap, he stands a slight 5-foot-6, weighs a mere 134 pounds and slouches like a puppet dangling from a string. All in all, he resembles a swarthy Pinocchio."

More recently, Iris Schneider, interviewing Dustin for *Rolling Stone* early in 1980, observed that "his Neanderthal slouch, unintimidating . . . frame, droopy brown eyes and unmistakable schnoz make him boyishly appealing." Reflecting on his own appearance, Dustin recalled: "In high school, the other guys had hair on their chests and played football. I played tennis, had a big nose and acne so bad my face looked like a rifle range." He once told Judy Michaelson, "I am the boy next door." Then, he added wryly: "Only the boy next door is not supposed to have pimples." In a more serious vein, he concluded: "I'm ordinary looking, I know, because people keep coming up and telling me I look like someone they know. I have to keep convincing people I'm not homely. I'm just average. Then, it occured to me that perhaps to be average is to be homely."

Even more than his "unhandsome" face, Dustin's self-image has been largely dictated by his size. Hoffman would appear to be a medium-sized man, except that he is so self-conscious about being considered short by others that in trying to compensate for it ("I'm five foot six—or six and a half, really—almost five *seven!*") he

begins to look shorter than he actually is. "A stump of a man" is how he once (jokingly?) referred to his height. The irony in his intense self-consciousness concerning his shortness is that the very first time he auditioned for a part in a play—Tiny Tim in junior high school—he feared he might be too tall. Having heard the role would go to the smallest boy who showed up, Dusty hunched down to make sure there was no competition. When he later heard that the part had always been considered his, he soon grew overly aware of his diminutive stature, and the awareness stayed with him—and grew more pronounced—over the years. "Grow, grow," Dustin would chant to his naked armpits and chest while standing in front of the bathroom mirror, waiting for some of the hair the other boys had to appear on him. He didn't develop physically as early as they did, and was overly aware of the braces on his teeth and the acne on his face. An extreme case of hero worship developed for his older brother Ronald, who was everything he wanted to be.

Mirroring the classic Biff/Hap emotional bond in *Salesman*, Dustin's relationship with Ronald ranged from idolization to envy. Ronald was the perennial "A" student; Dustin was always flunking something. Ronald went to a Shirley Temple type acting school for a while, and even worked as an extra in *Mr. Smith Goes to Washington;* Dustin had no such experiences. Today, as a federal economist, Ronald can boast of having sometimes served in the Oval Office with President Nixon, as a member of the Council of Economic Advisors. But Dustin is just as proud that Ronald was also arrrested in the great Washington peace march.

But back in the early days, going down to the beach with his brother was always traumatic for the young Dustin, because it happened to be the fabled Muscle Beach, where all the weightlifters congregated to flex their muscles for an adoring public of bikini-clad girls. In his mind, Dustin pictured himself getting smaller and smaller the closer they came to the beach. "There was so much muscle you couldn't catch a single brain vibration," he later joked. At twelve, he saved up his allowance for several weeks and sent away for some barbells advertised on the back of a comic

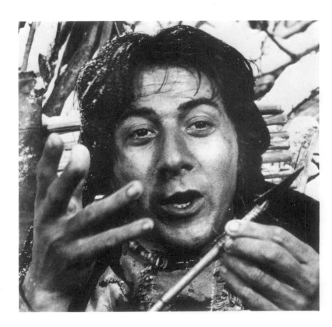

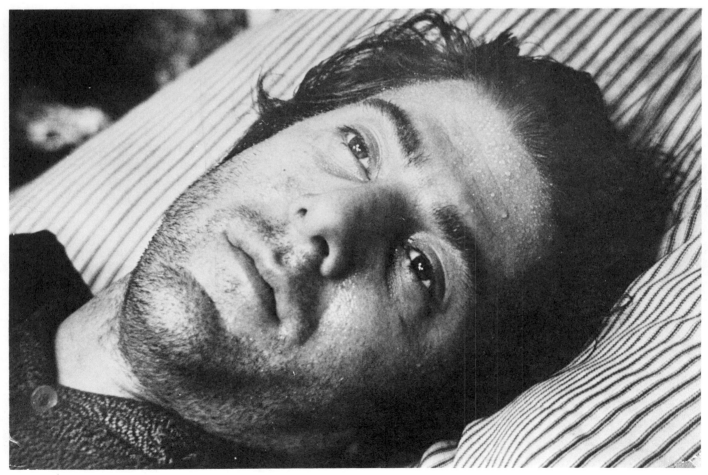

book. He was ninety pounds at the time and started diligently lifting the weights off and on over the next two years. At the end of that time, he was still ninety pounds, though he claims his neck had grown to an oversized twenty-three inches. He then developed an entire fantasy life while alone in his room; he was a great fighter, battling in the ring. In this fantasy, which he acted out elaborately, he would be knocked down to the floor again and again, but he would always come back and win by a knockout in the end.

In real life, though, he was—at least in his own estimation of himself—a living embodiment of the skinny little guy in that advertisement you see in the back of third-rate magazines, the guy who—in front of a pretty girl—gets sand kicked in his face by a muscle-bound moron. "In high school, I always envied the big, handsome guys, the *athletes*," he says. "I went through a very long period of wanting *terribly* to be a good-looking person." In the comic book ads, the little guy takes a Charles Atlas bodybuilding course and then returns for his sweet revenge. Hoffman got nothing more out of the course than an enlarged neck; as a movie star, though, he was able to become the idol of the very women who had once ignored him.

Above all, he was extremely self-conscious about his nose. If he spoke to a girl in the schoolyard, he would be careful to look her straight in the face, never allowing his profile to show. Then, in English class, the students were assigned to prepare book reports on famous people who interested them, and Dustin chose Gene Fowler's study of Jimmy Durante, called *Schnozzola*. This was an oral rather than written report, and Dustin had to stand in front of the entire class as he talked about the book. He found himself going into great detail about how conscious Durante had been about his famous nose, and how he had been so hurt in his youth by people making fun of it. Then Dustin shocked himself by weeping in front of the entire class. As people began to giggle or snort, he fled the room.

But an even more traumatic experience came when Dustin finally met one attractive girl who took an interest in him. Her name was Fran, and unfortunately for Dustin, there was a tall bully named Perry with an ugly mole on his neck who also liked Fran, and couldn't understand why she paid attention to the diminutive Dustin. One day, when all the guys were standing around—their jeans worn very low on the hips, as was the style at that time—the bully came up behind them and suddenly, in front of everyone, pulled Dustin's jeans down. The other guys began cheering him on to the tune of, "Fight! Fight!" But Dustin was too shocked to move. Then Perry knelt down in front of him, as if to make himself more equal in terms of size, and further taunted him. "Come on, Little Dusty," he snarled. "Fight me—now I'm even *shorter* than *you!*"

He was understandably miserable. His mind wandered in school. Once, when his class was covering geography, the teacher discussed the Rocky Mountains, but mentally, Dustin was farther away than that. The teacher could sense this, and suddenly asked, "Dusty, what is the name of those mountains?" The child sitting behind Dustin leaned forward and maliciously whispered the false clue, "George Washington." Dustin happily announced, "The George Washington Mountains!" and the class went wild. "I had this terrible feeling of humiliation," Dustin recalled some twenty years later, "and at the same time, I was delighted." He had been humiliated by being made to seem the village idiot, but he was delighted to have turned himself into the center of the universe, for the moment at least. That set him off on the course he would follow for the next several years: the class clown.

Actually, his compulsive sense of clownmanship has often threatened to interfere with his more serious ambitions as an actor, beginning with his very first role. When an older pal goaded the twelve-year-old Hoffman, rehearsing for Tiny Tim, to end their production of *A Christmas Carol* with the words, "God bless us all—goddam it!" there was no way Dustin could refuse—and he was suspended from school for what he said.

Later, in high school, he played the clown in order to get the attention he craved—and which did not naturally come his way. A favorite joke of his was forming a conspiracy of students to cough at a given moment in class and, inevitably, he got caught, and sent to the principal's office. But when the other kids innocently suggested he ought to become a comedian when he grew up, Dustin felt insulted. Didn't they consider him fit for a more respectable profession, like a teacher or doctor or lawyer or . . . ?

The actor in Hoffman has never been content to come forth only on the stage or in front of the camera. Robert Duvall recalls that in New York, they would ease tensions and frustrations over their lack of success by wandering through Greenwich Village, "performing"—terrifying women they passed by pretending to be sex maniacs. At that time, his need to relieve through humor the absurdity of his life often cost him his part-time jobs, as when he ran into trouble at the Macy's Toy Department shortly after one of his most outlandish stunts. When friend Gene Hackman and his two-year-old son Christopher showed up at the counter where Dustin was demonstrating playthings, Hoffman was seized with the inspiration to pass the little boy off to customers as a "life size, fully automated child doll" that was on special for $16.95. He got it from a lady customer, but he also got fired.

Even in recent, more successful years, this personality trait has stayed with him. When he received the Golden Globe Award as the screen's most promising male newcomer in 1968, he began his acceptance with, "I'm sorry I couldn't be here tonight . . .," and when he won more than ten years later as Male Performer of the Year for *Kramer*, he started with another gag: "I'd like to thank divorce . . ." Out shopping in Beverly Hills shortly after *Kramer*'s release, Dustin picked up a ringing telephone in a boutique, went into an extended imitation of the saleswoman's high-pitched voice and French accent, then made some off-color remarks to the caller. Dustin has said on several occasions that it might give him more pleasure to merely make people laugh than to move them to the complex emotions of a drama.

As the clowning suggests, Dustin's motivation for being an actor grew from his deep-rooted need for attention. "He has a great hunger that

he acquired in childhood," Murray Schisgal says, "a need for more affection, more love, more *every*thing!" An old friend who lived in the same apartment building as Dusty when he was a struggling would-be actor recalls him "sitting on my windowsill, swinging his legs over the street and calling to passersby, 'Do you know you've got a great ass?' " If one of those chic New York women who continued on down the street without so much as a moment's notice were stopped and told that this short, beak-nosed catcaller would in a few years emerge as one of the most significant male sex symbols, as well as one of the most respected actors, in America she would have laughed at the top of her lungs.

When he attended dances in high school, Dustin had formed the habit of waiting until everyone else had picked a partner, and then would walk over to the girl nobody else wanted to dance with—the fattest, or the quietest—and ask her. It gave him a pleasure to make her feel good, but also there was a perverse enjoyment in knowing everyone else was looking at them and laughing. After all, he was the center of the universe—for the moment. "I much preferred it," he admits, "to being ignored."

Being a clown let him feel as though he were the sun, around which the planets of his classmates circled, a concept which still interests him today. "When we're born," he claims, "we feel we're the center of the universe. Growing up is painful, because you discover that you're *not* the center. But when you become famous, you find you *are* the center. It's a suspect position to be in. I'm convinced that actors stay with movies not for the money but simply because of the power of the medium. None of us ever resolves a desire to be the center of the universe—that's *the* fantasy." Movie stardom can give you the illusion that has come true, but Dustin knows it is nothing more than an illusion: "I'm not the center of anything." The trick is to keep from buying the illusion yourself, when magazines put your picture on the cover, and people beg for autographs, and attractive women offer themselves for the taking.

One of the ways you fight that is by becoming a loner. In 1970, Dustin was quoted by *Family Weekly* as saying: "I never had any really close childhood friends, and I can count only about half a dozen friends now. The rest are acquaintances, mainly because I don't put myself in a position to make new friends. I don't dare, and I hate parties." As a child, one thing that led to his becoming a loner was that Dustin didn't enjoy eating, and barely touched his plate at dinner. "He was never like the other boys," Mrs. Hoffman has often told interviewers. "Dustin refused to go to his friends' birthday parties out of fear of having to eat the ice cream, cake, and candies." When Mrs. Hoffman approached a doctor about Dusty's eating problem, the man scoffed at her Jewish mother's concern and laughingly told her not to make the child eat. "When the boy needs food," the doctor insisted, "he'll eat it." Mrs. Hoffman followed that advice until one day, about a week later, she noticed Dustin's tongue was discoloring. A return visit to the doctor established that Dustin was suffering from serious malnutrition. From then on his mom fixed him whatever he wanted, as long as it encouraged him to eat. She also bought him a huge mongrel that was part German Shepherd, called Buffy, and allowed Dustin to have the dog seated next to him at the dinner table during family meals, with a napkin around his neck, eating off a plate like the rest of the family, if only it encouraged Dustin to eat better.

Some years later, there was a social club in high school called The Dragons, and Dustin wanted more than anything to join, to be *accepted*. But they rejected him: he didn't fit their "image." The experience jaded him and he became, in his own words, "an outsider, an *observer*." Looking back on high school, he has commented: "I don't think I had a single day that I was happy—I always felt like a misfit." Since then, his friends have been few, and he has chosen them carefully. As he puts it: "a friendship is pretty much the same as a relationship with a girl. You choose people whose response to life is pretty much the same as yours. You have the same kind of vision. Not that you verbalize it, but instinctively you react very similarly to anything that happens. The friends I have are all very different people, but we laugh at the same things. The people I feel closest to are people who don't ever compromise their basic nature,

don't ever compromise the way they feel. They're the exact opposite of the people who come out of the Dale Carnegie courses." Even from these few close friends, though, he often seeks privacy: "It's important to be alone sometimes. When I'm alone, I'm not necessarily happy. I don't feel like talking. I tend never to call a friend. There's an *ugly* part of me I don't want to share."

That "ugly side" surfaced while Dustin was searching for off-Broadway roles without much luck. He would wander up to Central Park on Thursday afternoons to watch the Broadway Show League play baseball, and envy them all terribly. On one occasion, he noticed Paul Newman playing left field, and was momentarily floored by the sight of the superstar. A high fly was hit in Newman's direction, and Paul began moving toward it gracefully—just as Paul Newman moves in a film. Somehow, though, he managed to miss the ball completely. A terrible sense of satisfaction came over Dustin, seeing Paul Newman fail at something as trivial as that. "It made my whole day," Dustin recalled years later.

He is consciously aware of the cruel streak in him ("I always had this desire to strike when I saw a vulnerable area!") and, he admits, "I have a perverse need to get away with as much as I can." It is not uncommon for him, while sitting in a classy restaurant with an attractive female interviewer he has just met, to lean over close to her and, without warning, pull her blouse away from her body, then peer down at her breasts— just to see how she will react. "I'm like a little kid," he insists, "and that's all it is—just curiosity. All my life, people have told me, 'Someday, you're going to do that, and somebody's going to whack you for it.' So far, nobody has."

His memory does not serve him well here: Katharine Ross whacked him—verbally, at least— when he pinched her rear end during the first day of rehearsal for *The Graduate*. And, like a kid who has finally been slapped for acting spoiled, he simmered down and treated her respectfully for the remainder of their working time together. But he remains a kind of "emotional outlaw," seeing how much he can get away with, then backing off, and behaving like a good boy after his hand has been slapped and he has been put in his place.

To friend Murray Schisgal, what Dustin calls his own "ugly side" is only further evidence of his essential honesty. "Dusty has a special way of looking at life," Schisgal told interviewer Martha Weinman Lear in 1968. "It's a way of cutting underneath the clichés and the formalities, and making fun of them." Other old acquaintances are less charitable, and insist Dustin's intelligent-seeming ability to quote intellectuals and classic writers off the top of his head does not bespeak the casual familiarity with their work it is calculated to create, but rather derives from a studied image he nurtures—despite his claim to being uninterested in a movie-star image. Such people insist he preps himself not by reading the works of those worthies, but only by skimming their books for usable, impressive-sounding quotes.

Dustin's admirers view his "anti-star" attitudes—his refusal to slip into the Beverly Hills status symbol lifestyle and insistence on remaining part of the New York scene—as the ultimate evidence of his essential honesty; his critics insist the anti-star image is nothing more than a pose, as self-conscious a case of image-building as George Hamilton with his mansion, his Mercedes, his hand-tailored suits and his perfect tan.

Donald Driver, who directed Dustin in Schisgal's *Jimmy Shine*, recalls that long after Dustin's finger—cut in an accident in Baltimore—had healed, Dustin still insisted someone announce, before the opening curtain, that Dustin was appearing with a wounded finger. "It was a blatant bid for public sympathy," Driver later complained. The producer of *Jimmy Shine*, Zev Buffman, has never forgotten that Dustin insisted on half the profits on the souvenir programs (which actors never normally receive) and got it on the grounds that they had forgotten to clear his biographical material with Dustin before going to print.

"He's very bright and he's very charming," former friend Ulu Grosbard is fond of telling

Liza Minnelli pays a surprise visit to the set of *Lenny* to kid with Dustin and Bob Fosse.

Dustin and director Ulu Grosbard prepare for a nighttime sequence during the shooting of *Straight Time*.

people, "but he can turn it on when he needs something from you and turn it off when he no longer does. It's not a conscious, deliberate thing on his part. It's just that he believes his own image, because he has a great need to believe in it. That is, after all, what good acting is all about, and Dustin is a *very* good actor—on the stage and on the screen, and also off."

When *Kramer vs. Kramer* was released, several magazines seized on the film's title as a means of commenting on Dustin's constant feuds. The New York *Times* published a story called "Dustin Hoffman vs. Nearly Everybody," and *Rolling Stone* went a step further by printing one called "Hoffman vs. Hoffman," implying Dustin's real conflict was with himself.

When *Us* Magazine asked Hoffman if he considers himself "difficult," he responded: "If that means I don't go along, then I've been difficult ever since I started. I got kicked out of acting class when I was twenty years old because I screamed at the teacher when she started talking to me in the middle of a scene. I got fired Off-Broadway and I quit shows. But I have always felt I knew what I was doing." Still, many of the respected directors whom Dustin has worked with express mixed reactions to his drive and energy and desire to be a full collaborator with them. Bob Fosse, who insisted on Hoffman and no one else for *Lenny*, speaks of Dustin with great admiration but tempers it by saying, "I'm not altogether sure his energy is always in the right direction. Much of it might be wasted effort. But the sincerity of his motivation to improve the film is unquestionable."

Another director, who wished to remain anonymous, is even more critical: "He's very difficult to satisfy. He insists on takes far beyond the necessity of them. He's driven to achieve perfection, and I don't know that he is the best judge of when it has been reached." John Schlesinger of *Midnight Cowboy* and *Marathon Man* has said, "He's one of the most inventive actors I've ever known. He's so full of ideas, he almost gives you *too* much. I loved working with him, but I'm not sure I'd want to do it again soon." When writer Joyce Haber asked a formidable director Dustin had once worked with what Dustin Hoffman "was *really* like," the director pointed to some expensively dressed, no-nonsense studio executives seated with him at lunch and said, "We seem like bad guys, but we're really nice. Dustin seems like a nice guy, but he's really bad."

But Meryl Streep, a defender of Dustin's, told interviewer Tony Schwartz, "Dustin is very demanding, but it isn't the 'star temperament' I'd been led to expect. It isn't vanity. He's a perfectionist about the film, and his ego is subjugated to that." Ex-wife Anne Byrne recalls that, "When we first met, he was a real slob." As a person to live with, she described him as "*very* difficult," though her explanation of that phrase is illuminating: "He demands acceptance of his way of life. He demands honesty. Dusty really believes your most important thing is to be what you are. That's very wonderful. And *very* difficult."

Dustin once made a statement that counters the comments of both Streep and Byrne: "I'm not easy to be around when I'm working. I'm also not easy to be around when I'm *not* working.

But when I am working, I'm just unable to function in any kind of normal way when I get home. It's not so much that I'm taking home the character as I'm taking home the disappointment, the fatigue. It's draining, working thirteen or fourteen hours at a stretch, doing maybe a two-minute scene." And when the two come into conflict—the success of one's art vs. the success of one's personal life—it is the art that, in Dustin's case, invariably wins out. This fact is at the base of the success of most all of Dustin's screen roles, and at the heart of the failure of his first marriage, as well as of many of his friendships.

In part, Dustin used *Kramer* as a means of being critical about people like himself, who want a career and a family and, in the end, let the family suffer for the career: "What we try to show in the film is how long it takes Ted Kramer to understand that he has not been what he has thought he has been. He's not been a good husband or a perfect father. It takes him a long

Dustin listens as John Schlesinger explains his concept for a *Marathon Man* sequence.

time to understand that he has not been, and *why* he has not been. People don't change out of anything but necessity." He is talking about Ted Kramer, but he knows that if you interchange advertising and moviemaking, he is in fact talking about himself: "You cannot be in show business or movies or advertising or public relations without sacrificing something. Either you sacrifice your work or your home. I don't think the men who say they split their time, half and half, are being truthful with themselves." At least, it was impossible for Dustin—who tried, and failed, to achieve such a balance.

Dustin's values about people and art became obvious in an impromptu argument that took place in a New York delicatessen in 1967, when Dustin and a friend were talking about movies and, in particular, about Elia Kazan, a director whose work Hoffman admired. Someone at the next table joined in without invitation, screaming that Kazan was not a legitimate artist because of his involvement with the Joseph McCarthy anti-communist hearings, when Kazan named names so he could go on working. "Elia Kazan is *so* an artist!" Dustin yelled back. "You can't be an artist and sell out your friends," came the man's angry reply. "One thing has *nothing* to do with the other," Hoffman chided with fervent conviction. "You *can* be an artist and sell out your own *mother!*"

The ultimate example of this attitude in action occurred during the shooting of *Kramer*. Dustin had come to deeply love little Justin Henry, the boy who played his son in the film. On the last day of shooting, they were about to do the scene in the arbor, in which Dustin tells the child he is going away with his mother. While the cameras were being set up for the shot, director Benton and Hoffman noticed that the child, just recovering from a sickness, was sitting alone in the arbor. Immediately, they realized the possibility on their hands. Benton began shooting film as Hoffman walked to the child, who had no idea that a "take" had started. Dustin softly began telling the boy that when a movie is finished, the "family" that has shot it breaks apart, and the child nodded; Dustin then promised Justin he would continue to see him regularly, and the child spontaneously broke into tears. With different dialogue dubbed in later, this became the devastatingly convincing sequence audiences responded to so strongly.

But if that is a fascinating behind-the-scenes story of how a great movie moment was achieved, it also reveals the kind of tactic Dustin's enemies attack him for. He saw nothing wrong in consciously manipulating the child's sincere responses for the good of the movie, and while the love he expressed for the boy was totally real, Hoffman had no compunctions about calculatedly exploiting their emotional bond for the sake of a scene—to get a "take" the way he wanted it.

But when people confront Dustin with the "dark side" of his personality, he laughs and says: "I'm a very nice man. *Really!* It's always bewildered me why more people don't like me." Certainly, one group of people that likes him well enough are the women. "It's not true that Dustin was ever a pre-med student," his brother Ronald jokes. "That rumor got started because he was always looking up the girls' skirts." Dustin puts it this way: "Women have a tendency to make me feel very vulnerable. I think men are scared to death of women, and with good reason."

In high school, his essential shyness spilled over to his early dating. When he took a girl out, his impulse may have been to kiss her, but he never did. "I was the king of Never Kissing"— wanting desperately to, yet too nervous, too anxious, to do it. Sometimes, he didn't even get as far as a date: he remembers dialing the phone and not being able to get to the last digit, so afraid was he of rejection. Later, acting provided him with a perfect outlet. "In acting class," he has admitted, "I heard they did scenes where we were supposed to follow an impulse. *My* impulse was to take a girl in my arms and kiss her. I'd pick a certain acting class because of the girls in it."

Once he hit New York, his awkwardness around women disappeared. He was always known as a swinger, constantly in the company of attractive women—especially "long legged, intelligent, artistically ambitious women," as one friend from that time recalls. Even here, though, his old "ugly duckling" stigma would occasionally return to haunt him, as when a striking-looking sculptress called "Marisol" turned down his request for a date.

"Why not?" he asked.

"Because I think you're a creep," she answered flatly.

For the most part, though, he was immensely successful with women from the moment he hit New York City. "He had more girls than Namath," Robert Duvall recalls. In fact, as an out-of-work actor, Dustin's biggest problem was not in getting girls—they came around pretty regularly—but with their parents. One date invited him to her folks' home in Boston for a weekend. The stay was nice but when the girl's mother dropped him at the train station for his return to Manhattan, the woman looked Dustin in the eye and asked him: "Have you ever considered being a doctor?" "No," he admitted. "Well," she said, "if you ever do, let me know."

To this day, Dustin is amazed at his own sexual appeal despite the fact he cannot compete with a Warren Beatty or a Robert Redford in the looks department: "There is some fun in knowing you can get away with murder looking quite average." Getting away with murder means being able, by the presence of your personality, to get women to do pretty much what you want them to do—a situation other men can only fantasize about. Once, when a schoolmate from California visited New York and stopped by to see the as yet unknown Dustin, he was seized by the inspiration to convince her he had become a painter, and played the role so convincingly that very shortly he had her completely nude, posing.

Yet while he loves women, he has always seen a conflict between sex and friendship: "I've never been able to say of a girl, 'Gee, we're great friends,' and let it go at that. I've always had the urge to make love. I don't know any girl I've slept with about whom I can now say, 'She's still a good friend.' " Despite that, he is a verbal champion of the feminist cause: "I find it exciting to be living now. Very difficult, very painful, very confusing, but very exciting. Women's Lib has made me realize my ambivalence about women. But even if I live to be ninety, I'll die wishing I had learned more about what I feel and *fear* about women. I think I fear my own vulnerability. A woman is a prime example of what will open up my vulnerability. Womankind occupies my thinking most of the day. I don't think that I think about anything else more."

"Even if I live to be ninety" is a significant phrase in itself, for Dustin's various comments over the years demonstrate he is obsessed with death, which helps explain his need to immortalize himself on celluloid while still alive. But even that has its drawbacks: "When you're a movie star," Dustin once said, "you're already dead, you're embalmed in a way, fixed forever on celluloid—and you can see the dream of living much more vividly than other people." Like everyone else who hits forty, he suffered from mid-life crisis. "Something we all do," he explained to writer Wayne Warga, "is double our age. At thirty, I thought of sixty and knew I could still play baseball. At thirty-five, I thought of seventy and all the things I'd still be able to do—go to the theatre, take a long walk, maybe even act. At forty I thought of eighty, and—I'm no longer sure. What makes forty so different for people is that you necessarily confront your own mortality. I personally find it unhealthy *not* to think about death—my whole feeling about life springs from the knowledge I'm going to die." Mentally creating possible obituaries has always taken up a certain amount of Dustin's time. One favorite goes this way: "Died in his nineties. Started out to be an actor, went on to be a director, and wound up doing . . . something else." The something else, he adds, would be of *practical* use to mankind—and that mother of a former girlfriend may yet find Dustin Hoffman, M.D., at her doorstep to, as she put it, look her up.

After playing the 121-year-old Jack Crabb in *Little Big Man*, Dustin's view on death mellowed slightly: "The ideal way would be to call your own death," he said, "to fear it all through life, and then reach an age where fear disappears, when you could say: 'I'm ready now. I'm tired, I've had my life.' " For someone as death-obsessed as Dustin, it was natural that he would be attracted to the Indians' attitudes when he learned about them during the filming of that picture: "To the Indians, death was a very simple thing, for life was just an appetizer." But his preoccupation with death grates against another personality trait, his "loner" mentality: "It's very hard for me to be alone. As long as there's someone in the house somewhere, it's very comforting. Because you can die at any time, you see, and it's my desire not to die alone."

But if he is death-obsessed, he is also, importantly, a born survivor, whose fascination with death only makes him appreciate life all the more, and cling to it with bear-hug indomitability. This is best illustrated by an experience that occurred about a year before he achieved fame. To celebrate getting a good role, he and a girlfriend were cooking dinner in her apartment, when a fondue pot full of grease exploded. Instead of rushing for the phone and calling the fire department for help, Dustin attempted to squelch the flames himself, and in the process his arms were burned badly. When the fire was finally out and a doctor called in to check his condition, he told Dustin to enter a hospital at once. Dustin refused—he wasn't going to miss the first day of rehearsals. He showed up at the theatre the following day with long sleeves rolled down so the rest of the cast wouldn't realize the terrible condition he was in. He suffered this way for the better part of a week, when infection set in and he collapsed.

When he woke up in the hospital, he was shocked to learn from the doctor who examined him that, without an immediate operation, it was doubtful he would live through the night. As the hospital attendants hurriedly prepared him, then wheeled him toward the operating room, Hoffman reacted to the surrealistic nightmare quality his life had suddenly taken on, first by making small talk with them, then off-color jokes, finally doing bizarre shtick—until, as in a scene that might have been lifted out of an off-Broadway dark comedy, the men in white were convulsed with laughter as they entered the operating room. Only later did Dustin admit to himself that his crazy behavior had been his only possible reaction to the craziness of the situation he had found himself in, that he covered his fear of death with strained humor, and in so doing stated his frenzied hold on life.

It was a hold that soon caused him to believe the seemingly in-control anesthetist, who was having difficulty inserting a tube down Dustin's throat that would keep the patient from choking on his own vomit during the operation, was in a "hyper" state, and incompetent to care for him properly. With no way of knowing for sure if he were correct in his assessment or merely acting out of paranoid fear, Dustin seized control of the situation, going in a matter of moments from passive patient to the "director" of the entire affair, insisting he would wait till morning when a new man would arrive for the operation—fully aware of the high risk involved. All that night he, in his own words, stayed alive only by "willing myself to do so." In the morning, following a successful operation, the doctor who had performed it confided to Hoffman that the actor had been right, and if the anesthesia had been improperly administered—as it probably would have been—Dustin would almost certainly have died. If Dustin has always lived in utter dread of death, he clearly also possesses a fervent and positive urge for life, as well as, beneath his veneer of charming craziness, a sharp, rational approach to any situation, however bizarre, that arises, demonstrating at such times his ability to, in Kipling's words, keep his head while all about are losing theirs.

But his obsession with his own eventual death carries with it overtones of another of his basic obsessions. "The minute you're famous," he once told *Newsweek*, "you can see that obituary: 'Dustin Hoffman died of a heart attack at 73. His first movie was a success.'" Death obsession, yes, but also another kind of obsession fused with it: the notion that failure is inevitable. "Hoffman," according to Richard Meryman, "is driven by a perfectionist's sense of failure." Murray Schisgal says, "He never felt he's truly put it all together. He will continually hack at the weaknesses and not see the strengths of his work." And Dustin complains, "You look at your work and say, 'I had a moment here or there,' but the rest of it you wish you could do over again. What you're reaching for is never what you get. Then you go into a screening room, and look at what's up there on the screen, and you know what you wanted is not there. But everyone else says, 'What's the matter? It's all right! Why can't you ever be satisfied?' But you were going for something way past what the other people are going for." Initially, one reason he wanted to go to New York was because, in his own words, "it's easier to fail 3,000 miles away from home, and I was sure I would fail." In 1974, he was both a bankable star and a critically acclaimed actor, but far from being satisfied at long last, he often seemed more morose and malcontent than ever before. As Howard Kissel commented: "Hoffman should, by the standards of our popular mythology, exude confidence and satisfaction. But his tone is largely one of frustration. Though his performances generally are praised, he feels he is capable of better work than often appears on the screen."

The bearer of both a Jewish guilt complex and a Puritan work ethic, Dustin likes to romanticize his plight, to see himself as a tragic performer in the tradition of Eugene O'Neill's father, potentially a great actor who gave up the complexity of Shakespearean roles to become a matinee idol with *The Count of Monte Cristo*, only to later regret his own commercial success. "Had I never gone into movies," Dustin sighs, "I could have been a great actor today." Perhaps. And, perhaps he might have burned himself out on the off-Broadway stage, found himself giving acting lessons to up and coming younger performers, or directing at the regional theatres around the country. Still, he complains: "In a way, I feel I've wasted the last ten years." And despite his continuing popularity, he works at psychologically preparing himself for the failure he ardently believes is eventually going to come: "If you can wake up tomorrow morning and be a failure, no longer adored in the public's eye, and still enjoy life and want to go on working, you're home free." But he fears the worst. "Show me somebody who's in menial labor," Hoffman once commented to a companion while walking through Greenwhich Village and noticing a former member of Sammy Davis's Will Mastin Trio shining shoes, "and I'll show you somebody who was an actor once."

Though Dustin received countless rave reviews for *The Graduate*, one critic called his performance an "in-and-out" one, and it was the single review he could quote from verbatim.

"Sure, it affects me," he admitted. "Somehow, it all brings my insecurities to the surface. There's a part of you that wants to believe the negative. Everybody likes to get good reviews. It's just another stay of execution, as far as I'm concerned. You still have to look forward to the worst, which will come maybe with the next review, when it will finally be revealed to all—including yourself—that you are a fraud." Dustin's fear of failure (and fraudulence) is matched by his at best ambiguous attitude toward success.

After the release of *The Graduate*, success brought some unexpected side effects, such as a lookalike impersonating Dustin in Las Vegas, New York cabbies going out of their way to stop for him instead of tearing on by, maitre d's in restaurants ushering him to the best instead of the worst tables, and Petrocelli suits offering him a job as a male model for their new line of clothing. "My biggest pitfall," he announced at that time, "would be to grab the fat movie contracts, do commercials, go on *The Johnny Carson Show* and be a pompous ass who pretends he knows everything about sex, religion, philosophy, you name it." In fact, while there were plenty of potentials for movies and commercials, there was little danger of getting stuck on *Tonight*, for Carson rejected Dustin as a possible guest, claiming he was "too low key and normal acting."

People couldn't understand why, despite a hit movie, Dustin continued to maintain the same three-room Greenwich Village apartment he had been living in. There was a good reason: he was afraid of being overwhelmed by his own sudden popularity. His brother gave him some sage advice from an economist's point of view: "Don't raise your standard of living." If he did, then the new lifestyle might threaten to become an end in itself. Dustin took the advice, and while he was shooting *Midnight Cowboy*, interviewers were aghast or delighted—depending on their own scheme of values—to find a $250,000 a picture star living in a $125-a-month flat. "When I was unemployed, I didn't like my apartment that much," he said. "Now, I like it." The reason was simple: now he lived there out of choice, not chance; because he wanted to, not because he had to. Still, less than a year later he was living in a more expansive and expensive brownstone—$400 a month—directly across from his original apartment, in a sense announcing he was attempting to move up without moving out.

Hoffman noticed his success caused a sense of discomfort with some of his old friends who, like him, were actors, who had been around as long (in some cases longer) without enjoying that modicum of success, and Dustin feared his own sudden success "magnified their own feelings of failure . . . there is always that edge of anger." But he was able to achieve the next best thing: a consciousness of the danger, as well as the pleasure, of "overnight" success. "I just have to get over this period," he confessed to *Look* Magazine. "Never in my life have I been so in love with myself."

"In many ways," Dustin wrote in *Playbill* in 1968, "being an overnight success is like being the victim of a disaster. I know some of my friends respond that way: 'How are you taking it?' I'd have to assure them I was okay." Even his ability to talk with strangers on the street reminded Dustin of the situation that exists during times of disaster, such as the aftermath of Jack Kennedy's assassination, or the day of the blackout, or even the New York City transit strike. At such heightened moments, everyone finds the need to drop the usual aura of standoffishness and, in a way that is most peculiar for New Yorkers, to assume a sense of community with everyone and anyone who passes. For Dustin, that unusual and heightened quality became a fact of everyday life.

But when Dustin and Anne took off for their honeymoon, Dustin found that no one in England recognized him, and he was highly pleased to rediscover the luxury of anonymity. Then, unconsciously, he found himself humming a song, louder and ever louder, as they walked through the streets of London. Finally, Anne stopped and asked if he knew what he was doing. "No, what?" he replied. "You were singing," she explained, " 'So here's to you, Mrs. Robinson . . . hey hey hey, hey hey hey. . . .' " After three days out of the limelight, he was unconsciously trying to reestablish his public identity. So, if being recognized brought with it head-

aches, Dustin admitted to missing it when it wasn't there.

One day in 1975, he and his wife sat in a café enjoying some pasta, when a woman walking by their table suddenly stopped, turned to Anne, and said, "Excuse me, but weren't you a dancer in the 'Nutcracker' ballet?" Anne, used to being ignored by autograph hounds interested only in her husband, was in shock. Half kiddingly, Dustin piped in with, "Do you realize that your recognizing her and not me may lead to a divorce?" "Oh," the woman replied shortly, "*The Graduate* was okay."

In time, he came to completely understand his love-hate attitude toward stardom: "The day is going to come when the whole world will be falling apart, and I'll open the paper to the entertainment page to see if my name is there. You'll always be able to find people who are willing to tell you that you're great. You don't really want that, yet it gets to be like an addiction. Suddenly, you need a fix. What I'm trying to do is get beyond the point where I need a fix, where I can say that sort of thing is destructive, and walk away from it. Once you are in the public eye, you think you *are* something. But you just happen to be a commodity they want. When you get into the bind of simply re-creating that which is pleasing and saleable, then growth stops. Success can really cripple you."

"The thing I have to guard against," he said as early as 1968, "is losing perspective. Off-Broadway, the recognition I was getting was in *balance* with what I was doing. I could take it nice and slow and not feel my soul being stolen. If you live for a long time with a fear that you're nothing much, and then are suddenly told you are everything you feared you weren't—well, I think it's very easy to go overboard and believe it all." In a phrase, what he feared was being seduced by success, and he began consciously, carefully guarding against it. This guarding process started even before the success actually came. Dustin insisted that a clause be written into his contract for *The Graduate* stating that producer Joseph E. Levine had no "options" on him. Dustin did not want to risk getting railroaded into making a series of pictures to cash in on *The Graduate*, did not want to become, in his own words, "The Andy Hardy of the Sixties," playing a series of "synthetic Benjamins." He was perfectly willing to take a small salary and sign to do any publicity stunts the studio wanted, but when the project was finally over, he would be able to leave it with his freedom for future creativity intact.

Just how much he was actually paid for *The Graduate* is a matter of some slight debate— different "official" figures range from $17,500 to $20,000. But most of it disappeared quickly owing to various expenses from his newfound status and also payment of old debts. In the interim period between the picture's completion and its official release, Dustin was still an unknown commodity who did not get offered interesting film parts. Ironically enough, the soon-to-be-star could be found standing on unemployment lines, waiting patiently for his check for $55 a week. Even after *The Graduate*'s premiere, Dustin still showed up at the unemployment office, only now people stared at him

in amazement—and, embarrassed, he decided to stay home.

He was amazed to realize that people stopping him on the streets for an autograph were shocked, even disappointed, to find he was "just a person." "What did you *think* I was?" he asked, dumbfounded. He himself had never felt that kind of extreme awe for movie stars, perhaps partially because he grew up near Hollywood, where they were highly visible. "Why should I get more press coverage than Christian Barnard?" he speculated, marvelling at that man's ability to save lives, and what seemed his own insignificant contribution beside it—echoing his mental obituary in which he claimed to hope he might someday do something "important." Hoffman is one of the few movie stars to openly admit his own mixed feelings about the experience of one's face being known to almost everyone. "It's boring to have it always going on," he once confided to a friend, "but when it doesn't, I have to admit I get worried. When I'm

Sam Peckinpah gives Dustin advice about how to play an upcoming scene during a lull in the shooting of *Straw Dogs*.

someplace and *nobody* notices me, I feel something's missing, and I want to talk a little louder, start acting a little flamboyant."

Perhaps no single anecdote so perfectly captures Hoffman's ambiguous attitude toward fame as this one: after filming of *The Graduate* was complete, Dustin flew back to his life—and soon-to-be-terminated obscurity—in New York. At this time, an interesting obsession took hold of him. In the evenings, he would walk the streets of New York, staring into the faces of the people he passed. They would momentarily glance back at this earnest, intense young man, then walk on. At each encounter, Hoffman would take a perverse pleasure, thinking to himself that in just a few weeks, anyone who passed him on the street would recognize him as the star of the year's big film. Hoffman wasn't satisfied with the void of obscurity he drifted in before *The Graduate*, nor has he ever been completely comfortable with the vast attention he has received since. Actually, during those nightly odysseys around Manhattan in the final calm before the eternal storm of recognition began, Dustin may have been the happiest he has ever been: like the virginal bride-to-be who, walking down the aisle in church, is happy her spinsterhood is over but dreads what the night will bring. If he could only have lived forever in that moment—much as the figures on Keats's Grecian Urn live in eternal bliss—he might have been in paradise. *You don't know me,* he must have thought as he stared into one set of eyes after another, but the machinery is already set in motion, and in a short time all of you will have paid to see in a theatre the man you are now passing by.

Only a day or two after the film opened, Dustin's life was forever altered—and the immediate impression was, of course, ecstasy. He recalls being stopped by someone on the street, who said: "You know something? *You* look just like *Dustin Hoffman!*" "What the man said to me," he told friends later that day, "that was just like saying, 'You look just like Gary Cooper.'" When newfound fans began swiping the plastic namebar on his mailbox, Dustin bought a hand label machine in order to replenish them daily. Dutifully, he read all his fan mail each evening and answered, in longhand, all except the quirkier ones. Of all his early fan letters, the one he enjoyed most was a brief note from a little girl in Duluth who wrote: "Please come and share Passover with me and my family. P. S.: If you're not Jewish, tear this up."

Hoffman's first reactions to those New York fans who began mobbing him on the street—"To be in a position, especially in *this* town, that suddenly you can talk to strangers!" he mused—was boyishly innocent, charmingly naive. "As if making up for long years of Kafkaesque confinement," Mel Gussow said, attempting to analyze it, "he loves to be recognized . . . for Dustin, this part of fame is a pleasure." It would not be for long, but at the beginning, Dusty really did stop on street corners, attempting to establish a human rapport with everyone who recognized him. "Aren't you Dustin Hoffman?" a cute teenage girl, a middle-class housewife, a businessman in a polyester suit would ask. "Yes," he would reply, genuinely flattered and, more important, genuinely interested in *them*, and he would ask, "Who are you?" "What do you do?" "Did you enjoy the movie?" If fate had cast him as a movie star, then he would teach fate a lesson by being approachable and agreeable in a way no movie star ever had before. But it turned out he was the one with a lesson to learn—that there is a very good reason why most movie stars are so unapproachable. He would learn it, and learn it the hard way.

"It may sound silly," he said some time later, "but when it's something you live with every day, it becomes a pressure. When your face isn't well known, you can go walking with a girl, have an argument with your wife, eat in a restaurant, but no matter how many people are around you, you've got privacy. Suddenly, for me, that just doesn't exist anymore." Dustin had braced himself, just before *The Graduate*'s release, to handle the attention of his fans *his* way he would not become Bob Hope, sending the butler out to shoo the wide-eyed, hang-jawed, awestruck multitude off the movie star's front porch. And, for a while, Dustin was as good as his secret pledge to himself. By the time he even thought to call the phone company and have them "unlist" his existing number, the new directory was already out, listing not only the number (he would soon become involved in long conversations with fans, especially those younger ones who felt he was "really Benjamin Braddock," the then-current generation's answer to Holden Caulfield, and as such able to solve all their problems) but also the address where he and Anne lived. Sixteen-year-old girls who got the shivers just tracking down his house and standing on the front steps were shocked to be invited up to the apartment for milk, cookies, and conversation. Eventually, though, he realized intelligent talk was impossible: the adulation in their eyes negated any kind of real human communication. They saw him as a god, would take anything he said as gospel, and after the first flurry of power pleasure, he found the experience decadent—threatening, even. For one moment, they looked at him as though he were above and beyond them; the next, the look in their eyes shifted, and he sensed they felt they *owned* him.

All at once, the offers of refreshments and conversation stopped. But by that time it was too late: the notion that Dustin Hoffman was now in the public domain had spread like a cancer out of control, through all levels of society. While filming an on-location scene for *Midnight Cowboy* in New York—a key scene which required intense concentration on the actor's part—the crowd, kept just beyond the film crew by guards, grew ever more unruly in their demand for autographs. One woman waved a piece of paper she wanted signed with fervent desperation, until her attitude sharply shifted to outraged indignation. "Mr. Hoffman," she screeched angrily at the artist who was unwilling to jump out of his character's mood in order to entertain the public, "I *paid* for you!" She had, after all, once purchased a ticket to *The Graduate*, and considered that she now owned a piece of the action.

"The jealousy I've seen!" he commented some time later. "People on the street, coming up to me with hatred in their eyes that says, without words, 'You've got it made—you're a star!' The terrible thing about it is, I can understand their resentment, because I've been there, too." Now, when he went into a restaurant, he would ask for a table that allowed him to face the wall. But if he dared to go to the bar for a drink, someone would inevitably grab him, insisting he come over to the table and wish someone else a "Happy Birthday." Or want to shake Dustin's hand. Or have his picture snapped with an arm around Dustin. And as a person who does not like to be touched by strangers, or have his "space" invaded, it was exasperating.

Hoffman tried to keep his chin up even when it all made him feel down. And in time, he realized that that precious quality of anonymity was never going to come back, that *this* was his *life*. So he devised a new tactic, as when he ignored a young girl who stood by the restaurant table where he was dining with Anne for as long as he could, and then, when she insisted he talk to her, told her she had lovely breasts. After a mildly shocking statement like that, there was really nothing more for her to say, so she left—feeling flattered. He hoped he had found a way to let the public know they were annoying him, but also communicate at the same time that he did appreciate the attention.

Asking for an autograph is, to Dustin, "dishonest—I don't think they really want it. They want something else, some kind of fantasy. It's not the autograph itself, it's the taking up of your time, it's talking to you, it's confronting the thing they have so many mixed feelings about. You represent many things to them, least of which is yourself." This attitude grows from an unpleasant experience: when he nearly chopped his right index finger off during a pre-Broadway road show engagement of Schisgal's *Jimmy Shine*, the nurses at the hospital he was rushed to tried to remove the blood-stained towel from his hand— not to operate on it, but to find out whether it still worked well enough to allow him to sign autographs.

One part of the adoring public is, naturally, the attractive women of the sort he remembers scorning him in high school, though he doesn't allow himself to "get even" by exploiting the possibilities now, even when they approach him on the street. "Every time it happens I'm flattered, though I know it has nothing to do with me. These young girls feel they can act out their fantasies at me because they know I'm inaccessible. I'm not going to do anything." But one night at the theatre, a girl came backstage and threw her arms around Dustin, insisting that she wanted him. He wheeled around and asked her to come back to his apartment, just to see her reaction—and she was terrified, as he knew she would be.

Another reason why he cannot relate to such women is that they are not relating to him, as a person, but to what he stands for: stardom. Al Pacino or Robert Redford would get the same reaction from them: they are not reacting to Dustin, per se, but to the idea of a star he, among others, stands for; and while they might not know it, they are operating out of a "groupie" mentality.

Finally, Hoffman's honeymoon with his public came crashing to an abrupt and official end on March 6, 1970, the day his apartment building at 18 West Eleventh Street was racked by an explosion next door where, unbeknown to Dustin, some Weatherman maniacs were busily constructing bombs meant to threaten the Establishment, and only managed to blow themselves to smithereens. As Dustin and Anne attempted to salvage what they could of their possessions from the carnage, celebrity gawkers began to line up outside. Dustin wandered into the still burning building to retrieve a few personal items and, stopping a moment to gaze out the window, noticed a crowd smiling and waving at him, as though they were lined up outside a theatre and he was arriving for a premiere. They were, he recalls, "really knocked out, because they were getting their two favorites—a disaster and a celebrity—at the same time." He became convinced the public took a horrible pleasure in seeing him, a movie star so seemingly removed from ordinary daily problems, brought down as low as he could go, in the same way the audience for a Greek tragedy simultaneously experiences both a terrible delight and a delightful terror at witnessing the fall of a prince. Hoffman developed a near-Shakespearean sensibility about the crowd, overly affectionate one moment and, like lap dogs that turn before your eyes into hunting hounds that have sniffed blood, ready to go for your jugular a moment later.

"There's a lot that stars feel that other people don't feel, except maybe very pretty girls. Very pretty girls walk down the street and they must feel just like stars do, because they constantly wonder, 'Are people looking at me?' They're really stars every day of the week, those girls. Well, being a movie star is like being a pretty girl. You are constantly bothered whether you like it or not. You cannot go through the day without someone hitting on you in some way. It's an invasion or privacy, but it's part of the deal." And no matter how annoying it can get, if it is suddenly gone, that too is a terrifying experience.

Even more touchy than his relationship to his public has been Hoffman's on again, off again love affair with the press. Doing publicity for *The Graduate* was in his contract, so he had very little to say about all the interviews. "I have to admit," he later confessed, "there was a part of me that *wanted* to do it, wanted to use that free million dollars worth of p.r. to try and make myself a big star. It was only after I read the way it all came out in print that I began to hate it." He was besieged by a bevy of interviewers, hailing from literally every publication imaginable—big and small, Establishment and Underground, intellectual and popular. His favorite of the early requests went like this:

Dear Mr. Hoffman, I am a student at the School of Visual Arts. My friends have bet me five dollars I couldn't get an interview with you. Would you help me win this wager? I'd be willing to split the profits.

Anyone with a sense of humor as keen as Dustin's would, naturally, appreciate that note. The girl got the interview and, what's more, got to keep the entire five dollars.

Unschooled in the fine points of being interviewed, and with a strong instinct for the honest reply, he spoke off the cuff about any subject asked him. The writers, relieved to be talking with someone who said what he thought instead of mouthing the jaded old clichés that usually come from movie stars who know the ropes, were thrilled with the interesting copy they got on everything from politics to art to personal matters. Interviewer Beverly Solochek put Dustin's style this way: "There is nothing self-conscious about Hoffman. . . . It's simply a happenstance that you're there as he mouths this long-standing, on-going dialogue he's been having with himself." But the constant repetition of the questions, and of the interview situation, eventually became a routine—and, in time, a less than pleasant one. Worse still was the prospect of reading what was written about him. Unable to rationalize it is a necessary evil that kept him in the public's eye and mind, Dustin grew ever more uncomfortable with the understanding this person in print was not him, but an extraction of him—an extraction the public would uncritically accept as the whole man. The thought depressed him.

He realized the interviewers were recreating him in their own images, *using* him in a sense by filtering his comments through their own consciousness. One article that did him in was a piece in the London *Telegraph* in which Dustin was quoted as calling something "groovy"—a word he despised and never used. It was the interviewer, he insisted, who had used that word throughout the interview, and in the end half a million readers experienced what they assumed was Dustin Hoffman but which was, more correctly, an androgynous combination of Dustin and the interviewer.

Worse still was the *Time* Magazine article/interview, portraying him as symbolizing youth and representing a new breed of Hollywood star. It infuriated Dustin so much that he considered halting the interview process entirely. He spent ten hours talking to a *Time* reporter, but in the end, the piece was written by someone else and all the quotes were mangled and misrepresented: *Time* quoted him as saying not what he actually said but what they wanted him to say in order to reinforce their preconception of what he stood for. "When I read things about how bigheaded I am, written by people who never met me," he complained, "it doesn't bother me. And I have read things about myself that I haven't liked but I have said, 'That's accurate—I *was* like that. I dug my own grave and I'm responsible.' But if I do an interview, if I give time, and then I find I have not been presented accurately, I feel disturbed. I feel *betrayed*."

For a short while after the release of *The*

Graduate, the press had been warm, and wrote that Dustin deserved whatever recognition he received, owing to his long period of apprenticeship. Then suddenly, "I was the Establishment, The Enemy. People started to write, 'Who *is* this guy, and how *dare* he?' Respect and admiration turned into—envy and ugliness." Soon, he feared each interviewer came to see him with a totally preconceived notion of what he would be: the shy kid or the jaded cynic, the offbeat sex symbol or the schlep, the clever intellectual or the confused, pretentious pseudo. He was particularly distressed when one young woman took the idea of an "angle" on an interview one step too far, showing up at his apartment with plans of seducing him so she could go home and write an article called "I Seduced Dustin Hoffman." Such an attitude didn't make him feel sexy; it made him feel like a thing, less than human, there to be used and manipulated and exploited, like one of those pretty girls whom Hoffman has always thought of as being very much like movie stars.

Like those reported cases of Jews in concentration camps who compulsively fashioned imitations of the Nazi uniforms of their tormentors, which they then fetishistically donned themselves, Dustin purchased a tape recorder identical to the ones carried by the endless interviewers, and took up the habit of taping routine conversations with anyone he came in contact with—the wardrobe girl on the set of *Little Big Man*, a stranger he sat next to on an airplane—drilling them with the same kind of abrupt questions he had so often been subjected to ("What's your relationship with your parents?"; "What's your objective in life?") and receiving the same kind of circumspect answers he had so often given. If Andy Warhol was correct when he said that in our time, everyone would be a celebrity for fifteen minutes, then Dustin Hoffman surely gave a number of people their shot.

"Almost always I have women interviewing me," he once bitterly complained, "women who look like they've always hated the pretty girls in their class." There is an unpleasant irony to the insensitivity of that statement in that Hoffman, alone among movie stars, should have been able to feel for those unhandsome women who were trying to achieve importance—a kind of beauty, even—through their writing: he was, after all, the kid who had always envied all the "walking surfboards" in California.

Dustin's most heated bout with the press came when *Playgirl* published late in 1979 what was purportedly an "exclusive interview" with him, in which that magazine quoted Dustin as saying Hollywood might force him "to give up acting." Hoffman later told Marilyn Beck of the New York *Daily News* that the quote, and others in the interview, were "untrue or garbled," that he didn't like or respect the magazine, and wouldn't have done the interview at all if he had been told by the interviewer just what publication she was representing.

But in late 1979, Hoffman knew that he needed a hit, and needed one badly. With his previous two pictures, *Agatha* and *Straight Time*, surfacing as box office flops—despite the fact both received relatively good critical notices—Dustin was fast beginning to appear passé, and despite his various statements over the years in which he denigrated movie stardom and looked back yearningly to the anonymity of live theatre, something in him did not want to relinquish the best movie roles to his lookalike Al Pacino, or Richard Dreyfuss, another adorably neurotic type. Hoffman wanted *Kramer* to be a film he could be proud of and, when shooting and editing were completed, he knew that it was. But he also knew that even excellent films, if not publicized and promoted properly, can die at the box office. However, if the press he had complained so often about got behind the film, they could put him back on top. So he willingly put himself through the longest line of press interviews since his debut film. As Wanda McDaniel wrote, "Hoffman, for the moment, had become Hollywood's most approachable star." And ironically enough, among those magazines that helped most was his old adversary *Time*, which featured him on their cover—and, in so doing, officially announced he was once more the reigning superstar.

Still, he remains uncomfortable about the power interviewers hold over him: "Most interviewers only want unrealistic, extraordinary statements on sex, on the movies and other actors, on life. But life is pretty everyday, even

for an actor. It's also so easy to be made to look a fool; a writer can rearrange things any way he or she wants. And those are the more conscientious ones—some just make up what they want."

But if a journalist can arrange things as he or she wants, so too can a film editor, and they hold a power over an actor that is far more significant than that of the interviewers. After filming *Papillon*, Hoffman was terribly frustrated for several months. "I don't know how I'm going to be in it," he told his friends. "I don't know what they're going to do to me in the cutting room." His anxiety over this situation caused him to reach for the metaphor that best allows him to explain moviemaking, that of the painter: "You decide on all the colors you're going to use, and you do all the sketches and get ready to put it on canvas, and someone comes up to you and says, 'Oops, thank you very much . . . these are the colors, these are the sketches, see you later' . . . and *they* proceed to do the painting. In a sense, that's what happens in the cutting room. I'd like to get in there and at least say what I think. Tell them, 'Use *that* take there, because in it, I set up something that I do twenty minutes later in the film, so please don't leave it on the cutting room floor.'"

Gradually, a need for collaboration grew out of his desire to protect himself as an actor and star. Hoffman fully revealed this in an interview with *Women's Wear Daily* in 1974, when he stated: "It's amazing what can be done in the cutting room to either hurt or protect an actor. When you do a scene, the director generally takes a master shot, a close up and some over-the-shoulder closeups. If you're an actor who's responsible to the moment, your takes will vary. A lot of nuances, shadings will differ from take to take. When he's finished shooting, the director will *whisper* to the script girl, "Print two, four, and six." You hear this. You feel you did your most interesting work in a take they're not even going to print. Somehow, you have to beg the script girl to print it . . . but even if you get the takes you want printed up and they look good in the rushes, you're not in the cutting room, and your best work can end up on the floor." Six years later, he felt confident that he was ready to assume a larger role, for he told *Redbook:* "Hav-

Producer Robert Evans kids with Dustin about an upcoming project.

ing done films now for a dozen years, the need to be more of a painter seems to be calling me. Until I satisfy *that* part of myself, so that what I'm doing is not just an acting job but represents pretty much what I feel about the subject, I'll continue to feel I haven't done anything."

The metaphor of "painting" films—of being the primary (or at least a significant secondary) shaping force in the creation of the work led to his desire to achieve the much-sought-after final cut of a film. But after the final cuts of both *Straight Time* and *Agatha* were taken away from him, owing to "fine print" clauses in his contracts, Aljean Harmetz of the New York *Times* reported Dustin sitting in his lawyer's office, "close to tears." And, once again, Dustin relied on his perennial metaphor of the painter to describe his emotional distress: "You put in a lifetime of work and training, and someone takes your paint brush away . . . whether I would

have made the pictures better or worse is irrelevant. It was my *right* to paint them."

While working on his first major film project, Dustin felt he had merely played a masculine Trilby to Mike Nichols' Svengali, claiming afterwards he deserved none of the credit for his brilliant characterization: "When I was making *The Graduate,* Mike Nichols wouldn't even let us use a 'but' if it was supposed to be an 'and.' " In all fairness, it is important to mention that Nichols insists it was Dustin who made the character of Benjamin click, and that Dustin improvised far more than he chooses to remember. But only one film later, Hoffman was anxiously trying to deliver more input into the creative process.

While shooting *Midnight Cowboy* in New York, he was seized with the inspiration to improvise a bit of business in which Ratso, eating in a lowlife Times Square joint, leaves in disgust

47

after a black man plops down next to him. To Dustin, this bit of business would provide the necessary "key" to his character, wordlessly illustrating the point that as far down as Ratso is in the world, he nonetheless considers himself superior to blacks; he has a sense of personal pride, however pathetically, narrowly, prejudicially misguided, and communicating this to an audience would open up new dimensions of his character. Excited, Hoffman confronted director Schlesinger with the concept, and stood there, stunned, as it was summarily dismissed, owing to the possibility such a scene might be misconstrued as a racial slur on the part of the filmmakers, thus needlessly offending possible black viewers, and that it would also make the Ratso character "too unsympathetic" in the eyes of the liberal moviegoers who would inevitably make up the majority of audiences for an art house picture. Powerless, Hoffman capitulated—promising himself that soon he would seize some of the decision-making power for himself.

Considering how creative, intense, and energetic Hoffman is, it's certainly understandable he could not long be satisfied with his role as star/performer. "If this is what film acting is all about," he had confided to his then close friend Ulu Grosbard after completing *The Graduate*, "I don't care if I ever do another picture." And while shooting *Little Big Man* several years later he announced, during a disgruntled moment, "What I can't understand is how anybody can *enjoy* film acting. I mean, film is great for the director—*he's* always cooking. But for an actor, there's just so much time spent sitting around."

"Sitting around" has never been Dustin's forte, and from the start he knew he could never be happy as one of the old-time movie performers content to kill time in their trailers skimming *Variety* or the stock market reports until needed on the set, at which point they would walk in and follow Spencer Tracy's dictum for good movie acting, which was to know one's lines and not bang into the furniture too much. "I have never done a picture with my own vision," he once complained to an interviewer. "It is always the director's vision, and his feeling for life, and it is never quite complementary to my own."

But unlike many actors, who want to direct themselves as soon as possible, Dustin felt directing a picture was something he should slip into gradually, and thought the best way to begin moving in that direction would be to work as both performer and co-producer on a project, which would allow him to have a great deal of input without yet seizing total control. Thus, on September 12, 1972, it was announced at the opening session of National General Pictures' International Sales Conference at the Beverly Wilshire Hotel that Dustin would become the fifth principal in First Artists Productions. At that moment, First Artists must have seemed like a dream come true for Dustin. It had been formed, in 1969, by Paul Newman, Barbra Streisand, and Sidney Poitier, when they tired of having their vehicles controlled by others and decided it was time to influence the projects with which they were to be associated. (More than half a century earlier, Mary Pickford, Doug Fairbanks, D. W. Griffith and Charlie Chaplin had founded United Artists for just such reasons). Steve McQueen had joined them in 1971. Dustin must have believed he was getting into an operation that was made to order for his collaborative dreams, and he understood and accepted the ground rules for participation. He would have to forgo the up front money—anywhere from one to two million!—he could now command per picture, and in its place receive instead a percentage of the profits as his financial reward, as well as "total creative control" over the pictures he worked on, including *final cut*, so long as he brought in a color film of not more than two hours, ten minutes, on or under the arranged budget, and according to the shooting schedule agreed upon, with himself in a starring or co-starring role.

"Within that simple framework," he happily announced to *Variety*'s Dale Pollock, "you could literally do anything you wanted to do. It was very exciting to be a painter, and not just a color on a palette." But the paintings would be smeared by the gallery owners, and the dream would turn into a nightmare. After forming First Artists amid much fanfare, those artists then did next to nothing to make their venture work as they had hoped it would. There was little interaction between them, and they quickly turned the business of running the company over to some of the same people who have traditionally run the movie business—a strange irony, since the reason for forming First Artists in the first place had been to get away from those very people!

Hoffman had hoped that his first film for First Artists might be an Ingmar Bergman picture, but the people running First Artists objected because Bergman films do not traditionally make much money: right then and there, Dustin knew he was in trouble. For one thing, their corporation had suddenly changed its image: moving more into the conglomerate category as, according to *The New York Times*, it became "publicly owned with interests in records and television as well as in movies." Ironically, the stars who had founded First Artists to create a greater artistic freedom for themselves were shortly reduced to mere stockholders in an ever-growing monolith and Hoffman, alone among them, wasn't even that—seeing as, having joined in only for artistic and not at all for economic reasons, he had failed even to pick up his stock options, and they had expired.

In February, 1978—some six years after joining—Dustin filed a $30 million-plus lawsuit against First Artists, its president Phil Feldman, and the distributing company, Warner Brothers, for seizing creative control of his two films, *Straight Time* and *Agatha*, from him. He insisted he had worked on those pictures virtually without pay because of the appealing promise of creative control, which had been denied him when he was not allowed to make crucial shooting decisions or to exercise final cut. Hoffman sought but lost a preliminary injunction to halt the distribution of *Agatha* by Warner Brothers. Then, in October of that year, First Artists filed a cross-complaint against him, arguing that he had "refused and neglected" to prepare a final cut of *Straight Time*, thus "forcing" them to take over this responsibility; that he refused to prepare the advertising and publicity materials for the films; that he made disparaging remarks about the pictures to numerous members of the press in an attempt to sabotage the films at the box office; that he had shot the film *Agatha* in "bad faith"

and with "improper motives" since the original script had contained no male part large enough to be considered "starring" or even "co-starring," and that he had refused to do the final looping (post-production dubbing of his voice onto the soundtrack), making it virtually impossible to ready the picture for completion and distribution.

First Artists sought an injunction to stop Hoffman from working on *Kramer vs. Kramer* for Columbia, in order to force him to return to work on the looping of *Agatha,* but they were as disappointed by the court as he had been in receiving an injunction against them. It's worth noting that Dustin never operated in quite the same manner as the other First Artists stars. They were all signed for three pictures apiece, he for only two; they were all to receive 10 percent of the gross receipts from their pictures, while his would be 12½ percent; they were entitled to 33⅓ percent of net profits, he to 43⅓ percent. Like the others, he was allowed to pick a member of the Board of Directors to First Artists and he named Jarvis Astaire, his business manager. Dustin began to believe that, after attaining this position, Astaire had operated out of loyalty to the company rather than to him, and was perfectly willing to make decisions against Dustin's best interests and in favor of the firm on whose board he now sat.

The major court case of *Hoffman vs. First Artists* has not been settled at the time of this writing, but it promises to become the most significant legal landmark case involving a movie star and a film company since Bette Davis went to court with Warner Brothers in the 1930's in her own maverick rebellion against being forced to appear in patently bad films according to the dictates of her long-term contract with them. A key word in Hoffman's suit is "conspiracy"; he charges that Astaire joined with company president Phil Feldman and First Artists to take his films away from him, and one either sympathizes with Hoffman's self-conception as an innocent victim at the mercy of cold corporate businessmen or conceives of him as a paranoid who cannot understand that they were perfectly willing to allow him indulgence in artistic freedom so long as they could do so without creating a dangerous financial bottom-line situation. Though Hoffman had signed a contract which did clearly specify that First Artists had a legal right to take the films away under certain circumstances, his case rests in part on his insistence that Phil Feldman had privately sworn to him on several occasions that Dustin need not worry about those clauses concerning shooting schedules and budgets, verbally promising that under *no* circumstances would the films be taken away.

"I learned not to trust anybody," Hoffman later said. But director Ulu Grosbard, who no longer speaks to Dustin since the completion of *Straight Time*, has only harsh words: "Dustin is a professional victim," he told *The New York Times*, "and when you put yourself in that position, you can make preemptive strikes against everyone and feel morally righteous. I think he *does* sincerely care about quality, but that's not a license for his behavior." Naturally, Hoffman's attorney, Bertram Fields, paints Dustin as a wronged martyr and crusading hero: "The Studios have an enormous amount of economic power. If you don't stand up and fight, you lose your rights. Mr. Hoffman is standing up and fighting." Dustin announced publicly: "It is a major disappointment, but both from being in the driver's seat, and in disappointment, you learn a great deal. I wouldn't trade the experience."

In other words, he learned from those two semi-disastrous film experiences how to go about getting the collaborative control he wanted; and having learned that, he was able to get first *Kramer* and then *Tootsie* done the way he wanted. And that is basic to the Hoffman character: why he not only survives, but survives with dignity. Years earlier, on the verge of Broadway stardom, he must have felt the world was coming to an end when hospitalization for burns caused the long-sought-after role to go to someone else. But it was only by being free then that he got his famed role in *Journey* and, on the basis of that, *The Graduate*—and everything since. Likewise, *Kramer* might never have been made—or, at least, made so successfully, and with Dustin getting pretty much the collaborative input he wanted—had it not been for the First Artists disappointments. In addition, he learned even more from *Kramer* and received even more collaborative power and responsibility on *Tootsie*. Though he may have been temporarily beaten, and beaten badly at that, in the long run he has not been defeated; indeed, it was only by experiencing the temporary beatings that he learned how to achieve his final victory, which he always seems to achieve in the end. The experience with First Artists must have, at the time, felt like an emotional Custer's Last Stand, but Dustin—much like his creation, Jack Crabb—proved to be a survivor.

His situation may have changed over the years—his status, his income—but his basic personality has not. He is, as always, an inveterate observer. Some friends insist Dustin never relaxes—that even while walking down the street, engaged in a simple conversation, he is hard at work, observing everyone who passes by, cataloging mannerisms, walks, gestures, speech patterns in his mind for future use in some film or play. That sometimes distresses Dustin, making him feel he is not "living in the moment" as fully as he should be. In the old days, while working odd jobs in New York, he was already, as Aimee Lee Ball once put it, busily "studying people, storing away mannerisms and behaviors like a cache for the winter, boning up on human misery and comedy and eccentricity for some once-and-future use in his work." According to Dustin, "I figure that if an actor can find the personal rhythm of the character he's creating, he's home free. And one of the best ways to do that is to follow a person down the street, unbeknownst to him. Pick up his walk, imitate it and continue it, even after he's out of sight. As you're doing it, observe what's happening to you. By zeroing in on a guy's personal rhythm, you'll find that you've become a different person."

Besides observing people in general, Dustin likes to research more specifically. For *Midnight Cowboy*, he hung around Times Square with the derelicts for several weeks before shooting; before the filming of *All the President's Men* began, he spent three months tagging after a Washington *Post* investigative reporter in order to fully understand the style of procedure; prior to starring in *Straight Time*, he had himself smuggled into the yard at San Quentin where, incognito, he literally became one with the convicts for an afternoon; with *Tootsie*, the unhappy early years of his own acting career provided him with all the research he needed to play the desperate difficult performer. Fans and friends speak highly of his desire for total authenticity; those more critical of Dustin consider it an attempt to legitimize his natural propensity toward voyeurism in the name of "art."

"A good actor," Dustin says, "is always working. In the back of your mind, you are thinking, even at a time when you have your own sense of grief, "this is something I can *use* at some future point." It's as if you were recording it, watching it happen, like a writer recording dialogue." For Dustin, a classic case of this happened in Boston in 1965. He and another young actor were invited by the lady who ran the theater in which they worked to come to her home for afternoon tea. It was a most civilized affair until her overly jealous husband returned home unexpectedly, saw the two young men there with his wife, pulled out a pistol and pointed it at them. When the man ordered both the stunned young actors to stand up, Dustin quickly slipped behind his friend and, wherever the boy moved, darted constantly behind him, again and again, until the man was at last disarmed by his wife. All the while, in addition to being terrified at the thought that this was it, and beyond the Keatonish comedy routine he was unwittingly improvising, there was a part of him that was busily filing the entire experience away in a compartment of his actor's memory bank, to draw upon at some future point in time when he would need to psychologically lock with an experience in his past in order to make a screen or stage character come vividly to life.

No actor/star of our time has ever attempted such a varied cast of characters in the canon of his performances, much less managed to carry most all of them through effectively. Psychologically *linking* to those characters—isolating and objectifying elements of his own self that are

Dustin and Sydney Pollack discuss an upcoming scene during the shooting of *Tootsie*.

present in the various characters, and correlating previous experiences of his own to those of the characters in question—he has created performances that are clearly "personal" even if they are just as clearly not "autobiographical." All the aspects of Dustin's personality discussed here, as well as all the significant experiences—the un-pleasant as well as the joyous—have in some way gone into his creations, those remarkable people he has brought to life onscreen over the years. This, then, has been an interpretation of the man behind the movies; here now are the movies that express the man.

THE FILMS

The Tiger Makes Out

A Columbia Pictures Presentation   1967

"The Tiger" (Eli Wallach) feels shoved aside by modern society.

CAST:

Eli Wallach *(Ben)*; Anne Jackson *(Gloria)*; Bob Dishy *(Jerry)*; John Harkins *(Leo)*; Ruth White *(Mrs. Kelly)*; Roland Wood *(Mr. Kelly)*; Rae Allen *(Beverly)*; Sudie Bond *(Miss Lane)*; David Burns *(Mr. Ratner)*; Bibi Osterwald *(Mrs. Ratner)*; Charles Nelson Reilly *(Registrar)*; David Doyle *(Housing Clerk)*; Dustin Hoffman *(Hap)*.

CREDITS:

Director, Arthur Hiller; screenplay, Murray Schisgal from his one-act play *The Tiger*; producer, George Justin; director of photography, Arthur J. Ornitz; music composed and conducted by Milton (Shorty) Rogers; editor, Robert C. Jones; running time, 94 minutes.

Anne Jackson and Bob Dishy find life in suburbia is less than bliss.

Dustin first met Murray Schisgal in 1966, when as an as yet unknown he was working in the Stockbridge, Massachusetts, theatre where one of Schisgal's plays was being performed in summer stock. The author came up to catch a rehearsal, felt an instinctual respect and immediate sense of emotional kinship for an inventive young actor in the cast, and a friendship quickly blossomed. After achieving movie stardom, Dustin immediately returned to live theatre in Schisgal's semi-musical *Jimmy Shine*, and later directed Schisgal's *All Over Town* with Cleavon Little. In real life, Hoffman and Schisgal appear a bit like a Laurel and Hardy team—the playwright being big and burly, the actor short and slim. They not only enjoy working together but have travelled extensively as a twosome, buying each other antique Americana for their respective collections.

What they share, essentially, is a view of the world best expressed in Schisgal's plays where he exhibits, in his own words, "the ability to make a world that is just a little off center," or in other words to show those of us who mistakenly choose to view the world as moving straight ahead and right on course the way things *really* run. Schisgal's is a vision of reality Hoffman shares, and that shared vision has always been at the heart of their warm friendship.

It strikes one as purposeful and pleasant, then, that Hoffman made his film debut (if an extremely abbreviated one) in a movie written by Schisgal, and in a project brought to the screen through the perseverance of talented people who had previously been "burned" by their experiences with Hollywood movies. *The Tiger* was originally half of a double bill of short plays (*The Typists* and *The Tiger*) which dealt, through the conventions of dark comedy, with the twin themes of conformity and individualism: *The Typists* concerned people who walk through their daily existences—and, beyond that, their entire lives—as office typists without ever comprehending each other's potential as a human being; *The Tiger* complemented that play perfectly by dealing with a neurotic malcontent who refuses to slip into just such a lifestyle. Though a popular hit off-Broadway, the brevity of the plays rendered their movie potential negligible. But Schisgal's next work—*Luv*, which brought him at last to Broadway—a full-length production, was soon snapped up for a possible film project.

Schisgal had toyed with the idea of fighting for artistic input, then finally gave up and sold *Luv* for the most money he could get—which was a lot. He would later regret that decision: Eli Wallach and his wife Anne Jackson, who had been the stars of the Broadway production, were dropped, as was the critically acclaimed Alan Arkin; instead, the film was restructured by some Hollywood hacks as a routine Jack Lemmon comedy vehicle in order to make it more "commercial"—the sad irony being it proved both a box office and critical dud. In order to enact some sweet revenge, the Wallachs bought Schisgal's short piece, *The Tiger*, hired Schisgal himself to flesh it out into a full length screen-

play, and produced it themselves at a cost of about $700,000. And while the film was not a smash hit by a long shot, the picture was none-theless made so cheaply it was nearly impossible to lose money; Schisgal and the Wallachs—as well as a bit player in the cast named Dustin Hoffman—derived great pleasure from seeing a Schisgal story brought to the screen with his vision intact.

The "tiger" of the title is Ben Harris (Eli Wallach), a middle-aged Greenwich Village mail-man, a semi-crazed character who bitterly insists life has dealt him a raw deal. When not working his route, Ben hides out in his basement apart-ment where he continues to pay rent to a former owner of the building—though the current owner now uses Ben's place as a storage room. Harris is a self-educated semi-intellectual and inveterate lecher who froths at the mouth when-ever he thinks of the superficial sexuality of the

The Tiger strikes again!

56

society around him, and is frustrated by the apparent fact he is the only man in Manhattan whom the sexual revolution has passed by.

In time, his path will cross that of Gloria Fiske (Anne Jackson), who at first seems as normal as Harris is odd, but whose middle-class existence is suffocating her. Husband Jerry (Bob Dishy) fights her decision to return to college and pick up a degree so she can do some useful and interesting work, and her appointment with the N.Y.U. Dean of Admissions (Charles Nelson Reilly) only proves totally frustrating. As she wanders back onto the New York street, uncertain where her future will take her, she discovers the answer to that question when she is kidnapped by Ben. For he has vowed to stop acting like an angry mouse and rather turn himself into a "tiger" by making off with one of those oversexed, mini-skirted teenieboppers but accidentally absconds with the equally distressed Gloria.

Rather than animal sex without commitment, what Ben finds is someone he can talk to, and as each challenges the other's values, they in the end touch one another deeply.

The short play opened at that point in the story when Ben carries the struggling woman into his apartment to discover—to his initial dismay—he has not made off with a sexy swinger but an equally troubled, equally frustrated, equally middle-aged person. For the film, Schisgal necessarily invented a series of episodes in which the backgrounds of Ben and Gloria are effectively established, creating sequences which ring with the wit for which he is famous: many of the vignettes are comic gems, loaded with Schisgal's humorously perceptive observations about the neuroticism of even seemingly normal people. But as the story progresses it becomes ever more clear that Schisgal's dialogue—theatrical in the finest sense of the

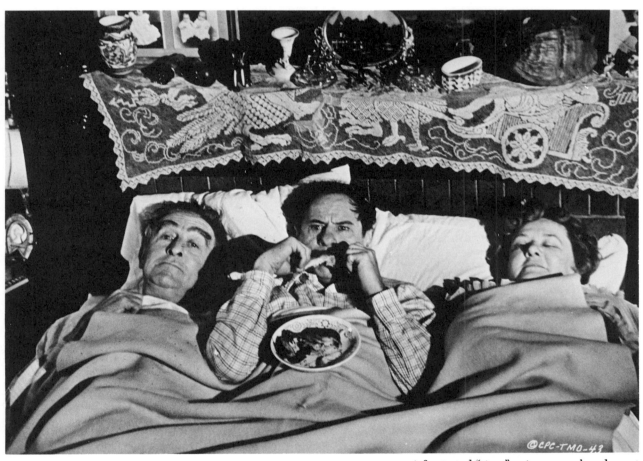

A frustrated "tiger" enjoys a snack and a rest.

term—sounds less suited to the screen than it did to the stage. And while this is first-rate Schisgal, done in the most uncompromising manner possible, the entire affair still comes off as a project that was more at home off-Broadway than it is on the motion picture screen. In addition, Arthur Hiller directed in such a manner that the film's style—its visual scheme, its pacing and rhythm—all call attention to the fact it is a stage play transferred (if never quite translated) to the screen.

A little more than a third of the way through the story, Wallach sets his sights on a pretty girl whose boyfriend is just then breaking up with her. The boyfriend is Dustin Hoffman, and though his character's name is never clearly heard in the film, he is listed as "Hap" in the credits. He appears for approximately thirty seconds, and he is not the dramatic focus of attention in the scene. Wallach is the observer, watching as Hoffman rejects the girl who will shortly become the temporary object of Wallach's attentions. "It's no good anymore, Rosie," Hoffman wails. "You mope around the house." "I'm not going to anymore," she insists pathetically. "It's just no good, Rosie," he continues. "You fill me with *guilt*." She desperately attempts to hang on: "I'm not asking you to marry me! I'm perfectly content to go on living with you under the original terms. We split all the expenses and live together. What's so terrible about that?" "What's so terrible?" he grimaces. "I'm the one who has to carry the *guilt* around. *I'm* the guilty one. Goodbye, Rosie Kriger."

Despite the brevity of Hoffman's moment, and despite the fact his role is intended more as a dramatic device than even a cameo character (he is there to provide the necessary bridge between Ben Harris and Rosie Kriger), Dustin managed to make the moment his, at the same time adding a more complex emotional depth to the scene than one might guess possible. For we are at once offended by Hap's coldness and unwillingness to show Rosie any feelings and at the same time sense his reaction is not entirely unmotivated. And while it would be pretentious to force a "personal expression" interpretation on so slight a role as Hap, it is nonetheless notable that in Dustin's first film, he played a man who

has power over women despite his average looks, and also is a person suffering from a strong sense of guilt—guilt all-encompassing but unspecified. Dustin's reign as a New York ladies' man is pretty much legendary, as is his intense sense of personal guilt over nothing in particular. Even in a role as relatively insignificant as this one in his premiere film, one senses he drew upon certain qualities within himself in order to make the character he played onscreen (however briefly) come vividly, if only momentarily, to life.

Naturally, the critics didn't mention Dustin in their reviews, but concentrated on whether or not the stage-to-film transition worked so far as they were concerned. In *Variety*, "Murf" argued that it did not: "Beware of the one-act play with apparent screen 'possibilities,' " he warned, calling it a "distended, uneven pic" and insisting that "Schisgal's screenplay in essence tacks on a long preceeding act, and an artificial closing bit." Similarly, David Austen in the journal *Films and Filming* concluded that "When Eli Wallach and Anne Jackson originally toured with this two-character stage play . . . it did tend to get somewhat lost in the vastness of such auditoriums as the Golden Green Hippodrome. There was every chance to improve on this trouble when it was adapted to the screen. However, it now gets a little dissipated with an over-enlarged cast . . . and suffocated by a camera which rarely backs away from large close-ups."

More often, though, the critics turned thumbs up. In the *Hollywood Reporter*, John Mahoney argued it was "Not a film for everyone—it may knock some attitudes out of joint—there is an audience which will identify with its bizarre, yet recognizable types and events as to the careening insanities of Mack Sennett." For Mandel Herbstman in *The Film Daily*, "It moves from incident to incident with a wild and zestful rhythm. . . . Discriminating audiences will find outstanding entertainment in the offering." Dale Munroe in the Los Angeles *Herald Examiner* said that "Schisgal's humor is rather like olives, an acquired taste . . . a painful reality that intrigues the spectator at the outset and holds his interest, sometimes against his will. throughout," while Kevin Thomas in the Los Angeles

Times claimed, "the way *The Tiger Makes Out* captivates an audience contains an objective lesson on how to turn a short play into a full length film." Bosley Crowther in *The New York Times* noted that "Schisgal is smacking with a slapstick of his own adroit device at the cliches of modern cultivation and the pomposities of bourgeois social grace," and in the *Motion Picture Herald*, Richard Gertner proclaimed it "A witty satire on modern day conformity, brightly acted . . . a delightful treat for sophisticated adults. To others it will probably seem pointless and absurd."

Eli Wallach and Anne Jackson move toward a meaningful relationship.

The Tiger makes out . . . but not quite the way he expected.

The Graduate

Released by Embassy Pictures   1967

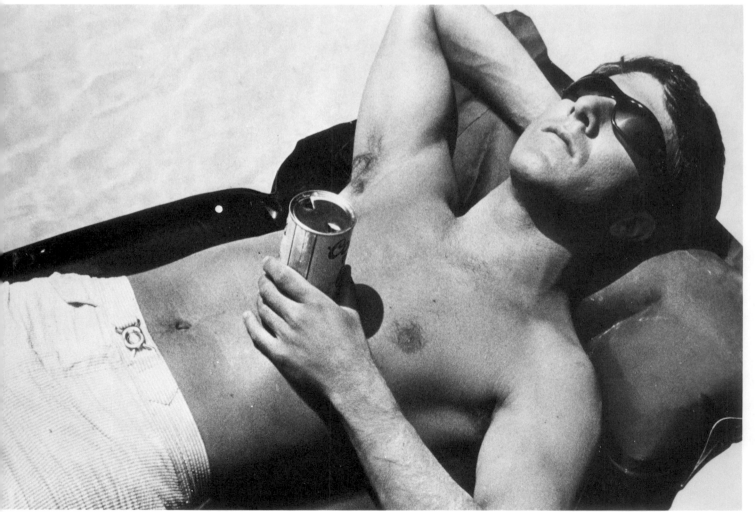

Dustin Hoffman as Ben—"floating."

CAST:

Anne Bancroft *(Mrs. Robinson);* Dustin Hoffman *(Benjamin Braddock);* Katharine Ross *(Elaine Robinson);* William Daniels *(Mr. Braddock);* Murray Hamilton *(Mr. Robinson);* Elizabeth Wilson *(Mrs. Braddock);* Brian Avery *(Carl Smith);* Walter Brooke *(Mr. Maguire);* Norman Fell *(Mr. McLeery);* Elizabeth Fraser *(Lady No. 2);* Alice Ghostley *(Mrs. Singleman);* Buck Henry *(Desk Clerk);* Marion Lorne *(Miss De Witt);* Richard Dreyfuss *(Student).*

CREDITS:

Director, Mike Nichols; screenplay by Calder Willingham and Buck Henry, based on the novel by Charles Webb; produced by Lawrence Turman; presented by Joseph E. Levine; music by Simon and Garfunkel; running time, 105 minutes.

After working off-Broadway in what was always a relaxed, family-style atmosphere, Dustin was shocked to find the Hollywood procedure something else entirely. What most bothered him was the sense of caste: "You walk into those shrouded studio temples, and nobody talks to the crew," he complained at the time. "And the extras are treated like scum. I got called 'Sir' so many times that I felt as though I were a Kentucky colonel." Besides, shooting a film for Nichols was not an easy experience. The director had never experienced a failure, which was a very different situation from Dustin's, who had lived with constant failure for years. "I never had the feeling he was happy with what I was doing," Dustin observed afterwards. "Oh, he would throw out a cookie occasionally, but I always felt like a disappointment. He walked around the entire time saying, 'Well, we'll never work together again, that's for sure. This is my most important work, and I'm going to get hit. I've done too many new things.' "

Eventually, even the thrill of starring in a major movie wore off, and it became a job—and a hard one at that. One day, Dustin couldn't get his juices going, and was giving Mike Nichols very little of what he has to give. The director took him aside and whispered, "This is the only day we're ever going to shoot this scene, and no matter how exhausted or lousy you feel, I want you to remember that what you give me is going to be on celluloid for people to see forever and ever. I know you're tired, but when you go to see this film, if you don't like your work in this scene, just remember always that this was the day you screwed up." The words went through Dustin like an electric shock; he went back on the set, gave it everything he had, and brought the scene to life.

After the film's release, those young people who thought Dustin was inseparable from Benjamin had no idea of the difficulty he had experienced approaching this role. In no way had he been able to relax and, as everyone assumed, play himself—Benjamin, as written, was that "walking surfboard" he had always been intimidated by. Besides, he was ten years older than the character he portrayed. "I looked at it as a character part, really, and tried to remember how I felt when I was that age back in 1958. I made no attempt at all to give it a feeling of the sixties. I've made a film that exploded, but I'm not responsible."

Now, fifteen years have elapsed since *The Graduate* "exploded" on the nation's theatre screens amid great hoopla and even greater hype; in 1967, the film proved so immediately influential—literally, a cornerstone of a movement in movies—that objective criticism was at first difficult, if not impossible. There was the flurry of early, laudatory reviews from the daily and weekly tabloids that confirmed the mass audience's wildest expectations about the picture. In *The New Yorker*, Brendan Gill called it "one of the liveliest gifts of the season"; in *The New Republic*, Stanley Kauffmann said "*The Graduate* gives some substance to the contention that American films are coming of age." In *Saturday Review*, Hollis Alpert described it as "the freshest, funniest, and most touching film of the year . . . the American film may never be quite the same again"; in *The New York Times*, Bosley Crowther insisted it was "not only one of the best of the year, but also one of the best seriocomic social satires we've had from Hollywood since Preston Sturges was making them."

Quite naturally, there followed more hesitant and analytical reactions in the monthlies and

Dustin Hoffman and Anne Bancroft.

quarterlies, publications which justified their existence by offering their more esoteric readerships voices crying in the wilderness. In *The Nation*, Robert Hatch argued that the film "is consistently funny and frequently ironic, but it lacks the aphoristic wit of Sheridan or Congreve, and as it wears on it forsakes cynicism for chase and begins to resemble more Harold Lloyd than Mayfair dandy." In *Commonweal*, Philip T. Hartung wrote that "the acting throughout is just fine, but one . . . begins to become aware that *The Graduate* is more like a comic strip caricature than a convincing portrait of youth-versus-elders. . . . Director Mike Nichols uses so many clever tricks in photographing all this and the pace is so rapid that the viewer hardly notices that this theme has been covered before by Harold Lloyd and other comedians."

In *The New York Review of Books*, Edgar Z. Friedenberg stated flatly that the film "presents itself as chic, comic social commentary. . . . But it is waxwork detail which the audience is expected to admire and marvel at. And a waxwork is precisely *not* social commentary because the realism is supposed to take the place of historical or political insight . . . even though it captures the look and sound of much of the contemporary California scene so skillfully, *The Graduate* seems to be basically a copout." By year's end, the film journals had their say. A cocky, cagey critic knows full well he can create an immediate reputation by totally devastating a contemporary classic; Stephen Farber and Estelle Changas did precisely that in a *Film Quarterly* article that concludes with the assessment that "The movie as a whole is a Youth-grooving movie for old people . . . bankers and dowagers know that it's 'in' to celebrate the young, and in *The Graduate* they can join the celebration with a minimum of fret. . . . Yet young people are falling for the film along with the old people, because it satisfies their most . . . simplistic notions of the generation gap."

The thrust of the piece—showing up the

Mrs. Robinson corners Ben on the night of his homecoming party.

movie as superficial beneath its shimmering veneer and the masterful timing of its release—rests on their notion of *The Graduate* as "Youth-grooving," just as the earlier rave reviews also derived from this conception—or, more properly put, this misconception. The idea of *The Graduate* as a youth film certainly did not come from Hoffman or Mike Nichols; rather from some desperate Embassy Pictures publicists who found themselves stuck with an offbeat product to sell. All around them, young people were suddenly transforming into self-conscious rebels against The Establishment, as the youth of the late sixties locked into a media-publicized and in some ways media-created Generation Gap conflict with their parents. This social calumny provided the perfect marketing pitch: *The Graduate*, with its tale of a young man who falls into an affair with one of his parent's friends, only to eventually find himself attracted to that woman's daughter, could be packaged and sold as the consummate generation gap tale. Understandably, the marketing technique worked on the public, and was probably more basic to the film's phenomenal success than any inherent qualities in the film itself.

But it's worth noting that when director Nichols spoke about his movie with college students of the time, who asked about the ambiguity of his ending ("But what's going to *happen* to Ben and Elaine?") Nichols shocked and angered his youthful audience by insisting the couple was definitely *not* going off to either make the world at large a better place to live or create the first hippie commune, but would rather "end up just like their parents in five or ten years." Young people wondered if it were possible Nichols didn't know his own characters, didn't comprehend the revolutionary statement his film made. Nichols, in fact, knew his characters full well—enough to separate them as they exist in the film as apart from the characters as they exist in the aura created *around* the film.

Nichols made absolutely no attempt to turn Benjamin Braddock into a representation of the youth of the late sixties, though he does work in a series of complex ways to *remove* Benjamin as much as possible *from* the youth of his time. Though initially hailed as a liberating break-

64

Mrs. Robinson waits for Ben at the bar.

through in film technique and later lambasted as displaying about as much depth as a Pepsi commercial, the movie's camerawork is completely functional at conveying the alienation of Ben not only from his elders but also from his colleagues. The opening shot provides a close-up image of Ben's face, then zooms out to reveal he is in a plane, surrounded by people of varying ages; at the outset, the point is made visually that even when surrounded by others, he is still alone. At the film's end, the reverse procedure is employed: we see Ben and Elaine on a bus full of people, but after revealing the couple in a two-shot, the camera then closes in on Benjamin's face to isolate him once again, insisting even after winning away the woman he wants from another man he is *still* alone. In between these two framing shots, further evidence of Ben's "aloneness" abound. During the title sequence,

for instance, Benjamin—having departed from the airplane that's carried him from an Eastern college back to California—rides the moving ramp into the lobby, and we view him as a singular figure again, as the camera slips in to isolate his image onscreen even though we know, from his context, he is surrounded by others.

It is in his room, the physical manifestation of the self he escapes into, that Mrs. Robinson (Bancroft) pursues him, and their first encounter is shot through a fishbowl into which Ben is staring, studying the occupants as he will shortly be studied himself when his father (William Daniels) makes him test out a new diving suit in their pool. As we share his plight through a point-of-view shot which forces us to view the world from his narrow focus, Ben submerges to the bottom of the pool—remaining there, so far

as we get to see, indefinitely. Realistically speaking, he must surface sooner or later; but by not allowing us to witness this act, we are implicitly led to understand that on some level, Ben never surfaces from that experience. The notion of a pane of glass (with water serving as a substitute symbol) which invisibly but irretrievably separates Ben not just from the older generation but from all normal human contact is repeated throughout the picture. As he makes plans for his first fling with Mrs. Robinson, Ben telephones her in the hotel bar from a booth only a few feet away to say he has the room key, as she—and we—see him peering from behind the glass of the booth; when at the end he arrives at the church where Elaine Robinson (Ross) is being married, he once again is separated from the object of his desire by a pane of glass—paralleling the glass that separates him from Mrs. Robinson, therebye suggesting the Elaine-Benjamin coupling will in the end prove no more satisfying than the Mrs. Robinson-Benjamin coupling did.

In addition, there are the constant visual reminders of Ben's unquestioning acceptance of the affluent upper-middle class lifestyle associated with his parents. He is throughout the neatest looking young person onscreen, and on his first visit to the Taft hotel for the Robinson affair, he is accepted without hesitation at a formal party he wanders into semi-accidentally, simply because he looks the proper Southern Californian. As Ben floats on the raft in his father's pool, sipping a can of beer and wearing dark wrap-around sun glasses that signal his unwillingness to make even eye contact with anyone or anything outside himself, he provides us with the most *passive* persona possible—and a total contrast to the youth of the late sixties which, if it could be identified by any single word concept, was certainly *activist*. In fact, on his first date with Elaine at a drive-in restaurant, the couple find themselves surrounded by typically hippie-ish youth, listening to loud rock music; rather than appearing at one with them, Benjamin orders—rather than requests—they turn the radio down. And when they ignore him, he pulls up the convertible top on his Alfa Romeo, isolating himself and Elaine from the young people of their time.

The music itself is important: one reason Benjamin was widely interpreted as a generational hero was the musical score by Simon and Garfunkel which, according to most critics, leant the film a sense of timeliness by employing then-currently popular songs instead of a more conventional soundtrack. Actually, the S and G songs were *not* current hits, but golden oldies from the recent past; soft folk ballads ("Sounds of Silence," "Scarborough Fair,") of the type that had been popular just *before* the folk-rock psychedelic sound eased such softer music off the air. The songs the hippies at the burger stand are listening to ("Big Green Pleasure Machine") and which is associated with them, not Ben, is strikingly different in style from all the other S and G songs in the picture, sounding as though it were devised as a satire on such songs.

Though Benjamin exists in a world of his own making, he walks through two distinct worlds—Beverly Hills in the film's first half, the Berkeley campus in the second, and while the two can certainly be taken as symbols of the political poles of the late sixties culture-conflict, what is significant is that Ben is equally oblivious to both. When he checks in at an off-campus rooming house in order to be near Elaine, the proprietor (Norman Fell) confronts him with 'You're not one of those outside agitators?" Ben doesn't so much deny being one as he appears uncomprehending as to what the man is even alluding to. Any of the students we see here would make far better representational figures of the new youth—they are both bearded and beaded.

Also important here is Ben's age. We witness his twenty-first birthday party: an aging boy or a young man, Ben is both and neither, not so much caught in the crunch of the Generation Gap as left out of it entirely. The point is driven home further by the pivotal scene in which Benjamin goes to the Taft Hotel for the first fling with Mrs. Robinson. As he opens the front door, Ben finds himself stuck holding it for a seemingly endless string of old people, an image which caused many critics at the time to perceive the film as a Generation Gap statement. The point

is, that is only *half* of the sequence; for when the old people finally do pass, a group of young people whiz by Ben from the opposite direction, and he is as excluded from their company as he was by the older generation.

But if the movie is not about what both its admirers and detractors have always agreed upon that it is about, what then *is* it about? Certainly something far less contemporary and more classical in its impact. When Mrs. Robinson first attempts to seduce Ben he fights her off, but only one scene later, we see him in a phone booth (his fish bowl again) desperately attempting to arrange a date. What transpires between those two moments must then be interpreted as supplying his motivation for making that call, and the only sequence onscreen between the two scenes is a conversation between Ben and Mr. Robinson, in which the man tells Ben, among other things: "In many ways, I feel as though you were *my* son!" It is, later, Mr. Robinson who mouths to Ben all those cliches we expect his father to tell him, Mr. Robinson who sees Ben as the young heir apparent "guarding the old castle," Mr. Robinson who whispers to Ben that he ought to "sow a few wild oats."

Later, then, the famous shot which carries Ben from his pool raft into a room of his own house that magically blends into the hotel room where he walks past Mrs. Robinson appears something more than merely a trendy transitional device when one realizes that at poolside Ben's mother was present, and during our view of Mrs. Robinson in what has metamorphosed into the hotel room, it's easy to momentarily think this is Ben's mother walking past him. Later, we are manipulated into an opposite confusion between the two women: as Ben stands shaving with the bathroom door ajar, we briefly assume it is Mrs. Robinson who appears next to him, then are mildly surprised to discover it is Ben's mother. Mrs. Braddock leaves the room, and Ben calls after her: "Wait—wait a minute, please!" But in mid-sentence, the scene blends once again, without warning, and though his sentence starts as an address to his mother in their home, it ends as an address to Mrs. Robinson in the hotel room. There is, under the bright chatter and slick surface of the film, a discom-

Mr. Robinson (Murray Hamilton) takes a "fatherly" approach to Ben's problems.

On his first trip to the hotel, Ben is ushered into a catered affair—but slips away to initiate his own "affair."

At the hotel bar, Ben and Mrs. Robinson discuss their upcoming indiscretion.

forting but intriguing sense of the tragic: this is no superficial comedy of modern sexual manners but an Oedipal myth played out in modern dress.

Even this important undercurrent fails to convey the full dramatic power of Ben's doomed affair with Mrs. Robinson and subsequent pursuit of Elaine. The relationship between mother and daughter is cemented by the device Mrs. Robinson employs to lure Ben upstairs at her home: the portrait of Elaine. Ben is noticeably unenamoured with her image, despite the fact that this painting not only captures the surface of Elaine's physical beauty but even idealizes it. Only later, when by accident the subject of Elaine arises during one of the hotel trysts, does Ben begin to show an interest:

MRS. ROBINSON: Don't talk about Elaine—

BENJAMIN: Why not? Tell me—why is she a *taboo* subject all of a sudden? (provocatively) Well, I guess I'll have to ask her out on a date and find out—

MRS. ROBINSON: Don't you *ever!*

BENJAMIN: (reasurringly) I have no intention . . .(hesitantly)Well, why *shouldn't* I?

Mrs. Robinson creates the attraction she fears by trying to deny even the remotest possibility of its existence. And when the first date transforms itself from an unpleasant experience into a delightful one, Ben tells the girl: "Elaine, I *like* you—I like you *so* much!"

The key to the meaning is that although he's apparently sincere, we have seen absolutely nothing that legitimizes his emotions: she appears only a pretty, superficial simp. Critics of the film have picked out this scene for attack, labelling it bad romantic drama, though this is in fact the moment that establishes Nichols' intentions. For it is not Elaine herself, but the impossibility of the entire situation with her that Benjamin is drawn to. Significantly, Ben cannot even discriminate between the two Robinson women: for the following day, as he drives through the

68

In their hotel room, Ben helps Mrs. Robinson undress . . .

. . . and then she finishes the job herself.

rain to the Robinson home and a woman's figure appears at the door of his car, even the audience has realized it is not Elaine but Mrs. Robinson before Benjamin does.

Notably, then, it is Ben who tells Elaine about the affair, for this is something he has been chafing at the bit to do—long before Mrs. Robinson threatened to tell Elaine herself. It is only by telling Elaine that Ben can achieve what he has been aiming at all along: he reduces himself to an observer. At this point, *The Graduate* becomes a case study of obsessive behavior. Ben drives by Elaine's house, taking both painful pleasure and pleasurable pain in seeing her but not being seen by her. And for as long as Elaine remains at home, this observation becomes Benjamin's life, or rather his unhealthy substitute for living. But when Ben notices Elaine being driven off to Berkeley by her father, everything changes. Since he can no longer lose himself in his preoccupation—the object of his *attentions* more than his *affections* being removed—he must necessarily act, though in a manner every bit as perverse as his previous inaction.

Benjamin's obsession grows in direct proportion to the apparent impossibility of achieving Elaine: he does not try to whisk Elaine off in the manner of a traditional hero in love. In fact, on the Berkeley campus, Ben does not approach Elaine at all, but rather resumes his observation of her from hiding—resumes playing out his obsession, rushing away whenever there is the possibility of being discovered. When Ben finally does approach her it is only when Elaine is totally out of her own element, and completely in his—travelling, in this case on a bus. From the very first shot of the film, it is Ben who has been associated with various modes of travel: the jet airliner that returns him to California, the sports car he zips everywhere in, the raft on which he drifts aimlessly, even the bus on which he (and Elaine) are travelling in the film's final shot. Elaine not only flatly rejects Ben, but does so in front of Carl Smith, a conventionally handsome man she's clearly more than mildly involved with. There now appears no way even a character as persistent as Ben can continue his obsession.

Necessarily, then, it is Elaine who at this point makes sure the obsession does not die, for she shows up unexpectedly, unannounced at Ben's room. The first time she does, he is shaving—an image previously associated with Ben's mother at a time when she was becoming confused with Mrs. Robinson, so that the shaving device ties all three women together for the first time. The next time Elaine enters Ben's apartment, she wakes him from a deep sleep—though by all appearances it is the middle of the afternoon.

The situation itself defines Benjamin: he is not living so much as sleepwalking/daydreaming his way through life in the most extreme and also most negative connotation of that term, consumed by his impossible dream of Elaine, whose name suggests she perhaps ought to be analyzed in relationship to Elaine, the Lilly Maid of Astelot in Arthurian legend. Ben is surely no Lancelot (at least not yet, though he will wield a cross like a broadsword by the movie's end) but more of a Don Quixote, travelling not through the world of his time like Lancelot but, like Quixote, through a dream world. In essence, the movie is *about* dreaming; moreover, about Ben's growing desire to turn the dream into viable reality.

But this he cannot accomplish without the cooperation of Elaine. Before she leaves, the girl drifts back into the room—more as women do in men's dreams than in men's realities—and, flirtatiously, asks him: "Will you kiss me?" The intense, immediate reaction of repulsion to his obsession has completely passed; noticeably, she is disturbed (but not unpleasantly) by his obsession and, when she kisses him, we see her clearly encouraging it, becoming a co-creator of it. As we will soon see, she does not love Benjamin—the *real* Benjamin—any more than Ben really loves her, though doubtless that is what each must surely believe about their own emotions for the other in order to legitimize those emotions to themselves:

> BENJAMIN: Marry me?
> ELAINE: (dreamily) I don't know . . .
> BENJAMIN: You *might*? You *might* marry me?
> ELAINE: (mildly encouraging) I might . . .

The dreamlike way in which she moves, speaks, and gazes at him tell us that in no way does she

At home, Ben shaves and finds the presence of his mother turning into a reminder of Mrs. Robinson.

Ben runs into the Robinson house and, rain-soaked, reveals his relationship with Mrs. Robinson to Elaine (Katharine Ross).

The landlord orders Ben out of his house.

The landlord (Norman Fell) finds Elaine in Ben's room as he shaves—an echo of the earlier shaving sequence.

71

Ben and Mrs. Robinson argue over Elaine's upcoming marriage.

hesitate because of any lingering bitterness or moral preoccupation over Ben's previous affair with her mother. She is in a state of rapture, as is he, over the purgatory they have fashioned. Never in the film does either appear so blissful, so entranced. Elaine becomes so adept at manipulating his fantasy—at first accepting, then totally embracing, his obsession—that she ultimately appears far more unhealthy than he. "Good God!" he mutters afterwards, and with good reason, having sparked the object of his neuroses into a grander, greater neuroses than even he was capable of imagining.

The Berkeley background then dissolves behind Ben and Elaine, as only their shared obsession counts. On a daily basis he proposes, and her ever more unlikely, untenable reasons for rejecting him elicit ever stranger comments from Ben:

BENJAMIN: Marry me today?
ELAINE: (flippantly) I just don't think it would work out.
BENJAMIN: (doggedly) Tomorrow?

All at once she is cool and casual again, as though such a mysterious change in mood might be needed to keep the obsession fresh and alive: he the masochist, she the sadist, they make a perfect pair in their glorious misery. Then she introduces an entirely new dimension by announcing the need to speak to Carl: "Oh, I said I might marry him," she calmly admits. And once more, we must reassess everything we have thus far thought and felt about the character. Rather than a slick, sappy story of modern day true love, the film is a put down of youthful romanticism, a pessimistic appraisal of it:

BENJAMIN: Are we getting married tomorrow?
ELAINE: No.
BENJAMIN: Day after?
ELAINE: I don't know . . . maybe we are . . . maybe we're not.

This sequence is filmed as in a dream—as if Elaine hadn't so much woken Ben that time in his room as she slipped into the dream he was dreaming. Finally, though, Elaine ceases to be the somnambulist long enough to let Benjamin know she ultimately wants a Lancelot, not a Quixote: "Why don't you just drag me off if you want to marry me so badly?" she asks testily.

At this point, Elaine abruptly stops being the woman that exists in Ben's imagination and now it is Benjamin who must enter into Elaine's dream of him. When he discovers she has left to marry Carl, we hear only the first words of her goodbye message: "I know what I'm doing is the best thing for you . . ." On one level the words provide the arch cliche, the ultimate Dear John

letter; in the film's unique context, though, it is a reminder of the challenge, and Ben accepts it on this level. The "best thing" for him is not to disappear from her life but rather to remember her request to "drag me off," make her fantasy a reality.

So Benjamin's "quest" continues—and the onetime Quixote/Benjamin, now the Lancelot/Benjamin, catches up with his Holy Grail—his Elaine of Astalot—where a grail is of course to be found, in a church. In the book he arrives just before the marriage and spirits Elaine away in the nick of time. Nichols' change is a drastic one:

Ben arrives at the church too late to stop the ceremony from taking place.

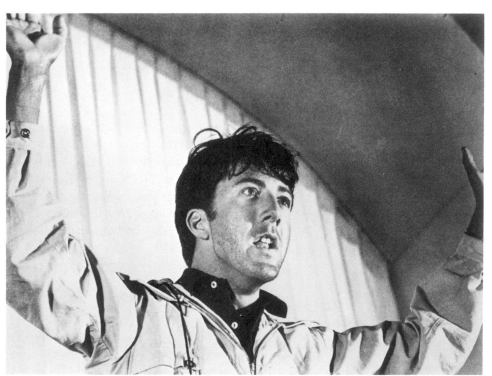

The hopeless Ben appears momentarily crucified at the back of the church.

Tug of war: Mrs. Robinson and Ben fight for Elaine . . .

as Ben rushes in, he witnesses the completion of the ceremony, sees Elaine kissing the groom—without regret, with a smile of pure contentment on her face. She is more impossible than ever—thus, more desirable than ever.

Lost in the grip of his old fantasy, he screams out her name. And now, the two fantasies—his and hers—at last come together. Hearing him, she turns, dreamlike, zombie-ish, the unwilling slave of a man who can make her fantasy a reality. "Why don't you just drag me off . . ." she earlier asked him. Now, at the most impossible—therefore, the most pleasurable—moment, here he is, doing just that: Ben has not been acting on his own accord, but merely following orders. Her slowly building scream—"Ben!"—is not an immediate reaction to a man she can't resist (he ironically is much less attractive than the man she has just happily given her hand to) but a call of recognition to and accept-

ance of the man who has overcome the challenge. She moves toward him as if driven by a power which controls her, and the basis of the moment's strength is that she is drawn not by a sentimental concept of true love but by the frightening concept of an irresistible compulsion.

Understandably, then, when they beat their way out of the church—leaving the people behind the great glass doors, finally completing the film's glass symbolism by reversing it, locking the world out instead of being locked out by it—and hop on the bus, their emotions undergo a sudden transformation. At first we watch them giggle and grin with victory: they have *won*, they have beat all odds and are together. Immediately thereafter, though, from their point-of-view shot we see they are in the midst of a crowd solemnly staring at them, grim and uninviting. The smiles on Ben and Elaine's faces disappear, for by com-

. . . and Ben wins!

pleting their fantasy—by at last turning it into reality—they have also destroyed it. No wonder, then, that Nichols had only cynical things to say about their possibilities for eventual happiness.

Throughout the movie, Ben wanted more than anything to talk: Mrs. Robinson's inability to respond to this need is part of what destroyed their relationship, while he and Elaine have been incessantly talking throughout every scene in which they were together. But in our last image of them, they at last have nothing to say: they are looking away from each other rather than, as in a conventional love story, into each other's eyes.

The film opened with Ben's first-class arrival in Los Angeles and ends with his de classe exit. The similar but opposing images are significant,

for Ben has at once come full cycle while reaching the diametrically opposed pole to where he once stood; he has won what he wanted and, by winning, lost it. If he is far less typical than he once seemed of the youth of his era, he is one of those rare, unique screen characters whose off-beat personal story is removed from any particular time reference altogether, and is capable of touching us as only the most universal of human fables, from *Oedipus the King* to *Hamlet*, do.

In addition to his acting ability, Dustin works so well in the part because he is so wrong for it. One pundit observed, with tongue firmly in cheek, that "*The Graduate* is a movie about a Jewish boy with gentile parents," but it is the ironic casting of Hoffman as the "walking surfboard" of Charles Webb's novel that helps trans-

The moment just *before* the final fade-out . . .

form a minor novel into a major movie, and in addition to playing this physical type he always considered himself the opposite of, living out on celluloid the fantasy of being what he thought he could never be, he also played a character who shared his tendency toward being an observer and also his need to be alone.

The critics were to a man impressed by his offbeat screen presence. Brendan Gill of *The New Yorker* said, "Dustin Hoffman makes a sensationally attractive movie debut as the troubled, virtuous (?) hero." Stanley Kauffmann in *The New Republic* described "Dustin Hoffman, a young actor already known in the theatre as an exceptional talent, who here increases his reputation." Robert Hatch of *The Nation* said, "Dustin Hoffman has the right manner as the highly moral and readily seducible Graduate; he is at once gauche, disconcertingly direct and well armed by incredulity. . . ." Hollis Alpert in *Saturday Review* proclaimed, "Dustin Hoffman is the most delightful film hero of our generation. Slightly undersized, totally unsmiling, he stares his way through a series of horrendous, harrowing experiences." And Bosley Crowther of *The New York Times* said, "With Mr. Hoffman's stolid, deadpanned performance, he gets a wonderfully compassionate sense of the ironic and pathetic immaturity of a mere baccalaureate scholar turned loose in an immature society."

. . . and the very different looks on their faces at the final fade-out!

Midnight Cowboy

A United Artists Presentation   1969

Dustin Hoffman as Ratso Rizzo.

CAST:

Dustin Hoffman (*Ratso Rizzo*); Jon Voight (*Joe Buck*); Sylvia Miles (*Cass*); John McGiver (*Mr. O'Daniel*); Brenda Vaccaro (*Shirley*); Barnard Hughes (*Towny*); Ruth White (*Sally Buck*); Viva (*Gretal McAlbertson*).

CREDITS:

Director, John Schlesinger; screenplay, Waldo Salt, based on the novel by James Leo Herlihy; producer, Jerome Hellman; a Jerome Hellman-John Schlesinger Production; running time, 113 minutes; rating, X.

With the success of *The Graduate* behind him, Dustin steadfastly refused to play the "synthetic Benjamins" that were his for the asking. "I don't want to be the Andy Hardy of the sixties," he told an interviewer. And to another, he complained: "People have me in a little pocket of their minds in that role, and they don't want to see me get out of it. Some people are waiting to see me fall on my ass." He strongly resented the typecasting offered to him, seeing that in *The Graduate* he had not played himself, as most everyone assumed, but the kind of "walking surfboard" he had always felt so different from; though Benjamin Braddock may have seemed like a conventional romantic lead, it had been for Dustin a difficult character role. But what he wanted now was to return to the kind of emotionally—and sometimes physically—demanding role that had made his reputation off-Broadway. Only problem was, few movies are made about characters who resemble the pathetic Russian clerk in *Journey of the Fifth Horse*, so Dustin instead collected unemployment checks and worked in a short film that a friend of his made on a shoestring budget.

Then, the right script was offered him, and while his professional advisors insisted he would be committing professional suicide if he played it, Dustin found himself drawn to the role of Enrico "Ratso" Rizzo in John Schlesinger's upcoming screen adaptation of James Leo Herlihy's acclaimed novel, *Midnight Cowboy*. His business managers insisted that it was a supporting role rather than a lead, and in Hollywood, where you are constantly judged by your last picture,

Dustin would be perceived as someone who had landed *The Graduate* by a fluke, and was now settling into his more proper station in life as an actor rather than a star. But the film, designed as one of the then-burgeoning American art house pictures, caught on with the public beyond anyone's expectations, emerging both as a major box office hit and the Academy Award winning Best Picture of the Year.

By winning this award, *Cowboy* established that the new wave of Hollywood films had at last been accepted by the powers of the Old Hollywood, and that even X-rated pictures (for that was what the film received during its initial release!) were no longer considered a passing fancy but a viable—and even artistically significant—aspect of the emerging movie scene. Still, the title was misleading to some people who expected from it a traditional western. In its opening sequence, *Cowboy* clearly established a distance from those pictures by putting them in a new perspective.

At first, one sees nothing but the white screen, as on the soundtrack we hear the pounding of hoofs and the ring of pistol shots echoing in the background. Then, the camera slowly draws back to reveal that the white screen we have been looking at is not merely the screen of the theatre we are in, but a theatre screen that has been photographed as the opening image of the picture we are watching. In a gradually evolving long shot we see an empty, broken down drive-in theatre on the outskirts of a small Texas town: the hoofbeats and gunshots were echoes—perhaps ghosts is the more correct term—of the old movie heroes who once rode not only the range but movie screens as well. They are all gone now, and the camera cuts quickly to the central character, Joe Buck (Jon Voight) as, in a near parody of Lee Marvin's elaborate preparation/ritual in *Cat Ballou* (itself a parody of Jack Palance's similar scene in *Shane*) he preens and postures in his cowboy garb and finalizes hopes to leave the small diner where he has been employed. He hopes to travel to New York City, where he feels certain the women will be more than willing to pay for a *real* man—a man of the west. The juxtaposition of the haunted drive-in with this naive would-be lover establishes at

Joe Buck (Jon Voight) and Ratso (Hoffman) check out an address.

once that he has been molded by the myths of the old, hokey movies, and the aim of this new, more realistic film is to follow him as those myths are shattered—as Joe Buck comes to realize that in real life, things don't work the way they do in romanticized movies.

The story line of the film parallels the plot of the book closely enough. Joe Buck boards a bus that carries him across the American heartlands, eventually arriving in Manhattan where he joyously flexes his muscles, flashes his grin and tries out his drawl for the ladies. Most are unimpressed. Though one (Sylvia Miles) does give him a turn in her Park Avenue apartment, she afterwards mentions that he looks far better than he performs. When he dares to suggest she pay him a fee, she quickly manipulates the would-be manipulator into giving her most of his money for "car fare." Shortly, Joe Buck is back on the street and, as his fortunes sink, he happens upon Ratso (Hoffman) for the first time. A Times Square street hustler, Ratso is a small-time con artist who quickly fleeces the drug store cowboy out of what little cash he has left. But when the destitute Joe happens to run into Ratso again, he is persuaded to allow the dying tubercular to work as his "business manager," ferreting around for customers. In time, though, Joe Buck finds himself picking up small change for homosexual encounters in 42nd St. grind house theatres. Joe and Ratso live together in a condemned tenement house, and though they mostly trade insults back and forth, we sense a growing bond between them as they learn to rely on one another for mutual survival—emotional, as well as physical, survival.

Eventually, Buck meets another classy lady (Brenda Vaccaro) whom he runs into at an Andy

Cleanliness is next to godliness: Ratso spruces up Joe's haircut.

Ratso and "the Midnight Cowboy" encounter a New York horse who seems unimpressed with the Texan.

Warhol party he has been invited to by accident. But she is even more critical of his performance than the first woman, and Joe distastefully returns to servicing gay men in order to earn enough money to take Ratso to Florida, where Ratso believes his ever-worsening cough may be cured by the climate. In time, Joe brutalizes a customer in order to extort the necessary money, but when he and Ratso finally arrive in Miami by bus, Joe Buck turns to his friend and discovers he is dead.

Since he expires at the finale, *Cowboy* might appear to be Ratso's tragedy, but it is not. Death appears as a merciful blessing to Ratso, and it is Joe Buck who serves as the tragic pivot of the film, for he must now face life alone, and thus he is the one our sympathy reaches out to. He is also a dynamic and growing character, for as the story progresses, he learns about life and his place in the universe. As he talks to Ratso only moments before his friend dies, Joe Buck abandons the nickname "Ratso" for the first time during the course of the picture (though Rizzo has asked him to do so on several occasions), calling him Enrico—and allowing him a bit of human dignity. Also, for the first time he openly admits what he has been suppressing the entire time; that he is not much good as a stud, and wants to find manual work in Miami. At that moment when he finally understands himself and his limitations as well as his true possibilities, he no longer has a companion to share his slowly acquired honesty with.

While filming in New York, Dustin told an interviewer that *Cowboy* was about "two men who love each other but do not engage in a homosexual relationship." That distinction is basic to the film, as the relationship between Joe Buck and Ratso grows constantly deeper and broader—in every aspect but the physical. The film deals with an almost platonic conception of love, as Ratso is the only person in the picture Joe Buck does not engage in sexual relations with, and yet the only person Joe Buck comes to feel a meaningful love for. Indeed, part of Joe Buck's tragedy is that he has clearly separated his ability to have sex from his ability to experience love.

All his sexual trysts—with men and with women—are performed in a passionless, unromantic way. And while he suggests a feeling of disgust at the homosexual relationships he has experienced in order to survive, the film suggests there is more to this aspect of his personality than he fully comprehends. When he is unable to perform with one of the women he meets, she laughs and suggests he may actually be gay. He quickly consummates the affair not so much out of desire or passion but out of anger at what she has said, as if to prove her wrong—and, in the process, perhaps proves her right. Even Ratso suggests at one point that Joe's cowboy garb is more appealing to homosexuals than it is to women, and the brief flashbacks we see give some slight insight into Buck's background, in which he was raised in a home without men—by a mother and a grandmother, each of whom may have been whores. Even his relationship with his girlfriend proved to be brutal and unsatisfying.

The film's biggest problem is that we don't learn nearly enough about Joe's background, certainly not as much as readers of the book did. Director Schlesinger's flashbacks are so brief and so uncomprehensible they seem more confusing than enlightening, and might have better been eliminated entirely. Schlesinger is guilty of the biggest blunder a film adapter of a novel can make: including scenes that are understandable only to people who have already read the book, rather than finding a way to dramatize the book so that the novelist's conception is made clear to everyone watching. The British Schlesinger had long since established himself as a leading director with such varied projects as *Far From the Madding Crowd*, *A Kind of Loving*, and his masterpiece *Darling*, but his approach here seems strained—as though an established filmmaker were attempting to go back and make a "first film" like those the youthful experimenters were turning out.

At times, the movie is artistically overdone, with gratuitously dazzling camera movements; at other moments, the style looks awkward and rough-edged. But the choice of a British director for so American a story had its advantage. Whereas an American director might have emphasized place over character, Schlesinger—be-

Joe Buck comforts a pained Ratso.

ing an outsider doing his first American film—naturally did it the other way around. For him there was a fascination in discovering the ambience of 42nd St., which he called "a mixture of violence, desperation, and humor all in one street," but his focus always remains on the offbeat relationship between the two unlikely antiheroes. His satire on American types is clearly the work of an outsider, unfamiliar with his subject matter, and instead of a knowing eye, the camera is an explorer, allowing us to share discoveries about New York.

Producer Jerry Hellman chose Schlesinger for this unique quality he could bring to New York's mean streets, and was willing to go with unknown Jon Voight because of his obvious abilities in spite of his lack of a name at that time. As for Dustin, Hellman took him not because of his success in *The Graduate*, but in spite of it—"because he was an actor, not because he was a star." And while critics generally noted the deficiencies in the directorial approach, they also noted the *Of Mice and Men* style relationship was the key to the film's success, the perform-

The death of Ratso foreshadowed in a cryptic scene.

ances by Voight and Hoffman the essence of the movie's magic.

Arthur Schlesinger, Jr., writing . in *Vogue*, noted that the movie "has the advantage of two entirely remarkable performances by Jon Voight . . . and Dustin Hoffman. . . . The two play together in superb counterpoint and make their odd couple explicable and convincing." *Time* insisted that "From his debut as the open-faced Benjamin Braddock in *The Graduate*, Hoffman has progressed by stepping backward—to a supporting part. It is an act of rare skill and rarer generosity." In *Saturday Review*, Hollis Alpert claimed that "Hoffman emerges with top honors, proving that his heady debut in *The Graduate* was no fluke." *Newsweek's* Joseph Morgenstern argued that Voight carried the picture, but added that "Hoffman's work is in no way inferior, but the script gives the movie to Voight" (he might have argued that Hoffman gave the movie to Voight!) In *The New Republic*, Stanley Kauffmann stated that Hoffman "proves again that he is versatile and gifted, no Mike Nichols creation."

But in addition to returning Dustin to those "cripple" roles he had cut his teeth on in live theatre, Ratso allowed Hoffman to come to grips, through his acting, with some important aspects of his own personality. One was the very significance for him of taking on a supporting role after having just played a lead. Dustin has commented often about the danger of perceiving oneself as the center of the universe. Another is the fact that the movie deals with the theme of friendship, and Hoffman has made clear that while he does not have many friends, those he does consider part of his select circle enjoy a profound emotional and psychological connection with him. Surely, he was able to draw on this personal conception of friendship to make the unlikely but unforgettable friendship in the film so believable.

And finally, it is notable that relatively early in his film career, Dustin played a character whose most obvious personality trait is that he is dying. In fact, Ratso is the *only* character Dustin has as yet played in a film who dies during the course of the story. Dustin's own near-obsession with death has caused him to write endless epitaphs

Joe and Ratso share a butt.

85

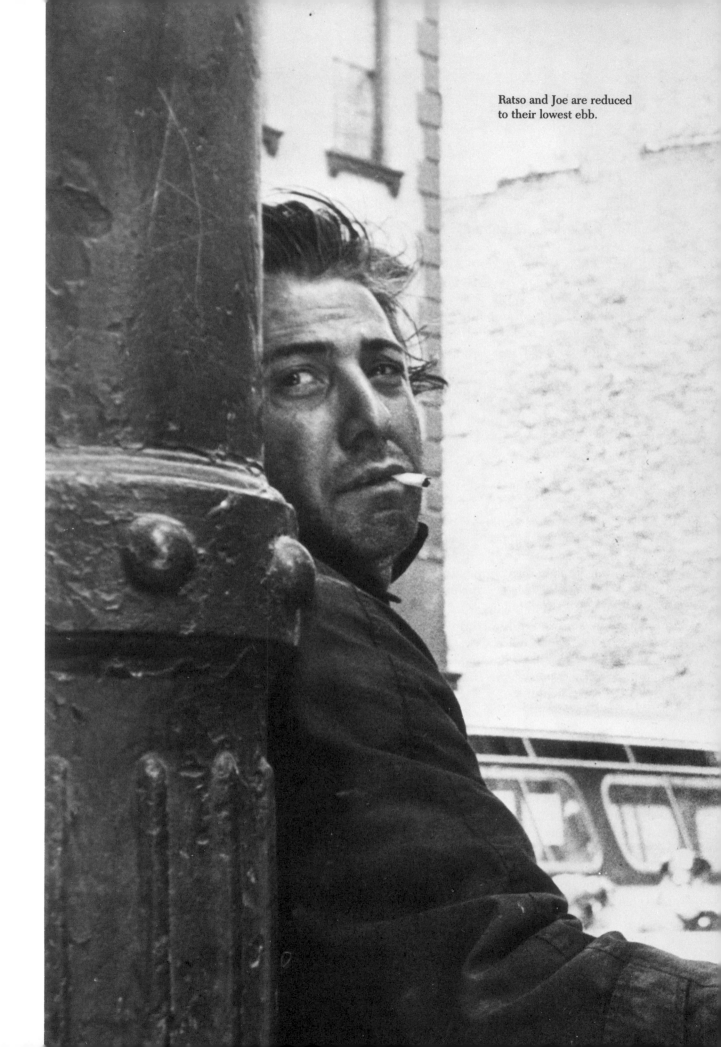

Ratso and Joe are reduced
to their lowest ebb.

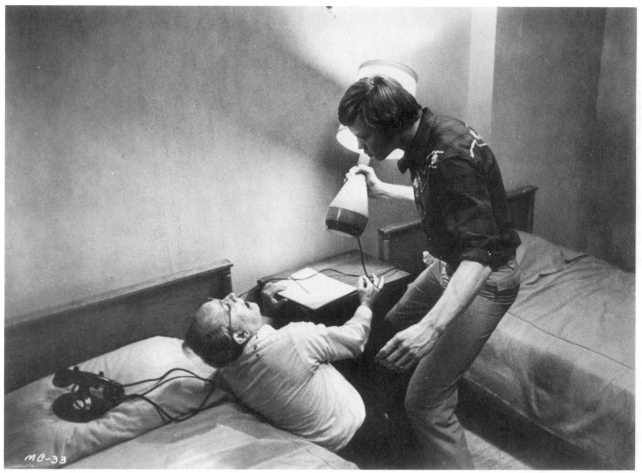

Joe (Jon Voight) beats a customer to procure "Florida money" for Ratso.

for himself, and by playing Ratso, he came to terms through acting with that final rite of passage, the one he fears most. By putting his own fears into the character and drawing upon his own obsession, Hoffman was able to make Ratso's death scene something other than a mere melodramatic contrivance.

In fact, Hoffman's identification with the role of the dying consumptive actually became a physical problem during the shooting. At one point, when director Schlesinger coaxed him to work on the element of the cough, Hoffman gave it so much concentration and energy that he literally fell down in the street vomiting. "Wow," muttered co-star Voight, who enjoyed a friendly/competitive relationship with Dustin, "how am I gonna upstage *that?*"

Interestingly enough, while Hoffman did *Cowboy* against the judgment of his advisors, he later came to see, and partially agree with, their point. "I used to say to myself that if ever I became a star," he commented after the film's release, "I would still be an artist—I would go after a particular role, and I wouldn't care how small it was if it was really good. But now I see that this isn't going to be so—I *do* care how small the part is. I saw *Cowboy* recently and sat there thinking, 'I wish I was on the screen a bit more. Jon Voight's on the screen an awful lot—this picture is really about *him*.' I think now that if a small character came along that I liked, I probably wouldn't do it, and I'd rationalize it by saying to myself, 'I'd rather save that character for a big part some day, and not waste it now.'" The anti-Hollywood rebel was beginning to comprehend—and, begrudgingly, accept—the Hollywood mentality.

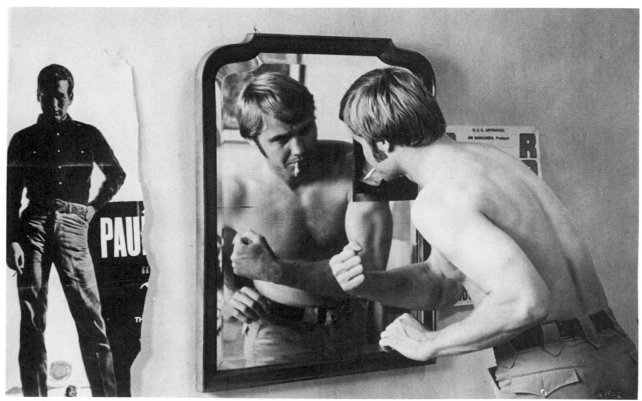

Joe Buck tries to emulate Paul Newman from the movie *Hud*.

Brenda Vaccaro is a New York sophisticate unmoved by Joe's performance.

Madigan's Millions

Released by American International Pictures
1969

The famous ad for *Madigan's Millions* and *Fearless Frank*, which
proved more memorable than either of the films.

CAST:

Cesar Romero *(Mike Madigan)*; Elsa Martinelli *(Vicky Shaw)*; Dustin Hoffman *(Jason Fister)*; Gustavo Rojo *(Lt. Arco)*; Fernando Hilbeck *(Burke)*; Franco Fabrizzi *(Condon)*; Riccardo Garrone *(Cirrini)*.

CREDITS:

Director, Stanley Prager; screenplay by Jim Henaghan and J. L. Bayonas; camera by Manolo Rojas; edited by Antonio Ramirez; music by G. Gregory Segura; a Westside International (Sidney Pink) Production; running time, 76 minutes; rating, G.

On the basis of *Midnight Cowboy's* extraordinary success, American International Pictures decided to capitalize on the fact that, several years earlier, the film's two exciting young stars had been featured in separate exploitation flicks. Hoffman's had been a minor entry called *Madigan's Millions,* and while he had already begun negotiating for *The Graduate* at the time he agreed to appear in it, Hoffman—having no idea of the stardom in store for him—regarded *Madigan* as a fast, fun way to see Rome and at the same time make several thousand much-needed dollars for a few weeks' work. Later, Joseph E. Levine—on the eve of *The Graduate's* release—would offer to buy up every existing print of *Madigan* and destroy them to save Dustin any possible embarrassment. Though Hoffman scoffed that such a move was a bit extreme, *Madigan* did surface briefly in 1969, with the promise that audiences could see Ratso and Joe Buck "back to back" or, if you preferred, "together (almost!) again—for the *first* time."

Madigan's Millions was one of a number of pictures turned out during the heyday of the made-for-TV movie, when television had gobbled up all the recent theatrical fare and still complained of a tremendous appetite for movies. Movies made especially for TV were soon the rage, and, at a time when theatrical audiences were shrinking, this new outlet provided a possible home for countless features—not to mention plenty of work for performers who would have otherwise been unemployed.

A Madrid-based American producer named Sidney Pink contracted a deal with the Westinghouse Broadcasting Corporation to complete 30 low-budget pictures, to be shot in various European locales, and, though the films were intended for American television rather than theatrical release, Pink was entitled to 18 months of theatrical release in Europe prior to Westinghouse's telecasting of the films in the U.S. For that reason, it was necessary to feature both a U.S. "name" to make statewide television bookings attractive and also a European "name" for the sake of the continental theatrical bookings, so Pink settled on a technique of pairing an American male personality with a European female in order to fulfill both those conditions. Thus, *Tunnels of Kaiserfurt* featured Gary Lockwood and Lucianna Paluzzi, *If the Shroud Fits* paired Tony Bennett with Elsa Martinelli, *The Bang Bang Kid* matched Rory Calhoun with Anita Ekberg and *Ragan* co-starred Robert Stack and Gina Lollobrigida. When *Madigan* was being readied, someone mentioned Dustin Hoffman for the male lead. Though he had never before starred in even a low-budget film, Dustin's reputation was known from his off-Broadway work, and was enough to qualify him as a "name" worthy of headlining the film.

The original conception had been to capitalize on George Raft's recent and momentary notoriety following his being canned from a job as "host" of a London casino, finding himself labelled "persona non grata" in England.

It was the nature of the cheapie-sleazeball film genre that any actor whose name had recently hit the headlines—however dubious the circumstances—was fair game for exploitation in a quickly produced picture, and Raft, not Hoffman, was signed for top billing and the title role, though he would have been able to wrap up all the shooting for his non-speaking cameo in a single day. However, problems developed concerning his willingness and ability to perform even that task, and at the last moment Raft disappeared from the cast, reportedly owing to "sickness." At any rate, it is Cesar Romero who in fact portrays Madigan and, in the film's wordless opening sequence, is seen staggering down a nearly deserted back alley of Rome, obviously

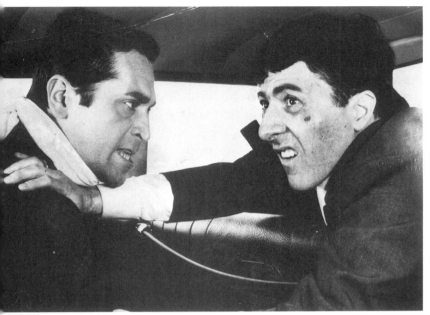

Dustin Hoffman holds off an attacking enemy agent.

dying from a previously inflicted wound. At a corner market, he grabs an apple from a stand and desperately shoves a key into it, then barely makes his way to an apartment where a pretty girl (Elsa Martinelli) and her child are sleeping, drops the apple beside the little boy, and trudges back down to the street where, after casting a mournful and meaningful glance at a towering billboard, he drops dead.

Though the filmmaking technique is even at this point obviously tacky, the opening is nonetheless economically shot and intrinsically interesting, suggesting the possibility that the film to follow will transcend its C-movie limitations and develop into a sleeper of sorts. And the plot continues to suggest possibilities for offbeat comedy when, after planting the Hitchcock-like MacGuffin (apple/key), the script sets up the premise of the caper to come: Madigan is an

Jason Fister (Hoffman) is threatened once again.

92

American gangster who years earlier was deported to Italy, reportedly with a great sum of money. But for the past several years he has been living in near poverty, suggesting his "millions" may be nothing more than a myth. Since the Italian police do not want American agents snooping around, the U.S. Treasury must send incognito an agent who doesn't look like an agent, and that turns out to be Jason Fister (Hoffman), a nondescript-looking bumbler. Even if he fails to recover the money, he will at least have been out of everybody's hair for a while.

Fister proceeds to drive the Rome police up the wall with his nutty behavior. In the process of discovering the apple that contains the key to the loot hidden behind the billboard Madigan looked at before he died, Fister manages to leave a succession of dead bodies in his wake, is pursued by both the police and the underworld, and romances (in his fashion) the woman believed to be Madigan's mistress, but who in the twist ending turns out to be the gangster's daughter. If at first the film seems to be shaping up as a mildly agreeable low-budget romp that borrows the Hitchcock formula of an unlikely hero beating out the slick professionals of espionage, that appeal lasts for less than fifteen minutes.

The plot soon goes from engaging to preposterous to ludicrous to unintelligible, and the humor just as quickly drops its brisk romp/caper quality, degenerating into non-stop mugging and mayhem of the most unappealing variety. Amazingly, Hoffman manages a number of good moments; unlike most performers in such a film, who woodenly walk their way through such trash and hope that the film never gets out of the can, Hoffman evidently cared enough to try and make something of, if not the project itself, than at least his participation in it. His timing of his gag lines is exceptionally good, which is all the more remarkable since this is one of those multi-language productions in which some cast and crew members were not even able to communicate with him. Dustin's ability to pose and position his body in such a way that it comes off as comically effective is used to good advantage on several occasions, and almost saves some scenes

that had little else to recommend them—if anything.

At other times, though, he apparently succumbed to the general slapdash mood of the project, and merely acts goofy instead of being funny. At such points, he is as broad (and bad) as everything else about the film, appearing a little like Arnold Stang doing an impression of Jerry Lewis. The film was not reviewed very widely on its initial release, but on its 1969 go-round with Jon Voight's equally unappealing *Fearless Frank*, a few critics did attempt to assess its worth. In *Variety*, "Murf" said: "Hoffman was 'introduced' in pic finished in 1967, shortly before *The Graduate* rolled; had it been released earlier, it might have finished him. . . . Hoffman appears to have mugged it up herein, with or without help from director Stanley Prager. There are performance flashes which have been put to good advantage in his three big pix, but essentially Hoffman plays the part like an Occidental version of Charlie Chan's number one son. . . ." More charitable by far was "Stein" in *Film TV Daily*: "No doubt about it, Dustin Hoffman is talented. He is so naive, nutty, clumsy, and talented in *Madigan's Millions* that he is the whole film. In fact, he saves the film. . . . His fans will love him—younger and a bit rough around the edges—but pure Dustin Hoffman. . . . Fister becomes involved in a kaleidoscope of events which could only be carried off by Hoffman." For John Mahoney of the *Hollywood Reporter*, Hoffman's predicament was a significant and recurring one faced by many movie stars: "Bette Davis recently lamented contemporary make-or-break showcasing in films, mentioning that today a young actor has to make it overnight like Dustin Hoffman, whereas her contemporaries had had the chance to develop and try again. In today's market, she reckoned that she wouldn't have been given another chance on the basis of her first film, *Bad Sister*. Fortunately for Dustin Hoffman, the film which introduced him to the world was not the film which introduced him to the screen, a film which might not have found its way to any screen but for the fame his second and third films excited.

... Hoffman does not rise above it, could not, though it is possible to see his promise, in retrospect only ... with color prints by Movielab, the film looks as if it had been photographed on rancid fettucini. ..."

The most interesting aspect of the film is what it reveals of Hoffman himself. Dustin's first attempts at entertaining were his famous clowning escapades, and there has been a certain element of the clown to him all his life. Though the character of Fister at first appears to have nothing to do with Dustin, it is nonetheless true that Fister also is a clown, perceived by everyone around him as a perfect fool even though he is intent on proving his worth—and does in time prove it.

Perhaps one reason Dustin was occasionally able to rise above the material at hand is that there is something in the character that roughly correlates to his own experiences as a man who was able to attract attention only by playing the clown, though he knew all along inside he wanted to accomplish more than anyone at first gave him credit for being able to do. In *Madigan's Millions*, Dustin was able to isolate the clown side of his own personality, forced to analyze such behavior by preparing to play it in a film, and brought a relatively lifeless and insignificant role to life by correlating Fister's clownlike reaction to the world around him to his own similar reactions—though his had been under drastically different circumstances.

Elsa Martinelli gives Jason one of his few pleasant moments in Rome.

John and Mary

20th Century Fox   1969

Mary (Mia Farrow) and John (Dustin Hoffman) meet in a New York City "swinging singles" bar.

CAST:

Dustin Hoffman *(John)*; Mia Farrow *(Mary)*; Michael Tolan *(James)*; Sunny Griffin *(Ruth)*; Stanley Beck *(Ernest)*; Tyne Daly *(Hilary)*.

CREDITS:

Director, Peter Yates; screenplay by John Mortimer, based on the novel by Mervyn Jones; produced by Ben Kadish; running time, 92 minutes; rating, R.

After foregoing the advice of all those managers, agents, and friends who insisted a role like Ratso would dim Dustin's chances for leading-man stardom, Hoffman followed their judgment with his next project, and went on to do *John and Mary,* in part because it allowed him to play a "normal human being" rather than another oddball. Ironically, though, the more "normal" the character in question was, the *greater* the challenge for Hoffman the actor.

"I've begun to think playing eccentrics all the time is, for me, a cop-out," he explained to reporters. "The *tough* thing for me is *not* to have a particular voice or gait for a part. I have this strong fear that if I am just myself, I'm going to be dull." The film's backers had no such fears, though, and wanted Dustin so badly for the part that, in order to free him for the daily shooting, bought out the entire matinee house on Broadway's *Jimmy Shine* for eight consecutive Wednesdays, at a cost of nearly $50,000. This allowed Dustin to shoot *John and Mary* by day, *every* day, and still show up at the theatre in time to go onstage each evening. Asked how he managed to do it, he laughed and said, "I'm a masochist."

Interestingly enough, this film designed with the new young audience in mind was shot at the famed old Biograph Studio in the Bronx, where people like D. W. Griffith had once plied their trade. Surprisingly, Dustin was not particularly impressed about working in the shadow of the man who literally created the movies, for this seemingly hip, literate actor openly admitted total ignorance about the golden days of Biograph: "The only thing I know about its history is that they shot some *Car 54* episodes here," he

said. But Dustin did know something about the classic screen romances, and did hope that *John and Mary* might click as a modern equivalent of *Seventh Heaven, Camille,* and *Casablanca.* That would have been a nice change of pace for him, opening up another whole side to his career. "I've always wanted to do a really great love story," Dustin's director, Peter Yates, said, "but it's hard to find one that's not hypocritical or saccharine." "I would like," Dustin admitted, "to be a character lover."

Certainly, the casting seemed right. After all, his co-star would be Mia Farrow, who had in 1967 achieved success as significant as his post-*Graduate* status with her *Rosemary's Baby* performance, which had won her an Oscar nomination and had tied with *The Graduate* as that year's most popular film with the new, emerging audience. Bringing the two of them together seemed as natural a stroke as bringing Clark Gable and Jean Harlow, or James Stewart and June Allyson, or Rock Hudson and Doris Day together; if each was so popular alone, imagine what the possible chemistry might be when they were onscreen together!

But if they were cast in an attempt to create the perfect screen couple for a new era, they couldn't have been further apart in terms of personal orientation. Mia talked constantly on the set about transcendental meditation, while Dustin was into psychoanalysis. Mia had romanticized notions about dying, like a gifted gothic poetess, at an early age; Dustin desperately wanted to live to be eighty. She was the Establishment WASP turned wild-eyed free spirit, he the uptight Jewish intellectual. "The Moonchild and the Fifth Beatle," *Time* labelled them. Another pundit laughingly described the new film as "*Rosemary* meets *The Graduate,*" and it certainly seemed likely that whatever happened with the critics, the film could not fail at the box-office.

But fail it did, because the calculation was all wrong and the expected chemistry did not click. Though Hoffman's career was continuing on the ascent, Miss Farrow's was already in decline. Her popularity had been something of an accident in the first place: after catching the fickle attention of TV audiences on the *Peyton Place*

The Mod Couple

series in 1964, she might have quickly slipped
into oblivion if not for her affair—and brief but
volatile and highly publicized marriage—with
superstar Frank Sinatra. There was a sensitive/
flakey quality to her that was vogueish in the
early flower power days of the late sixties: the
resemblance of her nonexistent figure to that of
popular models of the moment like Twiggy, and
her tendency to run off to study with the same
Mahareshi who had also raised the consciousness
of The Beatles. But *John and Mary*'s casting
suffered from the *Future Shock* quality of rapidly
changing styles: as the movie was being planned
she may have seemed a likely person to embody
the new, "now" woman, but by the time it was
released, she was already passé.

So observers took cynical pleasure in noting
that, during the obligatory nude scene, it was
impossible to tell whether one was looking at

Mia's behind or Dustin's—in spite of the fact that
as described in the original novel on which the
picture was loosely based, Mary's rear end is her
most attractively lush and womanly feature. But
little else about the book was kept intact. Changing the locale from England to New York, and
consequently trying to rewrite the dialogue,
making it idiomatically American instead of British, pretty much did in the book's conception,
which had been a study of the New Morality as it
had manifested itself in England.

In its American version, *John and Mary* attempted to turn a Hollywood movie cliche inside
out, thereby presenting it as something new and
daring. The title of the film hints at this: instead
of, in the old tinseltown fashion, exchanging
names at the beginning and heading toward bed
at the fadeout, the characters go to bed even
before the title sequence and finally get around

to exchanging names at the end. The basic problem is that the movie is so long—and the characters spend so much time together, as well as do so many things that in fact *require* the trading of names—that the premise appears a gimmick forced onto the storyline, rather than growing naturally from it. The filmmakers clearly hoped to provide a hip new variation on the traditional theme of boy meets girl, boy loses girl, boy gets girl. But their notion was not so revolutionary as the practitioners of the sexual revolution in the late sixties seemingly thought, for had they been a bit more well read, they would have realized Ernest Hemingway carefully scrutinized just such a relationship in his Lost Generation novel *A Farewell to Arms*. But in 1969, the Production Code that had banned such "amoral" couplings from movie screens was gone, and pictures were being marketed that promised a maturity never before seen on the screen.

But if the contents were indeed mature, the filmmaking was not. *John and Mary* was an overly trendy film for the youth market, and

Peter Yates designed his directorial scheme as an outright catalogue of all the then-popular filmmaking devices. Arch flashbacks reveal each of the principal's unhappy love lives, John's with a pretty model (Sunny Griffin) whose greatest fault appears to have been she couldn't cook as well as he; Mary's with a slick, phoney political-liberal (Michael Tolan) married to someone else. There are flashforwards, bizarre fantasy sequences, and freeze frames at intense moments, as well as voice overs which tell us what the characters are thinking as opposed to what they say. At the end, when no split screen has appeared, one wonders why it was overlooked. All this stylistic flamboyance has little to do with the story at hand, and is only so much cinematic window dressing—decorative rather than functional technical prowess. In retrospect, the film looks like a virtual encyclopedia of dead-end devices mistakenly believed to be the style of the future. And what the film failed to provide was something more basic but significant: an in-depth insight into the types of people who make up the emerging singles-

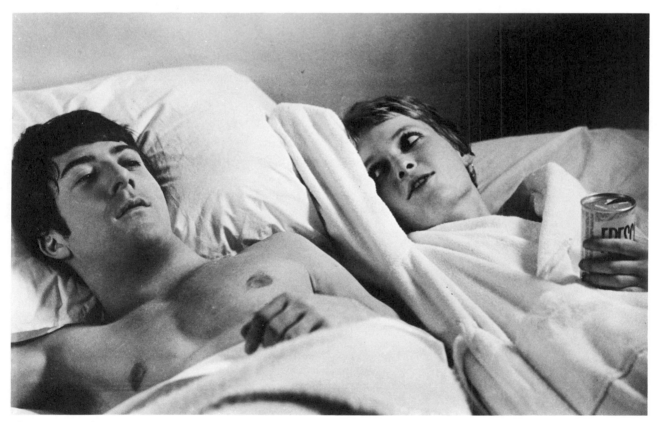

The Morning After.

John shows Mary his extensive record collection.

John's former love, Ruth (Sunny Griffin), in a warm embrace.

scene lifestyle.

All character motivations are simplistically Freudian: John's stand-offishness, like his love of cooking, derives from his political activist mother: he was always hungry as a child because she was off marching in protest over some social issue. The cartoonish portrait painted of the mother is a self-indulgent male child's nightmare vision of women who are interested in anything outside the home. We are asked to share John's grotesque conception of her as a fool who cared so deeply about the problems of the world when she should have had the good sense to stay in the home where she belonged—a notion outlandishly old-fashioned in view of the women's movement emerging even as the film was made. *John and Mary* eventually becomes as obsessed with food as John is: when the characters are not preparing food or devouring it, they are talking about it: theatre snack bars reported that, despite the low attendance, their sales went up.

The screenplay is meant to be sparse, only "suggesting" the characters through awkward attempts at conversation, thus forcing the actors to "fill them in" with gestures, postures, and body language. The less said about Miss Farrow's attempts, the better. But Dustin does very nicely: if in *Midnight Cowboy* he succeeded in taking one of life's cripples and showing that, on the inside, he happens to be a member of the human race, he here took the seemingly most normal and average guy in the world and demonstrated that, once you saw what was going on inside him, he might just turn out to be one of life's emotional cripples. But if Dustin succeeded in making John an interesting character, he was unable to pull off the larger task of salvaging the film itself.

For the most part, *John and Mary* is downright boring, concentrating on textures and subtle moods in the style of an "art film" while failing to provide the greater insight into human nature that should be at the basis of such a film's appeal. Besides, there is the commercial calculation always peeping out from behind the sheer banality: if *Pillow Talk* had been remade by Antonioni for post-Production Code audiences, the results might look something like this. And, toward the end, when the filmmakers try and relieve the tedium with some fast dramatic action, the results are even worse. When John turns Mary out of his apartment (she has made the "terrible" mistake of shattering their mood by calling her best girlfriend to tell her where she is) it seems unlikely; when he then grows despondent to see her again and searches all

Ruth converses with Charlie (Richard Clarke) as John looks on.

John and Mary prepare for one of their many meals together.

over New York in hopes of finding her, his concern is unmotivated and uncomprehensible; when he finally returns forlorn to his apartment and discovers she never actually left it, the revelation is unbelievable.

If *John and Mary* satisfied Dustin's advisors by reminding viewers he was a potential leading man, the film accomplished little else of artistic value other than his performance. This was the film, though, that allowed Dustin to deal onscreen with a man whose entire being—so far as screen time goes—is taken up by his relationship to a woman, and his difficulty in sustaining a satisfying one. One recalls Hoffman's oft-quoted comment, "I'll die wishing I had learned more about what I feel and *fear* about women—a woman is a prime example of what will open up

my vulnerability. Womankind occupies my thinking most of the day."

That comment, though uttered in an entirely different context, could be a summation of everything most interesting in *John and Mary*. For while Dustin's own relationships do not necessarily have much (if anything) to do with John's attempts to relate to Mary, Dustin could still draw on his own experiences, finding correlatives in the positive and negative relationships he had experienced, drawing on them to lend a sense of authenticity to what we see transpire. There is another "key" to understanding Dustin's relationship to John. If one recalls Dustin's problems with food as a child—and, beyond that, his need for a mother who remained at home with him, and prepared him the special dishes that John's mother did not—then John becomes a fearful projection of what might have been had Dustin's own mother been less dedicated to his well-being than she in fact was.

Too often, critics tend to overrate extreme and arch "character" roles such as Ratso, which are in fact fairly easy to do because they allow an actor so much invention and freedom, bordering on caricature as they do. The problem is that the same critics often fail to acknowledge the subtle and complex work that goes into creating a person on screen who does not seem (on the surface) to be anything but part of the mainstream. Yet Hoffman understood the formidable challenge of playing John properly, and if the film failed to meet the level of his performance, the picture did at least serve as a significant dry run on the way to the apparently everyday man—but in fact most difficult and complex character-Dustin would create onscreen: Ted Kramer.

Writing in *Life*, Richard Schickel called *John and Mary* "a mildly chic, mildly engaging little thing, played with admirable believability by its principals. It is aimed precisely at the squishy, romantic hearts of the under-25 set who now dominate the movie audience and it will surely provide them with some innocent pleasure." Tougher on the film but more aware of Hoffman's quality performance was Stanley Kauffman in *New Republic*, who said: "Whoever is managing Dustin Hoffman has chosen well for him. A light hip lover is a good change after *Midnight Cowboy*, which was a good change after *The Graduate*—and is especially good before his next appearance in the film of Thomas Berger's splendid novel, *Little Big Man*. . . . In terms of building his image as a versatile star, though on no other, this film was a good choice for Hoffman." Pauline Kael, who tends to be harder on Hoffman than most critics, at least paid him a backhanded compliment in *The New Yorker:* "Dustin Hoffman draws upon his astute knowledge of the audience's good will toward him and does well," though she went on to add that, "Reviewing this perfect nothing of a movie is rather degrading: it's like giving consumer hints on the latest expensive, worthless gift for the person who has everything." To be fair, the film had its champions, like Arthur Knight of *Saturday Review*, who found it successful and insisted that, "What makes it all work, above and beyond Hoffman's convincing performance . . . is the unobstrusive agility of Gayne Rescher's camera in such cramped spaces as Maxwell's Plum, the Fillmore East, and a Madison Avenue art gallery." More often, though, the film was chastized and Hoffman lauded. *Time* labelled Hoffman "one of the shrewdest young actors in the business" but insisted that "beneath the Manhattan chatter and the glossy confrontations, *John and Mary* is as empty as a singles bar on Monday morning." In a similar vein, Joseph Morgenstern of *Newsweek* argued that "Hoffman plays John simply and appealingly," but went on to complain that "Peter Yates's direction gives the illusion of intimacy without the delights of it."

John and Mary.

Little Big Man

A National General Pictures Release   1970

Jack (Dustin Hoffman) receives a lesson in cleanliness from the Reverend's
wife (Faye Dunaway).

CAST:

Dustin Hoffman (*Jack Crabb*); Faye Dunaway (*Mrs. Pendrake*); Martin Balsam (*Allardyce T. Merriwether*); Richard Mulligan (*General George Armstrong Custer*); Chief Dan George (*Old Lodge Skins*); Jeff Corey (*Wild Bill Hickock*); Amy Eccles (*Sunshine*); Kelly Jean Peters (*Olga*); Carole Androsky (*Caroline*); Robert Little Star (*Little Horse*); Cal Bellini (*Younger Bear*); Reuben Moreno (*Shadow That Comes in Sight*); Steve Shemayne (*Burns Red in the Sun*); William Hickey (*Historian*).

CREDITS;

Director, Arthur Penn; screenplay by Calder Willingham, based on the novel by Thomas Berger; director of photography, Harry Stradling, Jr.; music by John Hammond; produced by Stuart Millar; a Cinema Center Film Presentation; running time, 150 minutes; rating, PG.

Few actors appear less likely for a western than Dustin Hoffman; then again, no period of time ever seemed less able to support a western film than the early seventies, when a new America—and a new American cinema—were emerging. But as the most indigenous of all American movie genres the western is endlessly adjustable, its classic plots pliable enough to express the current mood of successive generations.

In the 1930s, Henry Fonda and Tyrone Power played Frank and Jesse James as outlaw heroes who, like the central characters in the then popular gangster pictures, expressed the antisocial attitudes of the Great Depression; in the 1950s, Jeff Hunter and Robert Wagner played Frank and Jesse as misunderstood youths, lost in the confusion of a post-war world, and second cousins to the alienated youth/juvenile delinquents of that period. During World War II, the steadfast heroes of epic westerns reflected our faith in American leadership, but during the following period of communist witch hunting the western hero was most often depicted as a decent man abandoned at a time of crisis by his community. In the flower-power period of the late sixties, Butch Cassidy and the Sundance Kid had been romanticized as essentially non-violent outlaws who try to drop out of the mainstream; in the early seventies, America was ripe for a new kind of western that would reflect the current concerns. It made sense, then, that Dustin Hoffman—the oddball character actor who had established himself as the reigning star of his time—would reinterpret the western hero in such a way as to appeal to the current mood of moviegoers.

But making a western proved far more difficult for Dusty than doing something like *The Graduate* or *Midnight Cowboy*. Learning to ride was hard because Dustin's legs are short, and every day, after spending time in the saddle, he had to bathe in epsom salts. The cold of the mountain country near Billings, Montana, was rough, but most unpleasant of all was learning to use a gun. He had to draw and fire rapidly, and when he did, he often pulled the trigger too fast, burning his leg with the powder from the blank cartridges. Besides, the film crew, used to old Hollywood stars, had to adjust to Dustin's unorthodox behavior. When a scene called for his character to sprawl face down in a muddy street for a shot that would take two full days to shoot, Dustin shocked everyone by refusing the obligatory stand-in, and instead lay there in the near freezing dirt the entire time. Occasionally, he fantasized about the ease enjoyed by a Frank Sinatra-type star, who shows up only for his close-ups and allows the remainder of a film to be shot "around" him, but Hoffman knew he could never go that route.

The most appealing aspect of the picture was the challenge of creating the 121-year-old Crabb for the movie's opening and closing, and Dustin still insists an Academy Award of some sort should have gone to makeup artist Dick Smith, who first cast a mold of Dustin's head and shoulders, then labored for three months making a foam latex mask for the actor. But if Smith could take care of the visual aspect, the voice had to be Dustin's contribution, and one he seriously prepared for. A doctor friend arranged for Dustin to observe some old people on Welfare Island, and Dustin tape-recorded one geriatric, but the fellow wasn't old enough, and Dustin felt the need to start over. Another doctor mentioned a newly developed drug which alcoholics used to dry

As an Indian, Jack fights against the cavalry.

themselves out and which did funny things with the voice but, after considering that possibility, Dustin decided against it as being dangerous to his health and also a cop-out: as an actor, he should be able to create the voice himself.

Before he had found his "key," however, he was out of Manhattan and in the middle of Montana, working on the picture. When he contracted laryngitis from the cold, he liked the way his voice sounded, but he was still playing Crabb as a young man, and he half-hoped that when the time came to play the older Crabb he would get sick again. When the crew had been shooting for close to six months and moved to Canada to finish the picture, Dustin became friendly with an Oriental crew member, and after being invited to the man's home for dinner one night, he met the crew member's father, a 104-year-old fellow. Dustin studied him carefully, and noticed he was always dressed with

dignity, in pajamas and a robe. In one hand he always held a cigarette, burning slowly, and in the other he constantly toyed with a paper napkin, which struck Dustin as being an old man's equivalent of a security blanket. For the old Jack Crabb Dustin knew he would do exactly that with each hand, and though the camera would most often be trained on his face and the audience might never see the hands at all, it would nonetheless help put Dustin in the proper mood, so that mentally he would feel secure in his part and, feeling that way, believe in the character and thus give a more convincing performance.

But when they reached Los Angeles and had to finally film the scene in which Crabb is 121, Dustin had not licked the voice problem. He locked himself in a room and screamed until he was hoarse, but the next day, when he was to shoot, his voice had gone back to its natural

Wild Bill Hickok (Jeff Corey) demonstrates his fast draw . . .

. . . and Jack learns to use a gun himself.

pitch. So the entire time he dressed and drove to the studio, he screamed at the top of his lungs. During the five hour application of make-up, he continued to scream. After make-up, he found a room by himself and screamed some more. At the Sawtelle Veterans' Hospital, where the scenes were to be shot, he found a padded room and sat in it, screaming, until several hospital guards came to see who the old man was who was making such a fuss. When Dustin met a 96-year-old patient and realized the man actually believed he was 121, he finally felt at ease with his role. All he needed now was his famous "key" to the character, the single element about Crabb's personality that would totally lock Dustin into Crabb, making him one with the complex character. What is this man's most basic problem? He mused. Then, it came to him: "I haven't had a decent bowel movement in 46 years" was the key. And, at last, the old man came alive onscreen.

Filmmaker Arthur *(Bonnie and Clyde)* Penn, working from a script by Calder Willingham, translated Thomas Berger's 1964 novel into a film featuring the gently mocking tone of a folk ballad, which moved with the meandering pace of a picaresque while establishing the mood of a mock epic. The picture begins as a young reporter interviews Jack Crabb (Hoffman), the self-confessed "sole white survivor of the Battle of the Little Big Horn, popularly known as Custer's Last Stand." Perturbed by the journalist's knee-jerk reactions and prejudicial attitudes toward the old west, Crabb relates his exploits beginning that day when, as a child travelling west by wagon, he saw his family massacred by Pawnees,

and was himself adopted by a tribe of friendly Cheyenne. In time, Jack came to love and respect his Indian grandfather, Old Lodge Skins (Chief Dan George). But upon discovering he is actually white, Jack feels the need to learn about his own culture.

Leaving behind the unspoiled innocence of the Cheyenne people, he soon finds himself uncomfortable with the ugliness and corruption he encounters on every level of white society: self-righteous hypocrisy of religous people in the form of a minister's wife (Faye Dunaway) who tries to seduce Jack at every possible turn; cold-blooded professionalism of the law 'n' order Establishment in the form of humorless gunman Wild Bill Hickock (Jeff Corey); the mercenary quality of American business in the guise of an amiable but shifty salesman (Martin Balsam);

Jack becomes a town drunk.

and militaristic racist-fascism in the guise of General George Armstrong Custer (Richard Mulligan).

Clearly, the film is not so much a movie *about* the old west as a film that exploits certain threads of history as a means of making a statement for and about the America of the early seventies. In 1970, most of Hollywood still backed off from addressing the Viet Nam War directly, but in a western, an inventive filmmaker could use the frontier landscape as an objective correlative for the current social consciousness. So the Indians are here romanticized as gentle, peaceful, even pacifistic, whereas white Americans—as symbolized chiefly by Custer—are depicted as natural destroyers, with only Jack—the counter-cultural drop-out, as played by "generational hero" Hoffman—is pure, because he was "spoiled" by the love and goodness of the plains Indians, and is thus unable to tolerate the hideousness of civilization when he does try to rejoin it.

The impressionable young Jack enjoys a heavenly choir with Mrs. Pendrake.

Jack returns to the Indians and takes a wife.

Jack becomes a travelling medicine salesman.

A terrified Jack flees some warring Indians.

All this makes *Little Big Man* a perfect mirror for the masochistic mentality of America at that time, as made clear by the fact that during the massacre in the Washita sequence, in which Custer attacks an Indian village including women and children, audiences responded (as they were meant to) by shouting out, "Mai Lai! Mai Lai!"; later in the film, they cheered Custer's death as a fantasy projection of what they might have liked to see happen to certain Viet Nam commanders. Today, though, that vision makes the movie seem overly simplistic, unfairly twisting history to fit in with the then-current value scheme; as far as history goes, one learns far more about the late sixties mentality that produced the film than the old west it is supposedly about. The movie is also dishonestly manipulative in its depiction of violence: when

Jack the muleskinner.

Jack and Mrs. Pendrake enjoy the simpler pleasures in life.

the Indians murder white women and children, Penn plays the scene as slapstick comedy so that audiences will be too busy laughing to sympathize with the victims. But when the whites are shown killing Indian families, the scenes are played as tragic in order to emotionally involve us on a realistic level. In reversing the old stereotype of good whites against bad Indians, Penn did not create a more objective or honest vision, but simply turned the old lie around and, by presenting it backwards, offered an equally extremist (and equally abhorrent) lie.

No critic of the time better captured this aspect of the film than David Denby in *The Atlantic:* "From the evidence of the movie, the whites didn't kill the Indians because they wanted the land, water, and skins, or because they were afraid of them, or even because they were racists. They killed them because it is the nature of white men to kill. And this sort of tautology is itself the essence of racism. Of course it's a new hip racism that will be very popular with certain sections of the young audience. . . . What starts as an elegy for lost values winds up as an exercise in white self-hatred . . ."

So instead of the complex, fascinating, ambiguous man history reports George Custer to have been, he is here reduced to a caricature,

112

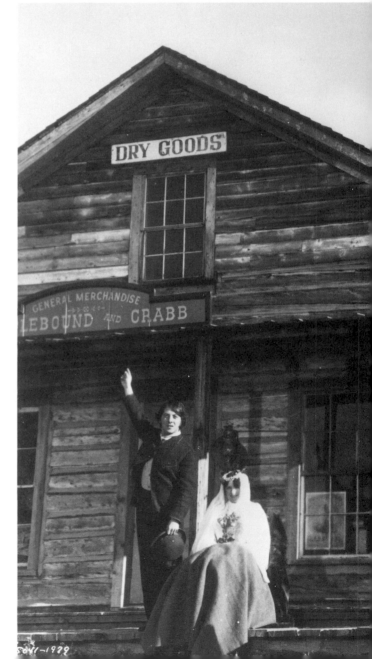

Jack's wedding.

and this might not be nearly so bothersome were it not that the film is 2½ hours long; in a picture of such enormous size and scope, we expect more character development than we get. A living cartoon is certainly an interesting conception, but the longer a film is, the less we can comfortably accept this quality, and while for a time we may continue to laugh, we eventually feel the necessity for something more, the desire to see these cartoons develop into real people.

Besides its epic length, there is the problem of the picture's inherent and unrelenting bigness in other ways. The massacre at Washita would be far more powerful than it is if it were the only such scene in the film, but in attempting to create a blockbuster, Penn felt the need to include an earlier, similar scene, and this diffuses

the impact of the later one. The film is uneven and overly moralistic, blending buffoonish comedy with outright didacticism in an awkward combination. But in spite of this it is undeniably an enjoyable film experience: exhilarating, entertaining, and exciting—all in all, far more effective than it has any right to be upon close examination of its faults.

And this is due to the sensibility and spirit Penn brings to it—ultimately, his understanding of how to play a scene for its most effective possibilities, coupled with his ability to encourage actors to be relaxed and honest for the camera, which often makes an unlikely moment metamorphise into a memorable scene. When Faye Dunaway lasciviously bathes a wide-eyed Dustin, muttering all the while cliches about the cleanliness of the body and mind while he sits pop-eyed and bemused, it is impossible not to howl. Hoffman is charming enough, providing plenty of good bits, but he doesn't create a real characterization any more than the other players do, even though he is onscreen more than most actors are in most films.

Early on, Jack is depicted as a kind of American Candide, an innocent pilgrim travelling through a series of adventures we expect will in time "educate" him. But we never see that education process take place, or really come to understand whether he has learned and grown from any of his encounters. Midway through the story, he poses and postures as a jaded gunfighter, but later on he is the innocent once again, as if the earlier experience did not take place. We see him survive one travesty after another, yet the script wants to have it both ways, wants to be able to play him as an innocent when it so desires, and as an experienced person if that serves the purpose—with no clear sense of development from one to the other. Dustin is not so much an actor playing scenes as a burlesque comic running through skits. No wonder, then, that he perceptively complained he feared "getting lost amid the scenery," and that he sensed he slipped "in and out of the role." For there was no role, really: one cannot say for certain what Jack Crabb is really like, only that he is a pleasant excuse for Hoffman to do shtik. We don't know what Jack Crabb's personality is because

Custer (Richard Mulligan) at the Little Big Horn.

the filmmakers don't appear to have made up their minds.

But Dustin was riding high with the critics at the time, and few had anything but positive things to say about him. Philip T. Hartung, in *Commonweal*, put it simply enough: "In the title role, Dustin Hoffman gives another of his superb performances." Stefan Kanfer of *Time* gave a mixed but ultimately positive review of the film, and commented that "In the title role, shuttling incessantly from the red to the white side, Dustin Hoffman adopts precisely the right attitude of bewildered reality lost in myth, a photograph projected on a Frederic Remington painting." However, *Saturday Review*'s Arthur Knight complained that "It is difficult to decide whether Dustin Hoffman's portrait of Crabb across generation gaps . . . is a personal triumph for the artist, or for the make-up artist, Dick Smith, who worked cosmetic wonders." And Pauline Kael, often a Hoffman critic, complained that "with his hopping walk and his nasal vocal tricks,

(Hoffman) is a good character actor, but one wearies of Jack Crabb's openmouthed bewilderment. One begins to accept handsome old Chief Dan George playing Old Lodge Skins as the central character, because his face draws the camera in a way Hoffman's doesn't; the chief has a radiance that the movie is starved of." But Kael's was a voice calling in the wilderness. Stanley Kauffmann in *New Republic* said of him: "He's short, he has a Feiffer profile, his voice is no great shakes, and, although he has charm, he has no great force of personality. What he has is instant credibility. It never seems to cross his mind that he is anything other than what he claims to be at the moment, so it never crosses our minds, either. . . . It's as if Hoffman were saying, 'What do you mean, I'm not a Cheyenne brave? I've been one all my life.' This ability to shut out objectivity—to shut out any view of one's self playing the part—is an essential particularly for "chameleon" actors, and it's Hoffman's ace." And for Paul D. Zimmerman of *Newsweek*,

"Hoffman's performance is a marvel, alive at every moment, generous to those who play opposite him, and full of dazzling surprises from the Keatonesque seriousness of his gun-slinger posturing to the sudden anger he unleashes as, in the role of scout, he counsels Custer to stand at Little Bighorn."

On the surface, *Little Big Man* is a movie about Indians and Viet Nam, about the frontier past as perceived through the prism of the then-current American point of view. Beyond that, it is a movie about culture shock and psychological disorientation. Momentarily putting aside the one-sidedness of the movie's obvious message, the fascination of the film actually rests in watching Crabb bounce back and forth from one sort of society to another, always feeling somewhat displaced: he is a white among the Indians and an Indian among the whites. Dustin surely locked in to his own similar experiences when, as a boy, his family moved back and forth from Beverly Hills to the tough downtown L.A. area, as his father's financial fortunes rose and fell during the Depression, and Dustin found himself enjoying the rough street style more than he did the "civilized" middle class life—just as Crabb comes to enjoy the Cheyenne culture more than

civilized whites. Later, when Dustin travelled to New York to pursue his career, he felt he had "discovered home"—the place where he really belonged, much as Crabb finds the Indians who take him in are more emotionally in tune with his values than the whites he was born among.

In addition to cultural displacement, Dustin shares another significant quality with Crabb: both are born survivors. Dustin "survived" the rigors of the New York acting scene at a time when other talented people were giving up and finding alternative professions; and, on a more literal level, he survived the burns from a cooking fire accident that the doctor in charge insisted would kill him. Crabb, of course, is the ultimate symbol of survival: the sole white survivor of Custer's Last Stand. Dustin's ability to play any role to the utmost depends on his ability to psychologically synchronize himself with the character by drawing on a parallel past experience—similar in emotional timbre, if not in surface details—in order to make the dramatized situation real rather than theatrical. Certainly, he had enough experience as a culturally displaced person and as a born survivor to handle the role of Jack Crabb.

Buffalo hunters load their wares.

Who Is Harry Kellerman and Why Is He Saying Those Terrible Things About Me?

A National General Pictures Release 1971

Dustin Hoffman as Georgie Soloway.

CAST:

Dustin Hoffman (*Georgie Soloway*); Barbara Harris (*Allison*); Jack Warden (*Dr. Moses*); David Burns (*Leon*); Dom De Luise (*Irwin*); Betty Walker (*Margot*); Rose Gregorio (*Gloria*); Gabriel Dell (*Sid*); Amy Levitt (*Susan*); Joe Sicari (*Marty*); Ed Zimmermann (*Holloran*); Candy Azzara (*Sally*); Robyn Millan (*Samantha*); Shel Silverstein (*Bernie*).

CREDITS:

Director-Producer, Ulu Grosbard; producer-writer, Herb Gardner; associate producer, Fred C. Caruso; director of photography, Victor J. Kemper; production designer, Harry Horner; sound, Jack C. Jacobsen; songs by Shel Silverstein; running time, 108 minutes; rating, PG.

Dustin's attraction to the *Harry Kellerman* project is completely understandable if far from justifiable. He had just finished two projects undertaken mainly on the advice of his agent and business managers: *John and Mary* (which was supposed to restore him to the matinee idol status of *The Graduate*) and *Little Big Man* (which was intended as proof he could dominate a big Hollywood epic.) The former was a box office dud and critical failure; the second was a runaway hit even if Hoffman inwardly feared that he got lost amid the scenery. What was needed to artistically satisfy him at this point in his career was a small film with a complex and clearly defined character, within the context of a film script as offbeat and original as an off-Broadway play. He satisfied himself that he had found both those qualities in Herb Gardner's *Who Is Harry Kellerman And Why Is He Saying Those Terrible Things About Me?*, the title of which certainly sounded more like that of an off (or off-off!) Broadway show than a major motion picture.

As an actor, the great appeal to Dustin was in playing a man who looked visibly different from himself—and, beyond that, playing a man at three distinct stages in his life. Though it may seem less of a challenge at first glance, playing a man eight years older than he was far more difficult than playing the 121-year-old hero of *Little Big Man*, for there, make-up and an affected vocal pattern could easily convey the illusion of age. But to play a man one step ahead of himself in maturity, Dustin would have to project into the near future, to study the way a man in his early forties moved and reacted, as compared to a man in his early thirties. Whereas *Little Big Man* had mainly bounced back and forth between the extremes of old age and callow youth, here Dustin would get to portray a man at seventeen, twenty-five, and forty, and have the opportunity to show not just a character—or even a character in transition—but rather the uniquely different facets of a man as he exists at specific moments in time. And while viewers still insisted on associating Hoffman with the perennially youthful *Graduate* image, he was interested in dealing with his own oncoming mid-life crisis by portraying such a syndrome on film.

"I've always been in awe of that period which goes from twenty to thirty-five," he told interviewers who visited him on the set of *Kellerman*. "Usually your dreams of what you would like to be—in terms of your marriage or your career—begin to flourish while you're around the age of twenty, then they are either fulfilled in the next fifteen years, or they begin to disintegrate by the time you're thirty-five."

At any rate, if the sensibility of the project was off-Broadway, the style and approach of the film proved to be nothing if not cinematic, for it makes use of split-second editing between past and present, as well as between reality and fantasy, in a manner that would be near impossible to pull off onstage, but which can be accomplished simply enough in the magical realm of movies just by editing two disparate pieces of film together.

The story begins as Georgie Soloway (Hoffman) sits in his triplex apartment atop New York's General Motors Building and dutifully composes his suicide note. Established immediately is the extreme dichotomy between Georgie's vestiges of commercial success and his spiritual sense of failure. He is an extraordinarily popular music business mogul, who can turn out over sixty songs a year, but he knows the terrible truth about himself: he is uncommitted and cor-

The young Georgie serenades an early love.

Success and failure in the music business: Dustin and Barbara Harris as a perennially hopeful singer.

rupt, for in one day he wrote both an anti-war peacenik hymn and an Air Force marching anthem. His popularity and notoriety—ranging from *Time* Magazine's Man of the Year cover to a triple decker sandwich named after him in his father's (David Burns) restaurant cannot belie his inward notion of being a popular fraud and a spiritual failure, so he leaps out the window and lands—on his analyst's couch, where he is, we realize, only fantasizing about suicide. Throughout the film, we are whisked back and forth between Georgie's fantasies and his realities, which often become blurred even for him. But one thing is made clear throughout: he is being exposed as a phony to all who know him by a mysterious, unknown man named Harry Kellerman, who has been calling just about everyone of influence in New York and spreading unpleasant—but mostly true—information about Georgie.

After studying Georgie's paranoid problems for nearly two hours, screenwriter Gardner reveals his "trick ending," which every viewer with the slightest power of elucidation has guessed after the first ten or twenty minutes: Harry is Georgie's alter ego; out of a terrible psychologi-

cal need he has formed a Mr. Hyde side of himself, for it is the failed idealist-artist in Georgie that most hates and despises the commercial sell-out side of Georgie, and wants to do him in. This notion might have worked if we had the slightest inclination that Gardner *assumed* everyone in the audience would grasp this truth before Georgie discovers it, until, along the way, everyone watching knew what only the central character didn't know: that he is his own nemesis. After all, this was precisely the kind of structural device that made the ancient *Oedipus the King* exert its tragic effect; it might have been spellbinding if it were understood and implicit in *Kellerman* that everyone is waiting for the fated hero to catch up with us, waiting for the moment when he will at last know the terrible truth each of us has grasped at some point in the proceedings.

Unfortunately, *Kellerman* is not constructed that way. The revelation appears to be meant as a cheap surprise ending, and for that reason comes off more as a failed gimmick than as a source of the film's dramatic structure. Indeed, the movie appears to have been "padded out"—as though Gardner came up with his trick ending first, then set about laboriously constructing a story leading up to it. Considering that Gardner's intended effect is based on his hope for a sudden shock ending, *Kellerman* might have been far more effective as one of those tightly constructed, thirty-minute TV dramas that had flourished on *Twilight Zone* and *Alfred Hitchcock Presents*. But as a full length film, it came off comparable to a decent short story idea mistakenly aspiring to be a full length novel.

The overall impact is not helped much by the uncertain direction of Ulu Grosbard, whose color scheme for the picture allows it a look that is far too lyrically lovely for its own good. Perhaps the prettiness is meant to convey some sort of an irony between the physical attractiveness of the lifestyle Georgie inhabits and his psychologically ugly perception of it, but if that was the director's conception, it does not work. For *Kellerman* looks as though the filmmakers were unable to fashion a visual scheme to fit the theme and mood of the story's central conception.

Even the fast cutting and blending of dream-

Dwarfed by his own image: The "real" Georgie and his media-created legend.

Even when surrounded by beautiful girls, Georgie still feels alone.

Georgie tries to write a new song and ignore the obvious distraction of an attractive onlooker.

like sequences with ones that are relatively realistic does not lend *Kellerman* the quality of an American arthouse film it was supposed to suggest, but seem more like stale borrowings of an approach the audience experienced as much as five years earlier in pictures like Bunuel's *Belle de Jour* or Antonioni's *Blow Up,* devices which had by the time of *Kellerman's* creation degenerated into cinematic conventions—cliches, even—meant to suggest instantaneous artiness, rather than experimental approaches to moviemaking art.

Kellerman's greatest irony appears, interestingly enough, an unintentional one, for this film finally seems like precisely the sort of picture Georgie Soloway would make if he were a director rather than a musician, as it cleverly, calculatedly rips off the current trends in popular art and turns them into a trendy product every bit as fraudulent as Georgie's musical creations.

To be fair, Gardner did write several funny scenes, especially the excellent one in which the successful but unfulfilled Georgie auditions a relatively talentless would-be singer (Barbara Harris) and finds himself attracted to her for everything that is genuine about this sincere but unsuccessful individual: her perseverance, her courage, her drive, her tenuous acceptance of her lack of commercial success, her unguarded human honesty. Most Herb Gardner plays have a single such scene that sets off the fabricated quality of the rest of the work. Surprisingly,

A flashback to more tranquil times.

120

Hoffman has claimed to be a fan of Gardner's writing, which is hard to understand in light of his great admiration for the plays of his friend Murray Schisgal, for while the two writers might at first seem to be dealing through comedy with the self-same serious issues—individuals struggling for self understanding in the face of a cold, unfeeling social system—the difference between their work could not be more marked.

Gardner supplies us with characters we are meant to feel sympathy for, to laugh along with, to care about and also enjoy, in both *Kellerman* and his earlier, more famous project, *A Thousand Clowns*, which starred Jason Robards as a self-confessed and self-righteous "non-conformist." The problem with Gardner is that he appears to take his characters' self-conception at face value, and fails to see the humor in their romanticized self-conceptions. But Gardner's "heroes" are not rugged individualists (for rugged individualists never conceive of themselves as rugged individualists) but phonies who play at non-conformity, and the essential emptiness of all his writing and the superficial, synthetic quality of his characters derives from this failure. When Schisgal, on the other hand, gives us characters who are self-conscious about being "individualists," as in the case of Ben Harris in *The Tiger*, he is always doing so to make them laughable—and to force us to laugh, in the process, at any pompous self-conceptions we may harbor.

Schisgal's writings present a man who, despite the evidence for pessimism he notices in the world around him, remains a touchingly charming romantic; Gardner's works reveal an embarrassing sentimentality shining through the surface sheen of pseudo-sophisticated cynicism. If Schisgal is a successful Neil Simon for hipsters, then Gardner is a failed Murray Schisgal for the masses. Thus, while *Harry Kellerman* is supposed to be a tragedy which presents itself to us in the guise of comedy, it is at heart only a soap opera attempting to pass itself off as comedy-drama, the "moment of truth" ending ringing as pure fabrication.

Amazingly, within this project Hoffman delivers one of his finest performances, one that is so perfect in suggesting the subtleties of the man

Georgie confronts his father (David Burns).

The first "urban cowboy": Georgie relaxes in his penthouse apartment.

121

Georgie's luxurious surroundings cannot quell his growing sense of failure.

Dom DeLuise and Dustin Hoffman in conversation.

122   Georgie exercises in his apartment.

Georgie cracks a rare smile.

that he breathes a life into Georgie that the character, as written, did not possess. Hoffman is well aware of the problem that his best work has often been done in films—including *Straight Time* and *John and Mary*—which were not seen very widely, and in which the film as a whole failed to support the level of his performance. His delineation of Soloway at three stages in his life is truly extraordinary, for he doesn't merely "suggest" these ages but literally becomes each of them on screen. Perhaps much of his conviction derives from seeing in Georgie a hint of what he himself might have become had he jumped aboard the commercial bandwagon available to him after *The Graduate*'s success. In a sense, Georgie was "The Road Not Taken" for Dustin; if he had failed to heed his brother Ronald's advice by keeping his lifestyle pretty much the same as it had been before stardom came, he might have turned out very much like Georgie, who enjoys success in the music business (the very business which, significantly,

Shel Silverstein and Dustin Hoffman in concert.

Dustin had originally planned to enter) and upgrades his lifestyle so much that he then has to compromise his artistic integrity and turn out junk in order to remain in that lifestyle. Dustin avoided such a mistake, but he understood the potential to go that route which had to be conquered. If Harry Kellerman is an alter ego for Georgie Soloway, then Georgie Soloway is just such an alter ego for Dustin Hoffman.

This is the single film in which he most clearly expresses his own mixed emotions concerning success, for as he told interviewers in a very different context: "I used to think that if I became successful everything would fall into place. I'd feel differently about everything—I'd be happy all the time. But that's not how it is. I have to tell you I don't feel different at all. When you are not successful, then you strive for success. After you are successful, you strive to stay that way." That is Dustin Hoffman talking to reporters shortly after *The Graduate* was released, but it could be Georgie Soloway talking to his psychiatrist. In addition, Georgie's fear that his work will be shown up as fraudulent mirrors Dustin's oft-voiced fear that someday everyone will discover "all your work is a fraud."

He ran all the way: Dustin as Georgie Soloway, a man in search of himself.

Ironically, then, his soul searching, near perfect, highly perceptive performance in this otherwise fraudulent film proves he has little to worry about in that department, for he provided the single saving grace to this otherwise misguided movie.

Mostly, the critics praised Hoffman even as they panned the film. Typical of the reviews was Hollis Alpert's in *Saturday Review*, wherein he stated: "In an earlier film, *The Graduate*, (Mike) Nichols brought to center stage Dustin Hoffman, who, in the interim, has become a superstar. . . . Hoffman is still a fine and engaging actor, but in this film he lacks the firm, guiding hand of his first film mentor. . . . What we like about Georgie is Dustin Hoffman himself, who keeps peeping impishly through the character's unhappy facade." Paul D. Zimmerman in *Newsweek* added that Georgie "is, beneath his mournful mustache, a cliche instead of a character, an amalgam of all those Hollywood heroes who realized the American dream only to end in alcoholism, insanity or suicide. Dustin Hoffman struggles valiantly to give his stereotype a specific resonance, his neck slanting out like a mon-

goose as he searches for meaning, his nasal voice wrought into a permanent question mark." In the *Hollywood Reporter,* Larry Cohen insisted that "Hoffman's portrayal of Georgie is the best single performance the actor has given in films to-date. The tremendous amount of feeling (particularly anguish) he invests in this character encourages rather than sucks at feeling; there are nuances here that Hoffman has never shown before." Winfred Blevins of the L.A. *Herald Examiner* concurred when she insisted "Georgie Soloway is one of his best characterizations—perhaps his fullest. He comes up with a large and telling vocabulary of physical movements (and non-movements) to give us Georgie's tension, fear, remoteness, and desperation. He brings an extraordinary range of nuance to Georgie's flow of emotions. . . ." One of the few critics who was not captivated by Hoffman's performance was Stefan Kanfer, who in *Time* wrote that "Hoffman's sluggish nasal metabolism is still amusing if familiar." Other than that one pulled punch, *Kellerman* was acknowledged as one of those Hoffman films in which his performance was not supported by the picture itself.

Resting along the way: Georgie grabs a rare moment of relaxation.

Straw Dogs

Distributed by Cinerama Releasing   1972

David Sumner (Dustin Hoffman) and wife Amy (Susan George) settle down for
what they believe will be a peaceful existence in a Cornwall village.

CAST:

Dustin Hoffman (*David Sumner*); Susan George (*Amy*); Peter Vaughn (*Tom Hedden*); T. P. McKenna (*Major Scott*); Del Henny (*Venner*); Ken Hutchinson (*Scutt*); Colin Welland (*Rev. Hood*); Jim Norton (*Cawsey*); Sally Thomsett (*Janice*); David Warner (*Henry Niles*).

CREDITS:

Director, Sam Peckinpah; screenplay by Sam Peckinpah and David Zelag Goodman, based on Gordon Williams's novel *The Siege at Trencher's Farm;* director of photography, John Coquillon; editors, Paul Davies, Roger Spottinswoode, and Tony Lawson; music by Jerry Fielding; produced by Daniel Melnick; an ABC Pictures Corporation Presentation; running time, 113 minutes; rating, R.

The period between 1967 and 1969—the period that, significantly, saw the release of both *The Graduate* and *Midnight Cowboy*—was a period of extreme transition in the movie business and, not coincidentally, society at large. Audiences witnessed the end of the Production Code restrictions and the beginning of the rating system; the auctioning off of the old studio accoutrements and the beginning of pictures shot entirely in "the real world"; the breakdown of the Hollywood assembly line system and the beginning of independently financed pictures. To a large degree, Dustin Hoffman's career (as a major star, if not as a working actor) was made possible by these changes. So too was one of the most overriding movie controversies of the time: the question of ever more graphic violence onscreen. At a point in time when political assassinations, ghetto burnings, and the escalating of both urban crime and the Viet Nam war made violence a depressing but inescapable fact of daily life, the movies which used the newfound freedom of the screen to reflect this violence were under constant attack, as critics and concerned viewers questioned whether the films were merely serving to honestly reflect the issue or were in fact a part of the problem.

In 1967, the year *The Graduate*'s sexual trysts proved controversial, the other most controversial single picture was Arthur Penn's *Bonnie and Clyde*, which employed an elongated slow mo-

tion/montage sequence to extend the deaths of the two 1930s outlaws. In 1969, the year *Midnight Cowboy*'s rough language and tough theme proved controversial, the other most controversial single picture was Sam Peckinpah's *The Wild Bunch*, which outdid *Bonnie and Clyde* by concluding with a literal "ballet of blood." It hardly seems coincidental, then, that an actor closely associated with his times would make a pair of extremely violent pictures, back to back, for these two directors.

While shooting *Little Big Man* for Penn, Dustin commented to reporters on the violence of the cavalry vs. Indian sequences, and his own mixed emotions about violence onscreen and off. "I'm not a violent person," he said then. "I don't shoot guns, don't fight, but I get excited by violence. I would like to investigate my feelings about violence in a role." Only one year later he was working for Sam Peckinpah in a film which did precisely that. And while *Little Big Man* and *Straw Dogs* are equally violent films, they are so different in terms of scope and theme and meaning that, if anything, they serve to complement rather than repeat one another. In *Little Big Man*, Hoffman portrayed an essentially non-violent character caught in a violent landscape, and as bloody as some of the film's scenes are, it moves inexorably toward an ending that is essentially anti-violent—even pacifistic—in outlook. But in *Straw Dogs*, Dustin's character ultimately unleashes more violence (he kills nearly half a dozen men in twenty minutes and derives great satisfaction from doing so) than any of the seemingly more violent characters in the picture.

Like D.H. Lawrence, Peckinpah presupposes that it is not only man's right but also his duty to sexually dominate a woman, despite her strong need to offer mighty resistance which she hopes he will be man enough to overcome. Like Ernest Hemingway, Peckinpah proceeds from the notion that to be a man, one must sooner or later test himself in violent combat and, like Hemingway's bullfighters and soldiers, know the moment-of-truth exhilaration of bloody victory. Though Penn and Peckinpah both analyze the quality of violence in our world, it is the presence of these themes that add a significant element to Peckinpah's pictures that is not present in Penn's: machismo.

David enters the local pub, where he sees Tom Hedden (Peter Vaughan) falling into an argument with bartender Harry (Robert Keegan) as Venner (Del Henney) looks on.

Little Big Man is an urban/liberal/intellectual filmmaker's attempt to work in what is essentially for him a foreign form: the western. *Straw Dogs* is a rural/conservative/anti-intellectual filmmaker's first stab at directing outside the western genre. If *Little Big Man* was a film by an artist who is revolted by the very violence he is artistically drawn to, *Straw Dogs* is the product of a man who sees in it a terrible kind of salvation. The only similarity in their treatments of violence is that neither director used it "gratuitously"—as a cheap audience turn-on—but rather treat violence as part of their world views. For Peckinpah, that view is summed up in a quote from Lao-tze: "Heaven and earth are not humane, and they ruthlessly treat all things in their scope as straw dogs."

Some three hundred years before the birth of Christ, "straw dogs" were oriental artifacts meant to be first worshipped, then afterwards put to the torch. For Peckinpah, that notion applies equally to the totems and taboos of civilized society, which the filmmaker views not as a monolithic, far-reaching positive force on our

David and Amy enjoy a country breakfast in one of the film's more relaxed moments.

Scutt (Ken Hutchison) and Venner (Del Henney) threaten David as Amy looks on.

lives, but as a flimsy, unsubstantial illusion. And while we pay homage to society on a daily basis through its economic, religious, and social institutions, this is all just an elaborate game, a hoax—for finally, we must put our civilized order aside and act as the Neanderthals we still are.

This vision borders on outright nihilism, but it is the way in which this vision shapes every aspect of the film that makes *Straw Dogs* an uncontestable work of art (however unpleasant) and not a bloody work of hack fiction like the minor novel *The Siege of Trencher's Farm* on which it is based. Peckinpah transformed the simple, realistic story, making it an ugly parable—a point made clear from his first shot, an out-of-focus image of what appears to be a swarm of bugs crawling all over each other: nature at its least appealing, survival of the fittest at its bleakest. But as the image sharpens, we see these are no insects at all but schoolchildren at play in, of all places, a cemetery. Shortly, we learn this setting is an isolated village in rural Cornwall to which a one-time resident named Amy (Susan George) and her newly acquired

The sexually charged Amy interrupts the complex mathematical thinking of David.

American husband, David Sumner (Hoffman), have just returned. In time, the village becomes so insistently isolated from the world at large (we never catch so much as a glimpse of anything over the big hill, never see evidence of even radio or TV input from the outside), that it ultimately *becomes* the world, in microcosm.

Likewise, the marriage of Amy and David is so unlikely that it cannot be accepted on a realistic level, but must be appreciated as a contrivance in the service of symbolism. She is a woman of the senses: half Lolita, half Constance Chatterley, she is part child-tease, part unfulfilled mature bride. He, conversely, is a man of the mind, the cerebral man married unwisely to the flesh-woman. Their moral opposition is made clear in the opening sequence for each: we watch as she walks bra-less through the rude town, exciting the yokels and taking obvious pleasure in the

animal instincts she raises in them; we see him walk nervously, a stranger in a strange land, into the pub where he apologetically asks for any brand of American cigarettes they might have. Immediately, Peckinpah establishes with his camera (which always seems to be precisely but effortlessly in the right place, looking from the unquestionably proper angle) and his consummate editing (the film's rhythm never skips a beat) that the village hates them both, for oddly different reasons, at once wanting the woman and unable to comprehend the man.

For the next ninety minutes—right up to the climactic siege sequence—Peckinpah builds a sense of tension, not only between the isolated couple and the potentially menacing populace, but more significantly still between David and Amy. He, we learn in time, came here not only to allow his wife a visit to her old home while also

Scutt (Ken Hutchison), Cawsey (Jim Norton) and Venner (Del Henney) surprise David and frighten the American intellectual.

131

David and Amy toast their future.

gaining for himself the peace and quiet needed to complete his book (a mathematical treatise on celestial navigation), but also to solve the problems in their marriage by "going back to the basics."

At home, he could not commit himself to any point of view or face up to the escalating violence around him. But the problems follow him to the very place he has retreated to hide from them. Dropping out, according to the film's vision, is impossible. This becomes evident when the workmen he hires to make repairs strangle his cat and leave it in the closet—"to prove they can get into your bedroom," in his wife's estimation. He tries to buy the friendship of the hard men by treating them to drinks at the pub, but they exploit his "friendship" by taking him off on a "snipe hunt" where several keep him busy holding a sack open for the "birds" he believes will run into it, while two others—one a previous lover of his wife—return to the house and take his "bird" sexually.

The sexual scene was one of the lengthiest, and most graphic, ever included in an essentially non-pornographic picture—simultaneously erotic and upsetting, raising the ire of feminists

Amy is raped and sodomized by Venner (Del Henney) and Scutt (Ken Hutchison).

who immediately labelled Peckinpah the ultimate male chauvinist moviemaker. For the sequence is both a seduction and a rape: the woman simultaneously entices the men into taking her and attempts to fight them off—effectively portrayed by Susan George, as an embodiment of Peckinpah's conception of women. Hoffman also sublimated his own personality for the filmmaker, by becoming the director's symbol for modern man—over intellectualized but still, in times of stress, a natural member of the animal kingdom.

It is a most interesting part for Hoffman because, like each of his other varied roles, it allows him to come to grips with a possibility within his own personality by isolating it from his complex self and analyzing this by playing it for the camera. As a teenager, Dustin feared he was one of those 90-pound weaklings who has sand kicked in his face at the beach; in the privacy of his own room, he allowed his imagination free rein, picturing himself punching them out and establishing sexual supremacy over one of the beautiful girls he wanted. *Straw Dogs* is then not only a film vision for Peckinpah but an actualization of Dustin's adolescent fantasy. As Pauline Kael put it in the *New Yorker*, "Hoffman, notoriously a cerebral actor, projects thought before movement; he's already a cartoon of an intellectual. There's a split second of blank indecision before the face lights up with purpose. He never looks as if he just naturally lived in the places he's stuck into for the camera; he always seems slightly the outsider anyway, and his duck walk and physical movements are a shade clumsy. Whatever he does seems a bit of a feat—and that, I think, is why we're drawn to him."

Time said Dustin's performance was "nervously cerebral and superbly realized," while Arthur Cooper in *Newsweek* claimed, "Hoffman's fine performance is all the more remarkable for the handicaps under which he labors. A superb character actor, he is called upon to play the kind of timid, repressed figure who requires a restrained, interiorized approach, depriving Hoffman of the bravura style at which he excels." Judith Crist, attacking the film in *New York*, complained that Dustin exuded a "catatonic sweetness." Most of the critics were impressed by the film's technical accomplishment and outraged at its message, and Kael spoke for many of them when she complained "I realize that it's a terrible thing to say of someone whose gifts you admire that he has made a fascist classic."

Ultimately, the final sequence is rendered with a moral ambiguousness that makes it unique among violent screen entertainments. The toughs attack the house late at night, and David is clearly not defending the "honor" of his wife—which he seems vaguely aware was lost long ago. He is to a degree defending the life of the village idiot (David Warner), who the townsmen are pursuing; they mean, at this point, no direct threat to David and Amy whatsoever, and would gladly leave the couple be if David would only turn over the idiot. What keeps all this from being a simplistic affair of good protecting innocence from evil is that the idiot is in fact guilty of the twin crimes—molesting, then murdering a

David and Amy attend the annual church party in their new home town.

David fights with Scutt.

pre-teenager—he has been accused of, so there is nothing particularly glorious about what David does. It is not the courageous defense of a wronged innocent but of a child killer. What the idiot-in-danger brings out in David is not the best in him, but the most primitive. And, to a degree, the idiot's well-being is of little interest to David, and is nothing more than the spark that sets him off.

What makes David fight is that the townspeople must enter his home in order to get at the idiot, and what David shouts to them is the key to understanding the scene—and Peckinpah. "This is my home—this is *me*—I will not allow violence against this house." The director is a great admirer of Robert Ardrey's concept of "territorial imperatives," the concept that what we fight for is the sanctity of our corner of the universe, the property which becomes an expression of the essence of ourselves. And in what becomes a twentieth century working-out of Peckinpah's frontier values, the man of the mind is instantaneously transformed into a cowboy-

134

style hero who fights to protect a wife who has turned her back on him and the safety of someone he hardly knows, for no better reason than that they have become a part of his territory—and, for that reason, are in his safe keeping. In so doing, the mouse becomes a man, learning not only that he is capable of violence but that it makes him feel good, feel fulfilled. "I got *all* of 'em," he says with a smile.

But there is no easy way back from the violence into which he has wandered. When the idiot complains, after the bloodbath, "I don't know my way home," David replies, "Neither do I." Despite the storm of controversy that surrounded it, the box office success of *Straw Dogs* further established Dustin as one of America's leading younger stars, while the quality of his performance reaffirmed his quality as an actor. Most important of all, the role further enhanced a unique quality that was so significant to the success of Hoffman's career, continuing his general acceptance as a symbol of the modern American male. In *The Graduate*, he had been perceived as a symbol of the sixties' restless youth; in *John and Mary*, he had incarnated the male

sector of the emerging swinging singles scene. In *Straw Dogs*, he was the urban, intellectual male, and that section of the audience perceived him as a representation of their own self-image onscreen.

Susan George as Amy.

The village toughs: Cawsey (Jim Norton), Scutt (Ken Hutchison), Hedden (Peter Vaughan), Venner (Del Henney), Riddaway (Donald Webster) and Bertie (Michael Mundell).

Papillon

An Allied Artists Release   1973

Steve McQueen, Dustin Hoffman, and other criminals are shipped out to Devil's Island.

CAST:

Steve McQueen *(Papillon);* Dustin Hoffman *(Dega);* Victor Jory *(Indian Chief);* Don Gordon *(Julot);* Anthony Zerbe *(Leper Colony Chief);* Robert Deman *(Maturette);* Woodrow Parfrey *(Clusiot);* Bill Mumy *(Lariot);* George Colouris *(Dr. Chatal);* Ratna Assan *(Zoraima);* William Smithers *(Warden Barrot);* Gregory Sierra *(Antonio);* Barbara Morrison *(Mother Superior);* Ellen Moss *(Nun);* Don Hanmer *(Butterfly Trader);* Dalton Trumbo *(Commandant).*

CREDITS:

Director, Franklin J. Schaffner; producers, Robert Dorfman and Franklin J. Schaffner; executive producer, Ted Richmond; screenplay by Dalton Trumbo and Lorenzo Semple, Jr., based on the book by Henri Charriere; photography, Fred Koenekamp; editor, Robert Swink; music, Jerry Goldsmith; A Corona/General Production in Technicolor; running time, 150 minutes; rated PG.

One of the advertisements for *Papillon* proudly announced to the public: "The *big* movie is back!" To a degree, it was no lie. The budget was big: thirteen million dollars had been squandered shooting the picture almost entirely on locations to authentically recreate the French Guiana settings. The screen image was big: a Cinemascope vision of life in the penal system of the early twentieth century that stretched so wide audiences never knew where to look first. The cast was big: thousands of extras, playing everything from shackled prisoners and strong-armed guards to tribes of natives and crowds of French citizens gleefully seeing convicted criminals off for Devil's Island. The running time was big: nearly three hours, with an intermission thrown in somewhere near the middle. But most of all, the stars were big: Steve McQueen and Dustin Hoffman—about the nearest thing to authentic superstars the

Papillon (McQueen) and Degas (Hoffman) arrive on the Island.

137

1970s had to offer, with the possible exception of Newman and Redford—matched together for the first time.

In just about all superficial respects, then, *Papillon* represented a return to the colossal adventure movies of the past. Part of its enormous success at the box office might be attributed to the movie-going audience's sudden nostalgia for such fare, having been glutted in the early seventies on a surfeit of post-*Easy Rider* low budget "experimental" movies, Hoffman's own *Midnight Cowboy* among them. And part of Hoffman's willingness to do *Papillon* may have derived from his tendency to balance, at that point in his career, each of his small, personal pictures with a big one—*Alfredo, Alfredo* opened the same week as *Papillon,* though with considerably less fanfare.

Surveying the unpleasant surroundings.

Papillon and Degas enjoy a moment's solace.

But in just about every respect that really matters, *Papillon* was actually a strikingly small movie: short on intelligence, on taste, and on imagination—in fact, all those elements which had, only a short while before, made *The Godfather* such a satisfying return to the big Hollywood superproductions, as it worked simultaneously as film art and film entertainment. *Papillon,* on the other hand, aped all the obvious, barren trappings of genuine epics, while missing entirely the basic ingredients which made them great.

For one thing, the extreme length of the film was in no way substantiated. The Henri Charriere book on which the film was based—a compilation of fact and fable about his days as a prisoner, concocted some thirty years after those incidents as an enjoyable exercise in self-aggrandizement—was surely no slim volume. But on every page the reader discovered some humorous aside, some wry observation on life, some acutely described detail, some stylistic flourish that made it rate, quite legitimately, as a "can't put down" book. Very few of those elements were captured in the film, partially explainable by the fact that it was scripted by Dalton Trumbo, who hadn't done a respectable screenplay in ten years, and whose lofty reputation rested more on the fact that he had been blacklisted years earlier, and that his screenplays always contained some semblance of a social message, rather than on any merit in the bulk of his writing. Just as culpable as Trumbo and his collaborator, Lorenzo Semple, Jr., was director Franklin J. Schaffner, the man who set George C. Scott's heels a-clicking in *Patton*.

Hoffman attempts escape in the night.

The beady-eyed McQueen and myopic Hoffman in prisoner's garb.

In that film, he had tried for a "big" approach and succeeded, mainly because the two main characters—Generals George Patton and Omar Bradley—were two of the biggest men of their time, and the overblown moviemaking style seemed particularly apt to express the essence of them. But unrelenting bigness was all wrong for a mostly straightforward story about two insignificant characters portrayed in *Papillon*. The result was a picture which, beneath its expensive and expansive veneer, offered little more than a run-of-the-mill "I Escaped From Devil's Island" B-movie story, dressed up in its Sunday best to look like something more than what it was. Actually, many such B-movie accounts of similar stories are far more satisfying than *Papillon*: they know what modest, limited little thing they want to accomplish; they announce it in an unpreten-

139

tious way; they carry it through in as sparingly short a time as possible. *Papillon* wanders on forever—and for what?

Steve McQueen is imprisoned, escapes with Dustin Hoffman's help, gets caught and is reincarcerated, only to escape again. Whenever he's on the run, things generally move briskly and the picture is engaging as yet another "great escape" yarn. But when he's in jail, the audience suffers even more than he does. Huge chunks of

Hoffman cares for his small garden.

Playing football with a cocoanut.

140

time go by in which absolutely nothing happens, except for McQueen sitting in solitary. That would be justifiable enough if only we felt educated, uplifted, or in some way enlightened by his plight, as was frequently the case in the novel. But that was not true of the film. Instead, it offered an almost pornographic depiction of human suffering, recorded dutifully as if the mere fact that some poor souls did indeed undergo such tortures justifies its endless depiction in a movie. The result proved to be an amorphous creation. A prison escape film like *The Great Escape* works skillfully as pure entertainment, whereas one such as *Grand Illusion* is clearly an in-depth intellectual tract. *Papillon* pretended to offer a bit of both, but failed quite completely as either.

"Henri Charriere escaped and lived the rest of his life a free man," the narrator's pompous voice intoned at the picture's end, "but the French penal system which imprisoned him did not survive!" This little ditty was superimposed over a long shot of McQueen leaving Hoffman behind and floating out to sea in one last desperate bid for freedom, a powerful image which might have been an effectively open-ended way to finish the tale. But the heavy hand of Dalton Trumbo couldn't resist making believe that the preceding story had some redeeming social value, that it could be used as a means of raising the audience's consciousness. So we had to hear an old-fashioned statement of the Stanley Kramer, mid-1950s liberal message-movie variety, booming out with the authority of the Voice of God. The implication is that Charriere's actions heroically helped to end such terrible forms of imprisonment, when in fact the two had nothing to do with each other; the French shut down their unpleasant penal colonies only when they ceased to be profitable, and not a minute before.

Schaffner was clearly aware the tale offered little in the way of visual excitement, so as a means of beefing it up somewhat he threw in close-ups of blood and guts. Interestingly enough, there was almost no critical or public outpouring against the graphic depiction of heads flipping from the guillotine, of open wounds offered to the audience and bodies being impaled on wooden spears. No one claimed—as they did with Arthur Penn's *Little Big Man* or Sam Peckinpah's *Straw Dogs*, two other highly violent projects Hoffman was associated with—that the bloodletting might have a negative effect on some viewers. Yet both those films employed violence as part of a consistent and effective artistic vision of life, whereas in *Papillon* it was purely exploitive—thrown in to make things appear less boring.

Caught!

A moment's rest.

Equally offensive were Schaffner's attempts to class up the picture with effects which bordered on the ludicrous. There were two "fantasy" sequences—one in which McQueen/Charriere envisions himself and his friend Louis Dega (Hoffman) receiving a heroes' return to Paris, and another in which he faces sentencing in a heavenly court. They look like someone's unsuccessful attempt to satirize the dream sequences in a Fellini flick. All the cliches which appeared in the films of the late 1960s, were subsequently beaten to death by overuse, and then disappeared from sight in the early 1970s were catalogued during the course of *Papillon:* two lovers running toward each other in slow motion—that sort of thing. In addition, these scenes jar so with the rest of the picture's down-to-earth realism that any sense of believability is shattered.

Equally lamentable is that despite the inordinate length, there were gaping holes in the story

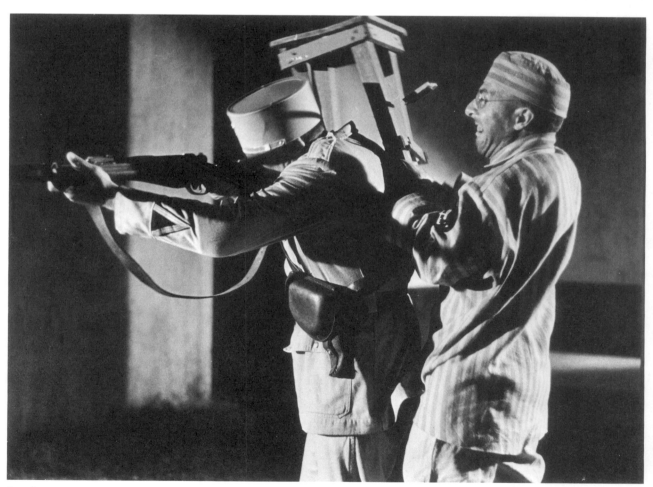
Another escape attempt.

Friends to the finish.

line, and character motivations were often non-existant. A group of headhunters wound McQueen with poisoned darts and we see him fall, unconscious, into a pond, where we assume he will drown if the poison does not finish him first. A moment later, he's somehow been saved and nursed back to life by friendly natives. And while we can certainly understand his burning desire to escape from the penal colonies, why does he leave the seashore village he has escaped to, and where he lives in freedom and friendship with plenty of food and an incredibly beautiful girlfriend? We know nothing of a burning desire to get back to France, and it is the Hoffman character who has people in Paris he wants to rejoin. We have been led to believe Charriere's only burning passion was to escape from the prison, and he has already done that—why take the risk of probable recapture by trying to return to the Continent, which he has no great love for anyway?

In a nutshell, this is *Papillon*'s problem: the film never lets us feel we are inside this fascinating and unusual man, which is precisely what the book accomplished on every page. We experi-ence only the surface of his reality, and therefore could consider ourselves lucky he was played by as powerful a presence as Steve McQueen, who only a few years earlier had seemed nothing more than a second-rate leading man. With *Papillon*, he matured into one of the most fascinating screen personalities of his time, with at least a trace of resemblance to the young Spencer Tracy. The electricity of his presence is what made the over-long starvation sequence bearable: he had one of those stoic faces which are so subtly expressive that he could make anything interesting. McQueen here managed to turn at least one unpromising moment into a personal triumph: in a midnight meeting with a group of lepers, he is forced to accept and puff a cigar that a half-decomposed man has been smoking. The string of emotions which criss-cross his face—beginning with fear and ending on arrogance—add up to a beautiful moment of wordless gesture.

Dustin Hoffman, unfortunately, did not fare nearly so well, as this was the performance which caused some of his most die-hard fans to at least temporarily reconsider the extent of his talent. The contrast between the two leads may have been responsible for this. McQueen was a movie star first, an actor second; his charisma was based on the cult of personality, which is why he could repeat himself endlessly without growing tiresome. Hoffman, on the other hand, had consistently striven to be an actor first, a star second. Without the benefit of a continuous persona, we expect something new from him each time. And, to succeed, he necessarily has to rise to the level of his own ambitions. But as Papillon's sidekick, his character appeared nothing more than an exaggerated repeat performance of his role in the off-Broadway *Journey of the Fifth Horse*. Perhaps he felt intimidated by McQueen's star presence, sensed the need to try and steal the show by continuously, consciously *acting*. Always, we saw the work, saw him thinking about what he would do next. Throughout the film, he appeared unable to say a line of dialogue without scrunching up his brow like some grotesque, deformed creature, and then spurting out the line as though he had a bad case of strep throat and found it painful to talk.

Louis Dega proved to be the last of the cripple

The shared fantasy of a triumphant return home.

roles Hoffman had been so successful with in the early days of his stage career, and which Hoffman himself had come to find unsatisfying. It was too easy to hide behind a mannerism rather than delineate the essence of a normal-seeming man, which is why roles in such films as *John and Mary* and *Kramer vs. Kramer* proved far more challenging and complex than the more superficially flamboyant roles in *Midnight Cowboy* and *Papillon*.

Hoffman was uncomfortable with the role of Dega almost from the start. A fictional character who is a composite of several prison-bound friends of the real-life Charriere, Dega had never been clearly defined as a person in the screenplay. To try and breathe life into him, especially his emotional reactions to the Devil's Island torturous, even hell-like existence, Hoffman borrowed an idea from his onetime acting teacher, Lonnie Chapman, who had always championed the notion of using great paintings as an inspiration—in effect, a possible "key"—to characterization. When Dustin had to find a psychological inroad to the prison lifestyle, he studied the tortured images of some of Francis Bacon's nightmare landscapes. But he knew it didn't do the trick for him. "I learned from that

experience," Dustin said later, "That you can't create more than is on paper, in the script."

To make Dega as interesting as Charriere, Hoffman himself created all the business about Dega wearing thick glasses, implying that the man was almost blind. But the script itself suggested no significance to Dega's problems with sight; if it had, then Dustin's characterization would have been legitimized. As is, it is baroque—ornamental and affected rather than a natural interpretation of the man as he was suggested on paper. "I learned," Dustin said, "not to build more of a character than the text can support."

The critics were generally less kind to Hoffman than usual, though there were a few flattering reviews, as the one in *Esquire* which claimed that Dega was "brought to wonderfully various, unpredictable, paradoxical—and thus thoroughly human—life by Dustin Hoffman, who gives a performance in which asperity and winsomeness supplant each other as quickly and dazzlingly as the faces of a spinning coin." Less poetic but almost as laudatory was Richard Schickel in *Life*, who claimed that "Hoffman submerges himself eccentrically and amusingly in his coward's role." Even Pauline Kael began

144

her *New Yorker* review with a backhanded compliment, for after knocking the film itself, she argued "I was grateful each time Dustin Hoffman turned up, simply because he tries to do something for his characterization. . . ." But quickly enough, the critical worm turned, and in this case at least, most critics agreed with her attack: "Hoffman seems to think he needs a physical gimmick for his characters . . . why does he go through the picture with his mouth open, like some adenoidal chinless wonder?"

Hoffman has often been the bright spot in a failed project; here, he was at the heart of the film's failure. Some of the blame may go, as he has claimed, to the way in which his performance was restructured and manipulated in the editing room. More likely than not, though, the real problem derives from an inability to find the "key" that would have unlocked Dega for Hoffman—and, in the process, allow Hoffman to find something of himself in Dega. There are, in fact, several similarities which might have provided the "key." Hoffman has always expressed a fear of eventual failure, and in the film his character eventually fails—in the fade-out, he is left on the prison island as McQueen floats away to success. Likewise, Hoffman has consistently talked about his fear of being alone, and basic to Dega's situation in the film is his being left alone in the final scene. But for whatever reasons, Hoffman does not appear to have locked in to the character despite the possible "keys", and his apparent inability to believe in Dega is basic to why audiences cannot believe in him either.

A terrified Hoffman undergoes harsh treatment at the hands of a brutal guard.

Shipmates—and prison mates.

Alfredo, Alfredo

A Paramount Pictures Release   1973

Dustin Hoffman as Alfredo.

CAST:

Dustin Hoffman *(Alfredo)*; Stefania Sandrelli *(Mariarosa)*; Carla Gravinia *(Carolina)*; Clara Colosimo *(Carolina's Mother)*; Daniele Patella *(Carolina's Father)*; Danika La Loggia *(Mariarosa's Mother)*; Saro Urzi *(Mariarosa's Father)*.

CREDITS:

Director, Pietro Germi; story and screenplay (Italian with English subtitles) by Leo Benvenuti, Piero de Bernardi, Tullio Pinelli and Pietro Germi; director of photography, Aiace Parolin; editor, Sergio Montanari; music, Carlo Rustichelli; a co-production by RPA-Rizzoli Films/Francoriz Productions; running time, 100 minutes; rating, R.

It's easy enough to understand why Dustin would have chosen to make *Alfredo, Alfredo* (originally to have been titled, "Till Divorce Do Us Part") for Italy's Pietro Germi. In the first place, Germi had a considerable track record, being the foremost among Italian cinema-social satirists who, in the early 1960s, eased out the earlier Neorealists (Vittorio De Sica, Roberto Rossellini, etc.) whose serious, probing, ponderous style had dictated that country's movie industry since the dawn of the post-war era. With *Divorce, Italian Style* and then *Seduced and Abandoned*, Germi had proven that Italian filmmakers could return to the métier of comedy without relinquishing their commitment to making films of social consciousness. Hoffman admired Germi's work, as most American intellectuals did.

Beyond that, though, Hoffman relished the idea of appearing in just such a film, and welcomed the difficult challenge of temporarily submerging his typically American personality so completely that he would be indistinguishable among an ensemble of European performers. After all, Dustin had earlier promised himself that he would not let his superstar status get in the way of tackling the kind of artistic challenges that, as an actor, he most enjoyed. Besides, he fancied the notion of balancing each of his big Hollywood pictures *(Little Big Man, Papillon)* with a smaller, more offbeat and personalized

project *(Midnight Cowboy, Harry Kellerman)* in order to satisfy the actor in him—just as the bigger films were satisfying that part of him which really did want to be a star. The script for *Alfredo* happened to reach Dustin just when he was on the lookout for a "little" picture, and the concept struck his fancy.

In it, Dustin plays a shy, reticent bank clerk living quietly with his father in a provincial Italian city. His deepest fear is that no attractive woman will ever give him a second glance, but there is something of the Walter Mitty in him, for secretly he dreams of being a playboy, a romancer, an "Alfie"—in short, a ladies' man. One day, a stunning female pharmacist (Stefania Sandrelli) visits the bank, and Alfredo nervously attends her, quite uncomfortable around such a magnificent-looking woman—and quite certain a lady of her beauty and elegance and social position would never give an at-best-average fellow like himself a second glance. But when he makes the most tentative of advances, he is shocked to find she responds by literally pursuing him, sweeping him off his feet and treating him as though he were a Greek God. Alfredo is flabbergasted, afraid to say anything for fear that in so doing he may make her aware of how ordinary he actually is, thus losing her forever. But she happily accompanies him to the altar, and he's thrilled to find himself married to a dream girl.

From the moment they begin their married life together, however, he realizes that he must deal with the reality rather than his fantasy of her, and she is not a dream but a person—with many flaws and weaknesses. She dominates him completely, taking over the house, sending him off to live in the cellar and moving her own hideous parents in upstairs. Sex between them quickly degenerates into a drudgery for him—a nightmare, even—and when their doctor prescribes that they must make love three times a day in order for her to become pregnant, he breaks out in a rash at her every touch. Ultimately, Alfredo yearns for a divorce so he can marry a quieter, seemingly more sympathetic lady architect (Carla Gravinia) he has since met and fallen in love with—his new "dream girl"!

Thus, the film deals directly with Italy's divorce laws, as did Germi's earlier films. It was

Alfredo enjoys a moment with his new mistress (Carla Gravina).

Alfredo receives a lecture from his new wife (Stefania Sandrelli).

148   Alfredo's marriage.

this very theme that lent those pictures their bite and wallop but which, ironically, caused *Alfredo* to seem inconsequential. On the one hand, Germi appeared to be only retreading material he had adequately covered already, though to be fair one must necessarily add there is nothing inherently wrong with a filmmaker approaching the same subject every few years, from his latest perspective—just as a painter might show us his development as an artist by the way that, at different times in his career, he paints the same subject. The catch is that a filmmaker doing this must necessarily show us how his attitudes about that subject have changed or, hopefully, matured during the intervening time, which Germi does not do here.

Another problem is that Germi dramatizes the

Alfredo tries to disentangle himself from a passionate moment in order to keep an important appointment.

bizarre situation in which his hero finds himself legally bound to satisfy his wife at her command or otherwise face prosecution in the courts, while being considered a criminal because of his affair with another woman, even though the same legal system sanctions his wife's taking of a lover! But by the time the film was finished and released, Italy had changed this law, permitting divorces under conditions like Alfredo's. There is nothing more stale than satire after the fact and, taken as satire, *Alfredo* was just that.

But if its satire came too late to be of any value, other elements of the comedy were more universal in their scope and intent—if also quite controversial. It is possible to interpret *Alfredo* as an arch misogynistic vision, for in many respects Germi appears to be the complete woman hater. The major complaint Alfredo lodges against his wife is that she's emotionally demanding and sexually aggressive. Her desire to run

149

their home is what characterizes her as the "villain" of the piece, putting the viewer in Alfredo's corner as he attempts to find some way to get rid of her in a country that doesn't provide the escape hatch of divorce. But Alfredo is a passive creature, and the wife necessarily assumed the active role in the house, if only as a result of her husband's lukewarm personality: *someone* has to run it. To a degree, he brings on her dominance by failing to be dominant himself—it is not so much basic to her character as it is a necessary state that arises from his submissiveness.

Within the framework of their marriage, he has created her—and if she is a Frankenstein's monster, it must be remembered that he is the Dr. Frankenstein. By the same token, she is depicted as being repulsive because she has a strong sex drive and never waits for him to make the first move in bed. When she screams with orgasmic pleasure, Alfredo does not feel all the more a man for having so fully satisfied her extreme needs, but is instead horrified at her enjoyment of sex. Amazingly enough, the film—released in 1974, at the absolute zenith of the feminist movement—was not singled out for attack by female critics as the ultimate male chauvinist nightmare vision of the female of the species, for in this interpretation at least, Alfredo serves as the archetypal arrested-adolescent male.

But such an attack may not be entirely justified, because the film doesn't so much *share* the male chauvinist's point of view as it *ridicules* it: the humor that is elicited does not so much cause us to laugh *with* Alfredo as *at* him. While Alfredo may be a misogynist who lives under the illusion that he loves women, the film is in fact harder on him than on either of the women involved.

George Bernard Shaw once said, "If you want to tell people the truth, you'd better make them laugh—or they'll *kill* you!" Alfredo offers a "truth" about men, and the dangerously romantic way they approach women. And as interpreted in the light of Shaw's advice, *Alfredo* presents the male viewer with an inglorious mirror image of himself—but one he cannot grow angry about since he is too busy laughing. For as Germi portrays it, Alfredo is not simply passing through a single bad experience, but

stuck on a merry-go-round he is doomed to ride forever. Interestingly, his second love is, at the end, going no better than the first, and Alfredo's female problem turns out to be not a single mistake but a recurring pattern. He has learned nothing from his tragically comic first marriage and, once again, he has fallen in love with a woman's image rather than the reality of her—which is why the picture suggests, at its closing, that he is doomed to yet another unhappy relationship.

Dustin Hoffman and Stefania Sandrelli in the early stages of courtship.

In the end, though, Germi's films are not anti-male any more than they are anti-female—but "anti" the institution of marriage, which he portrays as putting unfair restraints and responsibilities on both the men and the women involved. It is marriage in the most generalized sense—not just the specific marriage laws of Italy—that he takes to task, although, being an Italian by birth and upbringing, he naturally uses the specific situation in Italy as his particular case in point to comment on the broader concept of marriage

Alfredo finds himself being pushed aside by the woman he loves as she talks incessantly on the phone.

itself. In his view, marriage does not enshrine sexual love (as it is meant to do) but conversely destroys it.

In the vision presented by his films, Germi conceives of men and women as unwitting pawns, pushed about by this monolithic institution in a game they all try to play without ever understanding the true implication of the rules, and his comical attitude grows out of the offense he takes at what marriage eventually does to the human soul—male or female. This helps explain why his films have proven enormously popular outside of Italy, in places where his satire on the particulars of that country's divorce laws have little meaning.

In the final analysis, though, *Alfredo* is not as perfect a picture as Germi's earlier entries. It is a bit too slow at the beginning, building characterization at the expense of the story. Also, it was edited down more than Germi had hoped, with several key scenes missing—especially toward

151

Alfredo finds his work suffering as a result of his increased sexual activities.

the end—that would have served to make Germi's themes more focused and understandable. But the biggest problem of all, especially for the film's star, is the one of language. Dustin was delighted to join in an all-Italian production, and in his usual dedicated way, spent several months of intense work studying Italian so that he would be able to speak in that language along with the other actors. Upon arriving to shoot the film, he was terribly disappointed to learn he would be required to speak English. This was done for economic reasons, since films with English subtitles were not doing particularly well in America, and to succeed with the American audience the picture would have to be in English—with Dustin's voice recognizably his own. Though much of the pleasure of doing the film was therefore eliminated for him before shooting began, he begrudgingly went along with this approach.

Then, when the film was completed and in the can, it was decided on the executive level that *Alfredo* could be more quickly and inexpensively completed if it were all in Italian. Since Hoffman had long since departed for home and other film commitments, the only way to achieve this was by rushing in an Italian actor to redub Dustin's voice in the Italian language Dustin had so wanted to use himself. It was clearly one of those "no win" situations for him, and the actor who had been equally willing to do his voice either in Italian or in English had to suffer the painful experience of seeing the picture released in such a way that he delivered only "half a performance," as a strange, unlikely voice replaced his own.

In analyzing Hoffman's performance, almost every major critic cited this problem. "What are we to make," Richard Cuskelly of the L. A. *Herald-Examiner* asked, "of . . . Dustin Hoffman . . . not only playing an Italian (with florid body movements, oily black hair *et al.*), but doing it with somebody else's voice? Subtitles are nearly always preferable to dubbing, but in this case a voice as recognizable as Hoffman's is missed and so is much-needed intimacy with the character." Likewise, in *New York* Judith Crist wrote: "Since Hoffman spoke English during the filming, his words are dubbed and he seems to be miming the part. Nevertheless, he is completely charming as the pleasant, routine-ridden bank clerk. . . ." Not everyone was so charitable, though. In *Variety*, "Beau" complained: "Since the choked delivery has become one of his trademarks, it's not a little disconcerting to hear a smooth vocal style accompanying his post-*Graduate* body movements. With his own voice as backup, the 36-year old actor might not seem quite so strained in still milking certain 'boyish' mannerisms." Jay Cocks of *Time* said, "Robbing an actor of his voice is like chopping off an acrobat's legs. Hoffman remains undaunted, even though watching him is like seeing Jerry

Mahoney do a solo act." *Newsweek's* Arthur Cooper concurred: "Like a knish in a plate of *pasta fazool*, Dustin Hoffman is woefully out of place in Pietro Germi's *Alfredo Alfredo*. With slicked-back hair and tight-fitting suits, he looks the way cartoonist Edward Koren might draw Rudolph Valentino."

But Pauline Kael, a frequent Hoffman critic, found the situation an improvement. In the *New Yorker,* she wrote: "in general, dubbing is an abomination, but the stranger's voice does wonders for Hoffman—it brings him out. In American movies, he's the perennial urban weakling-adolescent, doomed to swallow spit forever, but here, rid of the frightened, choked-up voice that constricts his characters, he gives a softer-edged, more relaxed performance . . . he lost that self-conscious worry—'Who am I and what am I meant to be thinking right this minute?'—that makes him so tense an actor. Hoffman's acting along to the sound of someone else's voice makes

Alfredo goes to professionals to make himself more attractive.

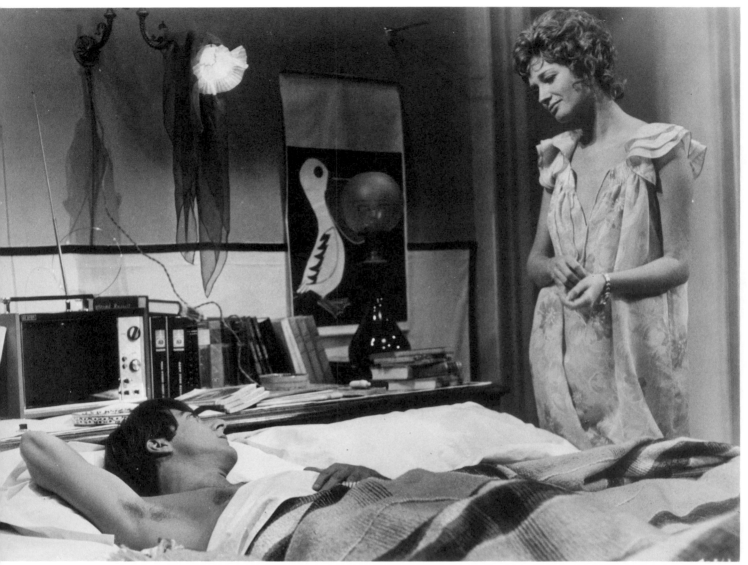

Alfredo relaxes in his mistress' apartment.

him seem like a silent comedian doing a routine."

There were also a few wholehearted endorsements: Charles Champlin writing in the L. A. *Times* noted: "Hoffman, his hair parted almost dead in the middle like an ad for greasy kid stuff, is very likable as the innocent to whom funny things happen (rather than as a performing comedian). He suffers nothing in translation." D.J.M. in *Cue* lauded him too: "Even in dubbed Italian, Dustin Hoffman is wonderful . . . with hair so greased one could ice skate on it." And Alan R. Howard of the *Hollywood Reporter* said that "Hoffman is wonderful, accomplishing the

formidable feat of becoming believably Italian in the English subtitled movie."

As far as personal expression is concerned, a Jewish American like Dustin may seem pretty far removed from the Italian Catholic he plays in this picture. But Alfredo is an average-looking fellow who succeeds far beyond his own comprehension with more than one gorgeous woman, and one recalls Hoffman's own statement: "There is some fun in knowing you can get away with murder looking quite average." Alfredo is obsessed with women, and Dustin has said, "I don't think I think about anything else more." Alfredo loves but fears women, and Dustin has mused:

"I'll die wishing I had learned more about what I fear about women." Hoffman's own lifelong fascination with the fairer sex has always been an essential aspect of his personality, and of all his films, *Alfredo Alfredo* most clearly allowed him to direct and channel that fascination into a screen performance.

Alfredo receives some important news.

Suffocated by love.

Lenny

A United Artists Release   1974

CAST:

Dustin Hoffman (*Lenny Bruce*); Valerie Perrine (*Honey Bruce*); Jan Miner (*Sally Marr*); Stanley Beck (*Artie Silver*); Gary Morton (*Sherman Hart*); Rashel Novikoff (*Aunt Mema*); Guy Rennie (*Jack Goldstein*).

CREDITS:

Director, Bob Fosse; screenplay, Julian Barry, based on his stage play; producer, Marvin Worth; executive producer, David V. Picker; editor, Alan Helm; director of photography, Bruce Surtees; running time, 112 minutes; rating, R.

At first, Dustin turned down the *Lenny* project for two reasons: he didn't like the way the

Dustin Hoffman as Lenny Bruce.

Broadway play had exploited certain elements of Lenny Bruce's life, and also didn't care for the initial film script he was offered. Besides, he felt the only good thing about the Broadway show had been Cliff Gorman's performance, firmly believed they ought to use him for the film, and told the producers so. But director Bob Fosse wanted Dustin desperately, so much so that at parties he would make a scene by half-jokingly falling to his knees, crawling to Dustin with his arms out, in the style of Jolson singing, begging the actor to take the part. Then, talk began to circulate that if Dustin didn't do it, his lookalike Al Pacino would. Shortly thereafter, Dustin signed for the role, and insiders insist he was still bristling about the fact the unknown Pacino had been picked for the role of Michael in *The Godfather* over him.

At any rate, when Hoffman did agree to do the film, he knew he needed a totally unique approach to the role, as apart from his previous fictionalized characters, and adapted an entirely new method of preparation. First, he bought a package of 3″ by 5″ index cards, and on each one he jotted down some significant bit of information he acquired about Bruce, along with his own instinctive observations about how the role ought to be played. These cards he tacked all over the walls of his avocado-infested office, so that wherever he looked, he would confront a possible "key" to the character. One card said "Leo Gorcey," because Dustin had noted from the filmed records of Bruce in performance that several of the comedian's physical mannerisms were not unlike those of the onetime Bowery Boy. "Jazz of Charlie Parker and Miles Davis," read another, mentally syncing Dustin to music that would convey the emotional temper of Bruce's era and lifestyle. Another read "Brando," reminding Dustin that Bruce had idolized the actor and, perhaps unconsciously, been influenced by his onscreen manner. What Dustin was perhaps less conscious about was the fact many of these keys to Bruce's personality also unlocked elements of his own self, which would be expressed in Dustin's characterization of Lenny. As a California teenager Dustin had always associated with the Bowery Boys when he saw their old movies; as a musician, he had grown to love the great jazz improvisational artists; and as a

157

Lenny is busted . . . . . . frisked . . .

. . . fingerprinted . . .

158

. . . and finds himself a criminal .

maturing actor, he had found much to appreciate in the films of Brando.

Naturally enough, the film works as personal expression for Hoffman as well as a created characterization, for there are some striking similarities between the two men: the offbeat sense of humor, the insecurity despite the enormous talent, the obsessive observation of people in order to create art that mirrors life, the pleasure of being a provocateur, the ability to seduce women without being particularly handsome, the almost crippling fear of eventual failure. And also the business of language: after all, Bruce did get busted for his vulgarisms, and Dustin has always been known as foul-mouthed.

Perhaps most important of all, though, is the basic fact that Lenny worked as a comic, a career many of the young Dustin's schoolmates thought he was destined for. In time, Dustin realized that if he had indeed become a comic instead of an actor, Lenny Bruce was the kind of comic he would have liked to have been. Thus, he sensed the need to be faithful to the truth about the real Lenny, and at the same time saw the danger of becoming a mere mimic, something he insisted he would not do. One way of solving the problem was to think of the picture not merely as a study of Bruce but as an indictment of the grayness of the Eisenhower era and the witch-hunt-

ing Joe McCarthy period of fear, which is what Dustin always conceived of Lenny Bruce as fighting against.

Still, he did spend over six months listening to classic Bruce recordings, trying to recapture the hysteria that ran through Bruce's voice—especially toward the end—and also some of his vocal mannerisms, including the nervous twitches that suggested a softness behind the tough exterior. Researching for Lenny also included interviewing more than fifty of the people who knew Lenny best, and much time spent with Lenny's mother, comedienne Sally Marr. But while shooting the film, he enjoyed telling interviewers he had never seen the real Lenny Bruce perform because, at that time, he had been a struggling, penniless actor who could not afford to get into the clubs where Bruce was playing.

... then is visited in jail by his wife, Honey (Valerie Perrine).

And when asked his impression of the film's overall theme, Dustin claimed: "He was just saying, 'Why can't we use the language on stage that we use in our daily lives?' "

Years earlier, when Lenny Bruce published his autobiography, he called it *How to Talk Dirty and Influence People*. In truth, though, Lenny Bruce never talked dirty. He talked clean because he talked honest, and that was surely the point of his remarkable career, as well as the

Lenny (Hoffman) and Honey (Perrine) in a happier mood.

Lenny in concert.

basis of the catastrophic (and often cathartic) effect he had on his audiences, and on the world of show business. Lenny has since been labeled a social satirist, but besides being a term he himself would have scoffed at, that was always of secondary importance in his work.

Mainly, he focused on language, not as an abstract concept to be debated by professors of semantics, but as the primary and most immediate force in our lives—the medium which predetermines how we see, what we think, the way we deal with the things we do. Whether he was burrowing deep into his scathing takeoff on *The Lone Ranger* ("Who was that mask man?") or singling out members of his audience as "niggers," "kikes," and "greaseballs," Bruce purified language by bringing it into the open. A word, he proved, was only vicious if used for a vicious purpose. Lenny said a word, said it over and over again, until it lost its capacity to shock—and lost its ugliness in the process.

Critics charged that he invented sick humor, but Lenny once insisted: "I'm not a comedian, and I'm not sick. The world is sick and I'm a surgeon with a scalpel . . ." The scalpel was his wit, a passionately cynical force he experimented

160

Lenny on trial.

with on every rung of the entertainment ladder, from sleazy strip joints to top-quality nightclubs. When he lost it—and, near the end, he actually bored people by reading them long-winded transcripts of his latest trial—his ability to simultaneously amuse and offend was gone. The problem wasn't that his talent had failed, but that he had been exhausted and embittered by a system which busted him time and again, and then put him through drawn-out legal hassles that broke him, first financially, and later, spiritually.

Fosse's film accurately recounted the entire process of Bruce's destruction. But the film was immediately attacked by the very people who might have seemed the intended audience: Lenny Bruce aficionados. Those who felt closest to the material were enraged by what had been lost in translation. Questions abounded: Did Dustin Hoffman color the way an entire generation would view Bruce? Were the most important bits of material (and every Bruce freak had his own opinion as to which ones they were) included? The point was, no major film—designed primarily as mass audience entertainment—could communicate the reality and complexity that was Lenny Bruce. For that, we need an extended biography (like Albert Goldman's *Ladies and Gentlemen—Lenny Bruce!!*), and even that raises questions. How much of what we read is objective, and to what degree has

Another view of Lenny (Hoffman) in concert.

162

Goldman recreated Lenny in his own image? It would be a mistake to take the film to task for what it could accomplish. Rather, like the stage success, also written by Julian Barry, who penned the screenplay, this is an exercise in myth making—Lenny Bruce is quite successfully turned into a modern American folk hero.

Lenny works largely because of Hoffman's rendering of the character. The two obvious approaches would be for an actor to retain his own star personality while delivering Lenny's material, or on the other hand to become invisible by immersing himself so completely in Lenny Bruce that he temporarily becomes the character. Diana Ross as Billie Holiday in *Lady Sings the Blues* would represent the first extreme, Hal Holbrook as Mark Twain the second. Hoffman cleverly mapped out a middle ground between the two, and it proved a perfect compromise. We are conscious of watching the likeable performer from *The Graduate* and *Little Big Man*, yet we feel the presence of Bruce himself, especially at those moments when Hoffman's eyes grow surly, his mouth hangs loose, and the resemblance to one of those old candid photographs of Bruce is uncanny.

Hoffman's Lenny retains much of the threatening quality that made audiences both fearful of and fascinated by the man who might say anything, and ultimately did. But he brought to the role just the right amount of warmth to suggest a person behind the persona. In so doing, he made this not just an extended impression of Bruce, but a dramatic interpretation of Bruce's personality. Lenny is suggested through a number of vocal and physical mannerisms, yet we are constantly reminded this is only an image of Lenny Bruce—a fiction inspired by his life—and not the real thing.

The critics were split down the middle on both the picture and the performance. In *Time*, Richard Schickel attacked the film as a cop out but asserted Dustin was "again asserting his claim to being today's great character leading man . . . what is awesome is the range of emotion he commands . . . he gives a complex and mercurial performance." Paul D. Zimmerman also attacked the film as shallow, but complemented "the rightness of Dustin Hoffman's look and

sound," nonetheless complaining in his *Newsweek* review that "Bruce was far more complex on a private level and far more dangerous in social terms than the brilliant but softer figure Hoffman has created." *The New Yorker*'s Pauline Kael argued that "Hoffman makes a serious, honorable try, but he's the wrong kind of actor to play Bruce. Hoffman ingratiates himself with an audience by his shy smile, his gentleness. . . . He wins people over by his lack of physical confidence; you pull for him because he's so nonthreatening . . his putziness is just what Bruce despised. Hoffman is touchingly childlike . . . there was nothing childlike about Lenny Bruce. He vamped the audience with a debauched, deliberately faggy come-hither that no one quite knew how to interpret; he was uncompromisingly not nice." More damning still was the *Esquire* review which claimed "Hoffman . . . manages very little. As young Lenny in love, he is the bumblingly coltish Graduate again. . . . As the adult Bruce, Hoffman is still too nice, cool, and lucid, with little of the madness and meanness that were mixed in with the messianism."

Interestingly, Hoffman and Fosse had worked hard to create this vulnerable side to the Bruce character, even though they were attacked for it. "Bruce was very naive," Dustin insisted in his defense. "His friends I talked to—fifty or sixty of them who knew him intimately—were full of contradictions about him but concurred on his naivete." He was also angered by the people who claimed he did not put the real Lenny Bruce up there onscreen: "A film is a film and should be viewed on that basis. I don't think George C. Scott's performance as George Patton is the true-life story of Patton, or that we caught the whole truth of Lenny Bruce. We tried for a certain color. Take somebody painting your portrait—if it's Chagall, you might look romantic, or Picasso might make you look neurotic." His point is well taken, though it's worth noting that this line of reasoning might also be used as a defense by the interviewers who present a portrait of Dustin in their newspaper stories that he complains is not "really him."

To be fair, the film does attempt to communicate Lenny's complexity. It is true that, at moments, Hoffman plays Lenny as an almost saint-

Valerie Perrine as Honey Bruce.

like character, a crusader for free speech who takes on the entire legal system and is destroyed for his efforts. At such moments, Lenny does cease to be the hipster those who actually saw him still remember, and is momentarily turned into something Bruce himself would probably have scoffed at: a liberal hero. But this is not the sum total of what viewers see. There is also the sequence in which Lenny turns his wife Honey (Valerie Perrine) on—against her will—to swinging (both sex and drugs), then abuses her when she gets hooked on the lifestyle. In another sequence that clearly demonstrates the filmmakers' desire to maintain integrity, Lenny sees Honey installed in a hospital following a serious automobile accident, then promptly makes love to one of the nurses. By the end of the film, Lenny Bruce does indeed emerge as a pop-hero. But what we have witnessed is hardly a whitewash job, and if we accept his heroic stature, we do so despite plenty of scenes that clearly show us his negative side.

Julian Barry's screenplay is highly effective, as his story cuts across three distinct situations. First, there is a single Lenny Bruce concert, in which the bearded performer runs through many of his classic routines. In fact, it's such a complete compendium of Lenny's most telling material that we cease to take it as an enactment of one particular performance, and begin thinking of it as the ultimate Lenny Bruce. From this point, the camera cuts to various people who knew Lenny: his outspoken show biz trouper mother (Jan Miner), his "shiksa goddess" stripper of a wife, Honey Harlow; as well as a fictional character, the agent-manager (Stanley Beck). Their reminiscences about the deceased entertainer are seemingly recorded by a biographer. And in between these sequences, there are episodes designed as a dramatic reconstruction of Lenny's life. The relationships between these three levels of reality are clear enough. If Lenny the performer talks about divorce, we can be sure the film will cut to an incident from his life touching on this subject, and then hear in the interviews his wife's explanations of this matter. It is an approach to Lenny Bruce not so very different from the approach this book takes toward Dustin Hoffman: a man's life and his art are inseparable.

Finally, there is Bob Fosse's fascinating direction. He completely abandoned the wild expressionism of Tom O'Horgan's stage show and instead filmed the story in the gritty,

164

black-and-white style most reminiscent of "serious" films of the fifties and sixties. *Lenny* was the first major production shot in black and white since Peter Bogdanovich's *The Last Picture Show* in 1971, and the images that cinematographer Bruce Surtees created proved highly appropriate, as well as aesthetically effective. In *Lenny*'s era, black and white was the convention for realism, as opposed to color for escapism. In 1974, the use of that convention purposefully called attention to itself, and its own artificiality reminded viewers how far from reality this film (or any film) is by the revival of a style that once caused audiences to expect The Truth.

Lenny Bruce was an innovator because he objected to the style of most nightclub comics—especially Milton Berle, caricatured in this film by Gary Morton—who perfected an "act" in the strictest sense of the word. Such people put on an ingratiating face for the public and spouted obscenities offstage. This was the concept Lenny set out to destroy. He didn't do an act at all, but instead walked onstage and began talking. He was damned as an oddball by the very same entertainers who unconsciously imitate his style today. To convey this, Fosse began his film with an enormous close-up of Lenny's mouth, as a voice-over narration by Hoffman as Lenny comments on the 1964 veneral disease epidemic: "Nobody wants to talk about it, nobody wants to say the word. Talking about it makes you the worst person in the country." Lenny was willing to become the worst person in the country, because he did talk about it. At his best, he did so with a natural sense of humor that allowed him to mention all the unmentionables and make people laugh at their own petty hang-ups. The essence of the man's life and his language was captured in this film.

The ugly side of Lenny.

The gentler side of Lenny.

165

All the President's Men

A Warner Brothers Release   1976

Carl Bernstein (Dustin Hoffman) and Bob Woodward (Robert Redford) begin work on "The Watergate Story."

CAST:

Dustin Hoffman *(Carl Bernstein)*; Robert Redford *(Bob Woodward)*; Jack Warden *(Harry Rosenfeld)*; Martin Balsam *(Howard Simons)*; Hal Holbrook *(Deep Throat)*; Jason Robards *(Ben Bradlee)*; Jane Alexander *(Bookkeeper)*; Meredith Baxter *(Debbie Sloan)*; Ned Beatty *(Dardis)*; Stephen Collins *(Hugh Sloan)*; Penny Fuller *(Sally Aiken)*; John McMartin *(Foreign Editor)*; Robert Walden *(Donald Segretti)*; Frank Wills *(Frank Wills)*; F. Murray Abraham *(Arresting Officer)*; Nicholas Coster *(Markham)*; David Arkin *(Bachinski)*; Henry Calvert *(Barker)*; Polly Holiday *(Secretary)*.

CREDITS:

Director, Alan J. Pakula; screenplay, William Goldman based on the book by Carl Bernstein and Bob Woodward; music by David Shire; director of photography, Gordon Willis; editor, Robert L. Wolfe; associate producers, Michael Britton and Jon Boorstin; A Wildwood Enterprises Production; running time, 135 minutes; rating, PG.

While promoting the just-completed film *The Candidate*, a picture which grew from his strong political convictions, Robert Redford overheard reporters discussing the Watergate situation, the Woodward-Bernstein investigation, and their own beliefs that Nixon would never be touched. Redford immediately contacted the two young reporters, who were still deeply embroiled in the day-to-day coverage of the scandal, and later they went so far as to credit him with influencing their eventual work. When their book, *All the President's Men*, eventually came out, Dustin Hoffman eagerly read it and at once contacted the two reporters with the concept of putting together a film version. They informed him that Redford was way ahead of him, had already contracted the book for his own production company, and Dustin had to settle for playing Bernstein in a film that was Redford's baby from start to finish.

But the two agreed wholeheartedly, early on at least, that authenticity was the keynote for success, and their studio complied. Warner Brothers spent close to $500,000 to recreate the Washington *Post*'s city room on their Burbank lot, going so far as to have trash from the baskets at the actual *Post* shipped west and stuffed into the trash baskets on the set. For research purposes, Dustin observed an investigative reporter named Fred Barbash, who had been working on a series of stories dealing with non-political corruption in Maryland, but using a similar procedure to Woodward and Bernstein's. Later, while he and Redford were shooting scenes in Hollywood, the two would dart constantly from the set between takes, find a phone, and call Woodward and Bernstein in Washington to make certain they were getting it all right—putting the story on film precisely as it had happened. Public interest in the project was immense, and screenwriter William Goldman labelled it "the biggest gossip picture since *The Godfather*," since during the shooting, rumors about the film circulated constantly. People were waiting with fascination for its release, in order to decide for themselves if it were a gargantuan hit or an unmitigated disaster.

All did not go well during filming. While most

Bernstein and Woodward confer on a possible lead.

agreement that they must avoid the two possible extremes: of a freewheeling *Front Page* newspaper comedy on the one hand and an anti-Nixon diatribe on the other, and somewhere along the way they settled on the notion of a "dramatized documentary." But their honeymoon with the *Post* people was now officially over, so much so that Hoffman—distressed at the lack of communication between the filmmakers and the journalists they were portraying—suggested, at one point, that they fictionalize the paper, giving it a made-up name, since the audience would implicitly understand it was *really* meant to be the *Post*. Redford and Pakula disagreed, and

of the *Post* people were initially infatuated with the idea of being portrayed in a major movie, the publisher, Katharine Graham, was uncomfortable with the project from beginning to end, and in time her resentment of Hollywood's intrusion into their sacrosanct world of serious journalism did spread to other staff members. A controversy developed over Redford's choice of Goldman for screenwriter. Both Redford and Hoffman had been delighted at the way Goldman whittled the complex, occasionally convoluted narrative of the book down to a relatively simple, straightforward story line, but they soon learned the *Post* people were less than pleased with the off-the-cuff, urbane humor, which turned Woodward and Bernstein into a latter day *Butch Cassidy and the Sundance Kid* team.

Goldman conceived of the project as a commercial theatrical entertainment, and the *Post* did not. Then, when Carl Bernstein himself attempted a rewrite, the script turned into an advertisement for himself—and his carefully calculated Playboy image. Redford tried a draft and Goldman tried another, as did other writers brought in, but in the end director Alan Pakula ended up improvising much of what exists on screen extemporaneously on the set, even as they shot.

Hoffman, Redford and Pakula were all in

Bernstein (Hoffman) in a tense moment.

Hoffman was voted down. In the end, the film was shot Redford's way—but at Hoffman's pace. Whereas Redford is an actor who comes to understand his role by the process of playing it, and instinctively learns about the character as he goes along, Hoffman likes to constantly discuss his character with everyone else involved, and do retake after retake—which had a great deal to do with the picture going more than a month over schedule and several million dollars over budget.

During the time span between the actual break-in on July 1, 1972, and the release of the movie less than four years later, a number of other filmmakers had beat them to it in a sense; for while there was no other film about Watergate *per se* at that time, the American cinema of the early seventies was literally composed of films which dealt, in disguised terms, with Watergate-style situations, as movie after movie depicted conspiracy and cover-up. *Chinatown*, ostensibly a 1930s nostalgia piece, concerned a private eye who crosses some powerful politicians willing to go to any lengths to keep their corruption secret; *Posse*, supposedly a western, concerned a law 'n' order sheriff whose own corruption is discovered and exposed by an idealistic newsman; even a disaster epic, *The Tow-*

Jason Robards and Martin Balsam as the editors the boys must report to.

ering Inferno, featured a Nixonish President of a major company who realizes the Establishment (in this case, a skyscraper) he has built is unsafe, but when a scandal (the fire) erupts, he sends two aids down to hush up the story with the reporters, even though the smoke eventually reaches all the way up to his position of power and he is necessarily removed. *All the President's Men* may have been the first film to deal with Watergate openly, but it did not mark the beginning of Watergate movies; if anything, this was the end product of an era of films whose mood and message, whose tone and theme, were all inspired by the monumental scandal.

Ironically, then, the only film which met Watergate face on proved the least effective in

artistically communicating what had been most essential about the Watergate era in America. Partially, this grows from the several months each of the stars spent researching at the *Post*, and each man's growing fascination with the newsgathering process. After all, the original inspiration to do this film had been to make the definitive movie about Watergate, but somewhere along the line, they both lost sight of this, stopped being able to see the forest so hung up were they on looking at trees.

The movie's subject is the way in which a reporter must persistently follow up dozens of leads, 99 percent of which take him nowhere, but finding, sooner or later, the single lead that opens a whole new area of investigation. Very often, the reporters must do a number on the people they question: browbeating them, pleading, manipulating, in the end creating a verbal and emotional torture chamber just to get someone to merely shake his head and confirm what the reporter already knows but cannot print without such confirmation. That is how the investigative journalism game is played, and both stars became infatuated with it.

Such situations are effectively conveyed in the film and, to be fair, are more accurately portrayed here than in any other American movie about journalism. Understandably, then, the film was, on its release, generally viewed by journalists as a triumph, and by the general public as something of a disappointment. Disappointment, but not a disaster, by any means. What the film does, it does well. Still, there is something clearly, naggingly missing, for one senses this is a case study of how any good, aggressive reporter works, but that it has very little to say about Watergate. What matter the authenticity of the crumpled papers in the wastebasket when we look at Washington, as depicted here, and see it as a series of pretty picture post card scenes (the exteriors mostly have the look of a travelogue) rather than the nightmarish city suggested by the original book, where behind the facade of business-as-usual normalcy, one could sense a shadow world of sleazy evil at work.

Goldman's writing was mostly scrapped as being too glib and flippant, so filled with humorous lines that, upon reading it, Carl Bernstein referred to the script as "a Henny Youngman jokebook." But perhaps the filmmakers were wrong in turning their backs on this approach. After all, the Ben Hecht/Charlie MacArthur newspaper comedy classic *The Front Page* had been inspired by an actual case. But director Pakula insisted instead on a scene by scene recreation of history, but with movie stars standing in for the real life people, though always mouthing the identical words—wearing the identical clothes, even—of the newsmen they stood in for. Pakula's approach harkens back to the state sponsored educational films of the Russian master Sergei Eisenstein.

Redford, meanwhile, claimed to view the project as a detective story of sorts, which makes a good deal of sense since the detective film, not coincidentally, bounded back into popularity following Watergate, with such items as *Night*

Woodward (Redford) leaves Bernstein (Hoffman) to question some more leads.

The growing importance of the story causes problems for the editors (Jack Warden and Martin Balsam).

Moves, Farewell My Lovely, The Black Bird, The Long Goodbye, and *The Midnight Man,* as well as the aforementioned blockbuster *Chinatown.* But a classic detective film is largely based on a richness of characterization, ranging from the detective himself to the fascinatingly quirky minor characters met along the way, and the flat, realistic style Pakula employed deflates such possibilities. The final film contains elements of all three approaches—the attitudes toward the material taken by writer, director, and producer—but not enough of any one approach to create a consistent and unique attitude towards the film.

All this seriously limits the performances of Hoffman and Redford. The problem is not that they are bad—if anything, each is quite good under the circumstances. But they are not really "acting" at all. Certainly, it's always nice to see big-name stars willing to sublimate their egos for the success of a project, the vision of which is larger than any particular characters; that is the basis of "ensemble" acting, and it often makes for acting at its best. But there is no sense of ensemble to the cast of *President's Men;* the performers are not allowed to create characters at all.

Hoffman stated outright that "this is not an actor's film," and his is almost an understatement. Whenever he and Redford walk down a

corridor in the newspaper office together—Redford shuffling in his self-assured, silver-spoon-in-the-mouth style, with the short-legged Hoffman hopping along twice as briskly just to keep up, with that comically intense quality of his—we sense what a wonderful team they had

the potential to be. The film was shot at a time when buddy-buddy films were at the height of their popularity—*The Sting, Scarecrow, Thunderbolt and Lightfoot,* Hoffman's own *Papillon*— and this might have emerged as the first thinking man's buddy-buddy film. An early scene, in which Hoffman/Bernstein and Redford/Woodward rub each other wrong, seems to be setting that up, though the chemistry of this first encounter is never properly developed.

While reading the book, we sense ourselves experiencing three levels of writing simultane-

Redford and Hoffman run, don't walk, as the story gets hotter.

ously: a perfect study of the newsgathering process, a shattering portrait of the Watergate scandal, and a fascinating analysis of a begrudging friendship, born out of an initial mutual wariness but cemented through respect of one another's work. In the film, only the first of those possibilities is ever communicated properly. Page by page, Woodward and Bernstein emerged in the book as knowable, likeable, even unforgettable people. Though they are played in the film by two of the country's most capable actor/stars, they are, with the exception of only a few touching scenes, question-asking machines. No wonder many critics pointed out that the real stars of the movie were the typewriters.

Understandably Hoffman received the most lukewarm notices of his career, instead of the usual accolades or attacks. *Newsweek's* Jack Kroll did comment happily that "with his long hair, his bohemian nattiness, his feverish, ferretlike drive . . . Hoffman becomes a clownish mixture of cajolery and clumsiness . . .," while Penelope Gilliatt of the *New Yorker* added the praise that "Carl Bernstein is played with intelligent nervous energy by Dustin Hoffman." In *The Nation*, Robert Hatch complained that "both Hoffman and Redford are far too recognizable, after too many hit pictures, to lure the most gullible of viewers into belief that what they are seeing is the real thing." Arguing from the opposite point of view, Tom Allen, S. C., wrote in *America* that the performers, "without denying their past screen iconographies, converge toward an unaffected naturalness . . . , Hoffman by shying away from the mannerisms of method characterization." Stanley Kauffmann of *The New Republic* put it perfectly when he described what he saw as "passable acting." Kinder by far was Harvey E. Phillips of *The National Review* who stated in passing that Woodward and Bernstein were played "with simplicity and tact" by Redford and Hoffman.

In trying perhaps too hard to not play up the Woodward/Bernstein team as modern media folk heroes but as two reporters who just happen to fall into the story of the century, the film fails to take properly into account the fact that the boys *did* become elevated to the level of folk heroes, and that a film about them ought to convey

something of the myth as well as the reality. But *President's Men* errs in the other direction: the surface of the investigation is portrayed perfectly, but the essence of it is just not there. And in admirably attempting to keep the film from turning into a simplistic attack on Nixon—which they rightly sensed would have been too easy, too trendy—they went too far in the opposite way, cutting off the story three-fifths of the way through the material covered in the book, and never properly establishing, in the context of the film, the ultimate significance of the case at hand: that the scandal eventually reached all the way to the top.

The movie certainly has its share of memorable moments: Redford handily trying to juggle two phones, and two important phone conversations, at once; Hoffman cleverly forcing his way into an office where he is clearly not wanted; the two of them together, smiling with mild shock as they believe they have at last encountered an insider who will willingly talk to them, only to gradually realize they are speaking to the wrong woman. But the narrative is so difficult to follow—and the film depends so completely on its audience's familiarity with certain key names and incidents—that, removed from the immediate viewing context of the mid-seventies, it is almost impossible to follow, even for people who kept abreast of the Watergate hearings at that time.

As always, though, Hoffman was able to use the film as a vehicle for personal expression. He has always described himself as an "observer" of life, and here he plays the most significant observer of our time; though Bernstein did not participate in any of the post-Watergate events, his acute observations of them had a major impact on the country, and a compulsive observer like Hoffman could find much to relate to in this aspect of Bernstein's personality. Beyond that, *President's Men* is the only one of Hoffman's projects thus far to openly deal with issues involving his own political beliefs and values in a dramatic manner, and it certainly is a film which expresses the attitude of a Gene McCarthy supporter from 1968. Thirdly, Hoffman has always insisted he very much wants to be a full collaborator on a project, and if his work behind the scenes on this film did not allow him that, his characterization at least did; for Bernstein is a full collaborator with Woodward in the creation of a work, the impact of which goes beyond either individual man.

Also, along with the later work *Agatha*, this film allows Hoffman to express his attitudes about that institution he has enjoyed such an irregular friendship with, The Press. Here he plays a reporter every bit as unrelenting in his pursuit of a story, and every bit as unconcerned with the privacy of others, as those journalists he has so often complained about.

Finally, this film stands—with *Midnight Cowboy* and *Papillon*—as one of a trilogy of pictures in which Hoffman has studied friendships between men, and like those other films expresses the notion of a friendship based on respect between two vastly different but equally worthwhile individuals.

The boys prepare their manuscript.

Marathon Man

Distributed by Paramount Pictures   1976

Dustin Hoffman as the Marathon Man.

CAST:

Dustin Hoffman *(Babe)*; Laurence Olivier *(Szell)*; Roy Scheider *(Doc)*; William Devane *(Janeway)*; Marthe Keller *(Elsa)*; Fritz Weaver *(Prof. Biesenthal)*; Richard Bright *(Karl)*; Marc Lawrence *(Erhard)*; Allen Joseph *(Babe's Father)*; Tito Goya *(Melendez)*; Ben Dova *(Szell's Brother)*; Lou Gilbert *(Rosenbaum)*; Jacques Martin *(LeClerc)*; James Wing Woo *(Chen)*.

CREDITS:

Director, John Schlesinger; screenplay by William Goldman, based on his novel; producers, Robert Evans and Sidney Beckerman; director of photography, Conrad Hall; editor, Jim Clark; music, Michael Small; running time, 125 minutes; rating, R.

The thriller, Graham Greene knew, need not be mere escapism. In novels like *This Gun for Hire*, *Confidential Agent*, and *The Third Man*, he dealt with the same themes that haunt his ostensibly more serious books: guilt, power, and morality. At their least presumptive, thrillers may well be nothing more than enjoyable trivia that allow readers and/or viewers to temporarily take leave of the problems of our time; but at their best, they can distill those problems down to their essence and, better still, present them in the context of a work that is, more than anything else, entertaining. Graham Greene had absolutely nothing to do with Dustin Hoffman's next film, *Marathon Man*, but he would have recognized in it—and no doubt appreciated—an indebtedness to his writings in the genre.

For this film is that most rare and remarkable of cinematic creations, a highly commercial picture (out to tap the same vast audience which was then flocking to *Jaws*, *The Exorcist*, and the *Airport* pictures) which nonetheless managed to communicate some unconventional, even controversial, ideas. William Goldman's script (based on his own novel) boasts the same quality which made his previous screen efforts (*Butch Cassidy and the Sundance Kid*, *The Great Waldo Pepper*, and the first, discarded draft for *All the President's Men*) the action-movie equivalents of Neil Simon's situation comedies: a crisp, clever, calculated approach to relatively mundane material. John *(Darling, Day of the Locust,* and Hoffman's *Midnight Cowboy)* Schlesinger's direction displayed his special talent for making us immediately feel at home with unlikely characters and the ambiguous relationships between them. Along with cinematographer Conrad Hall and an excellent cast assembled by producer Robert *(Chinatown)* Evans, they created a memorable motion picture about that most common of 1970s post-Watergate subjects: conspiracy.

When a movie is made by people who know their business, the opening scene does more than just start the story rolling: it sets in motion the mood and meaning the film will develop during its running time. *Marathon Man* offers a perfect example of this principle in action. Two elderly men, driving their cars through the streets of New York, find themselves locked into a duel neither really wanted. One cuts off the other's entrance into the flow of traffic, leading to an angry bout of name-calling, resulting in an even more heated race to the next red light, until the simple, everyday confrontation of disgruntled motorists escalates into an all-out fight to the finish.

The scene catches the viewer first of all because of its surface realism. Anyone who has ever suffered through a traffic jam—especially in Manhattan—knows how easily tempers can flare out of control, as normal people begin to behave like maniacs behind the wheels, and we are immediately involved in a situation that does not appear terribly far from our own experiences. Second, the scene works because it's funny. As the race grows ever wilder, the sense of realism steadily diminishes: the spontaneous drag race between the two old codgers becomes an exaggeration of a normal experience, and we begin to laugh because what we see is a caricature of a situation we all know. It's like those gradually escalating scenes of anger between Laurel and Hardy, when one wrinkles the other's jacket and, in retribution, has his sleeve ripped off; for revenge, he rips the other's jacket completely to shreds and so on and so on, until the stubbornness of each leads to a total humiliation both of the opposition and the self. Finally, though, our laughter is cut off as the cars suddenly crash into a gasoline truck, killing at least one of the men

Dustin falls in love with Marthe Keller.

instantly. That isn't supposed to happen in a comedy, where nobody ever *really* gets hurt. We must immediately reject our own earlier response of laughter, and feel an insecurity about it bordering on guilt.

At once, then, the picture makes the audience not just a simple observer, but an accomplice. And the film that follows proceeds according to the three principles of the first scene. *Marathon Man* whisks us around a complex triangle of characters whose lives are, at first, seemingly unrelated. Scylla (Roy Scheider) appears to be some sort of a spy, and his international-intrigue-type adventures in and around Paris strike us as falling somewhere between a James Bond yarn and a John Le Carré tale. Babe (Dustin Hoffman) is a Columbia University graduate student whose scholarly interests in recent American social-political history must share his time with training to be a marathon runner and involvement with an enigmatic lover (Marthe

The love affair turns into a passionate obsession.

178

Dustin fights back against the Nazi agents.

Keller). Szell (Laurence Olivier) is the one-time boss of a Nazi concentration camp who used his skill as a dentist to extract the gold from teeth of Jewish inmates, and has long since converted the fortune he amassed into diamonds which rest in a safe-deposit box in New York. But a fatal automobile accident which, at first glance, has nothing to do with any of them, will quickly tie the three characters together in a tale of terror and torture.

For in time, we learn that one of the old men killed in the initial automobile accident happened to be the brother of Szell, who has been acting as the custodian of Szell's fortune. And now, unable to trust any of his lackeys, Szell must himself leave the safety of his hideaway in order to come to New York and claim his fortune, putting him in conflict with Scylla and, after Scylla's death, Babe—whose pleasant businessman brother Doc, Babe suddenly learns, is actually an international agent known as Scylla. Babe had no previous inkling of Doc's actual profession until his brother stumbles into Babe's apartment, bleeding to death.

One effective shock technique of Goldman's book was naturally lost in the transition to the screen: the novel did not let us know that the government agent Scylla and the brother of Babe are one and the same man until that moment when Doc dies in Babe's arms, a trick that could of course not be duplicated on the screen, as we immediately recognize the two men as both being played by Scheider. In place of this bit of gimmicky suspense (perhaps even a dirty trick played by the author on the reader) is the impact of scenes which are far more powerful when rendered on film with full visual impact, especially that moment when Szell turns his destructive dental equipment on Babe in hopes of learning information the innocent Babe does not possess. It is one of the most bizarre, unforgettable, and, in some critics' opinions, overly sensationalized torture scenes in the history of

Dustin screams for help as two frightening agents (Richard Bright and Marc Lawrence) attempt to drown him in a bathtub.

movies. And at this point we realize that Babe's hobby of running is not just a way of characterizing him but a significant plot device (he will eventually run, not for a prize, but, literally, for his life) without which his escape on foot from a pursuing car would be less believable. It is in the end a symbol: he is a "runner" in more ways than one.

At any rate, up until the middle of the film, when we are finally allowed to understand the relationships between these men, the emotional and entertainment quality of their episodes are kept as separate as the men themselves: for half its running time, the picture is shot with three distinct tones to fit the three distinct characters. Hoffman's sections are done as the kind of comedy-drama at which he excels, and remind one of *The Graduate* or *John and Mary;* Scheider's are violent and fast-paced, just what one would expect from the star of *Jaws;* Olivier's heavy and sombre, with a glimmer of *The Boys from Brazil*.

In addition to the difference in mood, there is a totally distinct social concern developed in each separate portion. Olivier's character carries the none-too-subtle first name "Christian," and he is fictional incarnation of a factual evil, the surviving Nazi: old now, but not a whit less cruel and certainly no less frightening. As the war years slip ever further into past history, the villains from that era are in danger of slipping into the recesses of our memory. *Marathon Man*—like *The Boys from Brazil* and TV's *Holocaust*—insists on the old adage that those who cannot learn from history are doomed to repeat it, and reminds older viewers that the ghosts of that terrible time are with us still and could surface again at the least likely moment, in the least likely place. It also educates an entire new generation of people who barely comprehend, much less remember, the concentration camps that the scars are still deep, still visible, still able to affect us.

If Olivier stands for a frightening aspect of the 1940s, then Hoffman represents a holdover of

The murderous Nazi leader (Laurence Olivier) approaches Dustin with his dental equipment.

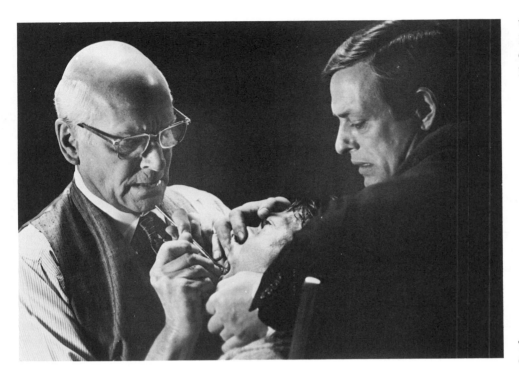

While Richard Bright holds back Dustin's head, Laurence Olivier uses dental equipment to torture the young man.

The love between Dustin and Marthe quickly turns to mistrust.

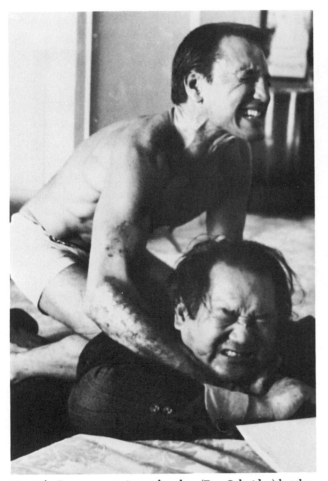

Dustin's Government Agent brother (Roy Scheider) battles a mysterious Oriental assassin.

the 1950s and the memories of Sen. Joseph McCarthy. For Babe Levy's dissertation is to be an exploration of the horrors of the black-list, yet his is no mere intellectual exercise. His real aim is to clear the name of his father, an innocent historian accused of having Communist ties and driven to suicide at the height of the witch hunt era. In a flashback, we share with Hoffman his misty memories of the man and the house they

181

lived in; Babe still keeps the gun with which his father took his own life.

Scheider's role is less clearly defined than the others, but eventually he comes to stand for the international intrigue shenanigans of the 1960s, that period of time when Sean Connery became a pop hero as agent 007, the ultimate amoral agent. That was a period when few Americans saw the need to question C.I.A. tactics; many even considered them a form of modern sophistication. It seems hardly coincidental that Will Devane, the actor who played Scheider's accomplice Janeway, bears a striking resemblance to the key figure of the sixties, Jack Kennedy, and in fact even played the late president in a TV movie dealing with the Cuban missile crisis.

At one point, Devane explains to Hoffman the special government agency, referred to only as The Division and existing somewhere in a nebulous middleground between the C.I.A. and the F.B.I., he and Scheider are members of; but much of what he says turns out to be pure fabrication and, by the movie's end, viewers are not sure whether the two were actually working for the government at all. The ambiguity so effectively communicated is at the heart of what went wrong with the dream of the 1960s.

During the picture's second half, the three plots tie neatly together. More important, though, is that as they do, the social periods the three characters represent also begin to blend. And significantly, it is in the cultural and psychic battleground of the 1970s (represented by things falling apart, as garbage strikes and crime in the streets form the background—and metaphor— for what we see) that our problems with the past must be resolved once and for all. So in the seventies, a ghost from the forties threatens a man haunted by memories of the fifties because of his relationship to a holdover from the sixties. The movie's last image represents Babe's attempt to put the past behind him, once he has squared off with it in the present, and find his future—looking forward, perhaps, to the 1980s.

As for Hoffman's performance, Jack Kroll in *Newsweek* wrote that "Hoffman is excellent as this marathon man, a little guy who runs miles in Central Park every day. . . ." Some critics found it impossible to separate the performer from the character he played, such as Judith Crist who in *Saturday Review* claimed that "Hoffman's persona is perfection for the young man. . . ." Pauline Kael, never a critic to overpraise Hoffman, once again attacked his nasal delivery of lines: "running around with cut nerves gives Hoffman more of an excuse for that gasping sound. Can you imagine what he'd do if he played in *Humoresque* or *Golden Boy*? With a violin to breathe to, he'd be the Paganini of snufflers." And yet, elsewhere in her review, she did say that Hoffman had "never before looked so fit, and there isn't a bum note in his performance." A number of critics felt the need to compare the two top-billed stars and, for Stanley Kauffman of *The New Republic,* Hoffman came out on top: "Hoffman, generally a good actor, does absolutely nothing wrong. Olivier, sometimes a great actor, does absolutely nothing notable." But Robert Hatch of *The Nation* found them equally disappointing: "Dustin Hoffman does again his impersonation of a homicidal mouse, and Olivier, with the help of a pair of very thick lenses, attains the final pinnacle of the master criminal cliché." On the other hand, Jay Cocks of *Time* heartily endorsed them both: "The movie offers Dustin Hoffman, giving one of his best performances, up against Laurence Olivier, who is in fine form playing an arch villain."

In addition to Hoffman's character going up against Olivier's, Hoffman's style had to go up against Olivier's, and one of the film's values is as a showcase of such different styles being practiced together. This difference in approaches was clear even on the set. As always, Hoffman wanted to understand everything about the character he was playing—in the true method acting tradition—in order to become the man and thus get him right. A polished technician/ craftsman like Olivier was a bit put off by that. "Why must he go through all the Sturm and Drang?" he would ask people standing about him on the set, while waiting for Hoffman to get into character so he could perform. "Why doesn't he just *act?*" The answer, of course, rests in the very different definitions of acting the two men subscribe to. For Olivier, acting is the mastery of a craft which allows one to suggest a character other than oneself; for Hoffman, it is finding a key that unlocks the character for the performer and allows them to at least temporarily become one.

In point of fact, there are many "keys" to this character—more qualities of the man playing the part that are basic to the role he is playing and can be authentically actualized onscreen by drawing from past experiences. Like both *Little Big Man* and *Straw Dogs*, the film allows Hoffman to play an essentially non-violent man forced by circumstances into violent acts. More significant still, it is the only role Hoffman has thus far played onscreen that studies and scrutinizes his own Jewishness: Hoffman has always claimed to suffer from an extremely strong sense of Jewish guilt, and Babe Levy is the archetypal Jewish sufferer, driven by demons and tormented by bad dreams of the twentieth century Jewish predicament. Although Hoffman has played Jewish characters in other projects, never

before had he approached a role that so analyzed the relationship of the modern Jew to his immediate past.

And finally, it is the only film he has done so far that concerns itself with a relationship between brothers. Like Babe, Dustin has a slightly older brother; like Babe, that brother "found himself" and proved successful first; like Babe, that brother is in government service; like Babe, Dustin both emulates and ènvies the brother. There is a Biff-Hap quality to the scenes between Hoffman and Scheider in the film, and if one remembers the importance of *Death of a Salesman* to the young Hoffman, that makes sense. When Olivier scoffed at Dustin's intense, inner-directed approach, what he failed to realize was that Hoffman was not, like himself, merely acting out one more role in one more movie. To a degree, he was coming to grips with his own story.

Roy Scheider as the Marathon Man's secret agent brother.

Straight Time

Distributed by Warner Brothers 1978

184   Dustin Hoffman as Max Dembo.

CAST:

Dustin Hoffman *(Max Dembo)*; Theresa Russell *(Jenny Mercer)*; Harry Dean Stanton *(Jerry Schue)*; Gary Busey *(Willy Darin)*; M. Emmet Walsh *(Earl Frank)*; Sandy Baron *(Manny)*; Kathy Bates *(Selma Darin)*; Edward Bunker *(Mickey)*; Stuart I. Berton *(Salesman No. 1)*; Barry Cahill *(Salesman No. 2)*; Corey Rand *(Carlos)*; James Ray *(Manager)*; Fran Ryan *(Cafe Owner)*; Rita Taggart *(Carol Schue)*.

CREDITS:

Director, Ulu Grosbard; screenplay by Alvin Sargent, Edward Bunker and Jeffrey Boam, based on Edward Bunker's novel *No Beast So Fierce*; produced by Stanley Beck and Tim Zinnemann; director of photography, Owem Roizman; editors, Sam O'Steen and Randy Roberts; music, David Shire; executive producer, Howard B. Pine; A First Artists presentation; running time, 114 minutes; rating, R.

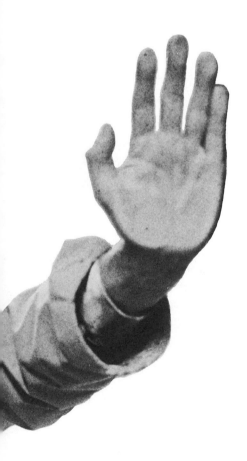

Straight Time should have been the experience of a lifetime for Dustin Hoffman. In the first place, he had entertained the idea of doing this film for nearly five years, ever since first reading criminal Edward Bunker's novel *No Beast So Fierce* and being deeply moved by the study of an ex-con struggling to survive under the current parole system. When he joined First Artists, the project seemed the perfect beginning for his relationship with a company which had promised him near-total artistic freedom. Yet somehow, nothing went right. Dustin employed numerous writers to do various drafts of a screenplay, after being unhappy with the first script he read. He was all set to direct himself and, considering his previous statements of envy for the director's position of power over the finished film, that should have made him happy.

Dustin began shooting in March, 1977, but after several dismal weeks went by, millions of dollars had been squandered, and almost nothing of worth was in the can. Dustin desperately contacted his old friend Ulu *(Harry Kellerman)* Grosbard, begging him to fly in and try to salvage things. Grosbard was hesitant, but felt he could not in conscience ignore the pleadings of so close a friend, and volunteered to at least try his best. But Dustin immediately began quarreling with Grosbard about the way he was treating the story, and their arguments escalated during the remainder of the filming schedule.

Their conflict was clear in statements each later made to *The New York Times*. "If he's so meticulous and such a perfectionist," Grosbard wondered, "why had he created such an enormous mess?" "I was doing the best work I'd ever done," Hoffman countered, "and I knew the film wasn't supporting the performance." Though their bickering could have forced a closing down of the production—rumors were rampant that Hoffman was acting absolutely "irrational" on the set—the picture was somehow completed, though in a far different form from what had been planned. Lost along the way was the great film that might have been, millions of dollars of investment money never to be recovered, Dustin's dream of collaboration on a project, and a longtime friendship.

Max heads for the prison doors and hopes he will not be back soon.

Max and his parole officer leave the prison.

Even after exceeding the 61 days approved shooting schedule by some 23 days, Hoffman and Grosbard still didn't have what they wanted, at which time Phil Feldman of First Artists suggested they stop shooting, prepare a rough cut of the film, study it carefully, and then proceed from there in terms of eventually shooting what they would still need to make a successful picture. Dustin was perfectly willing to go along with what sounded like a common sense solution; after all, some time and distance might give him much needed perspective on this project. Only after production had been completely shut down did Dustin learn second-hand that as far as Feldman was concerned, shooting was over—for good. "I would never have agreed to a hiatus had I known that," Dustin later insisted.

Meanwhile, Dustin had planned to shoot *Agatha* in England, then return to America in order to work on the editing and sound looping of *Straight Time*. Legally speaking, he had six months to complete *Straight Time* after principal photography on the project was finished. As far as he was concerned, it *wasn't* finished—they were only on hiatus—so he still had plenty of time. The problem was that the film, so far as First Artists was concerned, had "rapped" in July, so contractual right to supervise the film's

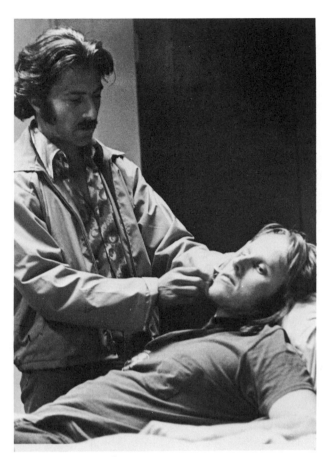

Dustin Hoffman and Gary Busey.

editing would be in January—at which point Dustin would still be shooting *Agatha* in a far-away country.

First Artists took the right of first cut away from Hoffman after he had edited only the first twenty minutes of the picture, even though he had completely bypassed his usual million-dollar salary for the right to cut it. The provision which allowed Feldman to take over a film alluded to the costs and time of the shooting schedule growing "out of control" during production. But while *Straight Time* did go over budget and schedule, Dustin felt strongly that he was treated badly by Feldman, who had encouraged him to begin shooting without a finalized script—which lead directly to all the problems. First Artists then allowed Warner Brothers to dump the film into an unimpressive release, without much fanfare or advance publicity.

"The film fails to lift itself beyond a kind of documentary reality," Hoffman later told interviewers. "That's done in the editing." Dustin had a strong point of view about the criminal activities portrayed in the picture, and it was the point of view—not the criminal activities themselves—that ended on the cutting room floor,

The first meeting with the girl (Theresa Russell).

Max Dembo in a tight spot.

leaving nothing more than a slice-of-life realistic study of a singular criminal. The story about this man contains what Dustin considers one of his own finest performances, but never really makes a fluent point about the criminal, or the courts and parole system, or anything else.

Tom Buckley, writing in *The New York Times*, did note that Warner Brothers opened the film in New York on a Friday, without advance screenings for critics. This is the approach taken by distributors when they fear they have a colossal turkey on their hands, in hopes of doing a solid weekend's business based on the star's drawing power alone, before the bad reviews come pouring in. As it turned out, though, *Straight Time* received mostly strong notices, the *Times* included. In fact, Dustin's lawyer in his case against First Artists, Bertram Fields, did mention that "one important critic pointed out that [the film] seemed to sag after the first third, which is exactly at the point the editing was taken away from [Hoffman]." And while the reviews for the film were understandably mixed, Hoffman's personal notices were mostly glowing.

In *The Nation*, Robert Hatch commented that

Max attempts a normal domestic life.

Alone and unloved in Hollywood.

A quiet conversation in the midst of a violent lifestyle.

streets, so long as he adheres to a strict code of behavior. At first, Max makes every effort to do just that, finding himself a sleazy but affordable room, trying hard to land honest work, and avoiding the lowlife temptations around him. In time, he even strikes up a relationship with a pretty middle-class girl (Theresa Russell). But his parole officer (M. Emmett Walsh) is a disagreeable sort, searching for some minor infraction in Max's pattern of living that will allow him to throw Max back into prison. He mistakenly thinks he has discovered Max shooting up drugs in his room, and rushes Max to the jail for purposes of observation. Innocent, Max is turned back onto the streets once again, but now his dedication to living the straight life crumbles,

even though he doesn't "have the strongest of narratives or many details of personality on which to build . . . he is an actor who, if so required and within his range of somewhat bizarre types, could work up a character from an ad in the phone book's yellow pages." Penelope Gilliatt of *The New Yorker* commented: "Ulu Grosbard has drawn a near-perfect performance of a very imperfect human being from Dustin Hoffman, an actor who memorably first enacted hatred of the unhazardous in *The Graduate*, and who here, in maturity, consummates that contempt." *Newsweek*'s David Ansen, in a review which praised the film as a whole, said that Hoffman "daringly and brilliantly" played Dembo, while *Time*'s Frank Rich, in a review which panned the film, at least conceded that Hoffman "works hard and well to create a man who lives in a state of constant punishment. It's an admirable job." Stanley Kauffmann of *The New Republic*, in a damning attack on the picture, was one of the very few to offer Hoffman a lukewarm review: "He does well enough" was all the enthusiasm he could muster up.

As the film opens, so too do the gates of San Quentin prison, as Max Dembo (Hoffman) is released after serving six years for armed robbery. The parole system returns him to the

Max reluctantly returns to a life of crime.

replaced by a terrible rage against a system which insists he go straight yet seems determined not to let him do it. While riding in the parole officer's car, listening to the man verbally abuse him, Max suddenly explodes—attacking the officer, and immediately returning to a life of crime.

Shreds of evidence remain throughout that the movie wants to communicate a single, significant message: far from being a means of possible rehabilitation, the parole system is nothing more than one more aspect of a great societal trap that serves the purpose of seeing to it criminals are never allowed to re-enter society, but instead are constantly forced—against their own wishes—back into, first, a life of crime, then a life in

prison. But this notion gets diffused along the way, for the picture's focus shifts to compulsive criminal friends of Max's. One (Harry Dean Stanton) is trying hard to adjust to a middle-class lifestyle with a regular job, barbeque pit, swimming pool and wife; the other (Gary Busey) is whacko-off-the-wall on drugs. As the three men plan a robbery together, both these supporting performances emerge as sharply etched and effectively rendered, but, good as they both are, neither performer can steal the thunder from Dustin. The viewer literally forgets that this is the boyishly charming movie star of such films as *The Graduate*, so completely does he create the characterization of Max Dembo.

Sadly, though, the case study of Max usurps center stage from the theme. *Straight Time* shifts awkwardly from being a polemical picture about an unfair system into a violent melodrama about a finely drawn but ultimately pathetic and incomprehensible man. Something about Max is self-destructive: more than the victim of an unfair system, he appears to cause himself to be victimized without even knowing it. There is a fascinating quality which suggests that the problem of being stuck with an obnoxious parole officer is a relatively minor one: he is actually forced back into a life of crime by a victim complex that causes him to bring out the predator in people. On this level, the film is relatively successful, for Hoffman makes Max one of the most complex characters he has ever played, believably bouncing back and forth from sincerity to dishonesty, from charming politeness to enraged anti-social behavior, from quiet passivity to volcanic action.

Yet even the quality of the performance damages the overall effect of the film, for as we become as involved as we do in Max's unpredictability, we adjust our expectations for the film, and progressively see it more as a character study of a unique (rather than universal) criminal. Thus, it becomes increasingly more difficult to understand whether this is meant as a generalized indictment of the parole system *per se*, or an offbeat case that has little to say about the system as a whole. For that matter, one never grasps whether the intention of the film is to indicate that Max's parole officer typifies parole officers in general, or that he should be perceived as an aberration in the system.

The filmmaking itself is essentially lackluster. Far from the symbolic flamboyance of *Harry Kellerman*, Grosbard settled instead for a kind of yeomanlike realism, which is functional enough but flat in effect—so low key it makes *Straight Time* look, from the outset, like a minor effort, a tawdry tale told to no specific purpose other than immerse us in the tawdriness of it all. The project is hardly served by a plot that is at once pedestrian and ponderous, following the central character around with gritty but unresolved cinema verité techniques.

At one point, Max's girlfriend abandons her normal lifestyle to run off in *Bonnie and Clyde* fashion, shooting up the countryside with him. If her personality were better explained, we might be able to rationalize this. But she is nothing more than a device, a diversion: the pretty girl who gets involved with the hero and will follow him anywhere, in order to make the movie more romantic and therefore more commercial. Without her, the film would assuredly be more tedious even than it is; with her, it seems somewhat contrived, the very thing an intentionally realistic picture cannot be if it is to succeed.

Certainly, *Straight Time* would seem of all Dustin's films the one least likely to connect with him as a person—a portrayal that has him imaginatively sketching his role rather than relying on correlating experiences from his own life. Yet there are some striking correlations all the same. One derives from that period when Dustin's family was, at the height of the Depression, forced to reside in a rough neighborhood where Dustin temporarily became involved with a street gang. In the movie, Max makes clear that his life of crime began with some small acts of vandalism as a juvenile delinquent. Had Dustin's parents not moved back to Beverly Hills shortly thereafter, then—who knows? Dustin might have, as impossible as it seems today, turned out like Max, and Dustin's ability to bring this character so sharply to life must in part have grown out of a realization that there, but for the grace of God, goes Dustin.

In addition, what eventually forces Max to turn outlaw is the fact he is a "difficult" personal-

Max and a companion (Harry Dean Stanton) pull off a robbery.

ity, and this quality puts him in conflict with whatever institution he works within. Though all the stars involved with First Artists suffered disappointments and lodged complaints, none of them went through the hell that Dustin—"difficult Dustin," as he is so often labelled by people who have worked with him—went through. In fact, First Artists appears to have done a number on him every bit as severe as the one the parole system does on Max in the movie. Dustin undoubtedly drew on the parallel situation he was experiencing while making the film, transferring his own frustration to Max and so channeling it in the most creative way possible. Likewise, Max's essential character trait—his victim complex—has often been seen as basic to Hoffman's problems; Ulu Grosbard is one of those moviemakers who has come to see Dustin as a "professional victim."

And finally, there is that sense of unpredictability about Dembo's personality, his bizarre changes in mood which make him so frightening a character; just as Dustin has commented upon his own "ugly side," so too have both interviewers and close friends of his spoken of his unpredictability, his own sudden swoops from elation to depression. Clearly, if the specifics of Max Dembo's situation had to be created for him, the psychological situation Max finds himself in was not too far from Dustin's own range of experience.

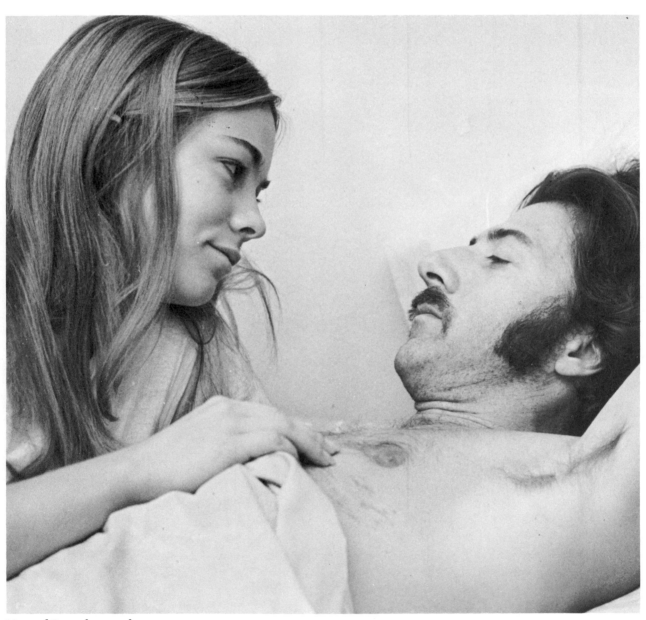

Max and Jenny become lovers.

Agatha

A Warner Brothers Release   1979

Dustin Hoffman as Wally Stanton.

CAST:

Dustin Hoffman *(Wally Stanton)*; Vanessa Redgrave *(Agatha Christie)*; Timothy Dalton *(Archie Christie)*; Helen Morse *(Evelyn)*; Tony Britton *(William Collins)*; Timothy West *(Kenward)*; Celia Gregory *(Nancy Neele)*; Alan Badel *(Lord Brackenbury)*; Paul Brooke *(John Foster)*; Carolyn Pickles *(Charlotte Fisher)*; Robert Longden *(Pettleson)*; Donald Nithsdale *(Uncle Jones)*; Liz Smith *(Flora)*.

CREDITS:

Director, Michael Apted; Producers, Jarvis Astaire and Gabrik Losey; screenplay by Kathleen Tynan and Arthur Hopcraft, from a story by Kathleen Tynan; music by Johnny Mandel; photographed by Vittorio Storaro; edited by Jim Clark; A First Artists Presentation; running time, 98 minutes; rating, PG.

Even as Hoffman was worrying over the uncompleted *Straight Time*, a major rift was arising with First Artists over the script for *Agatha*. With only weeks left before shooting was set to commence, the company complained that the project would give Hoffman what they considered to be a "supporting role" rather than what

he insisted was in fact a brief but full "co-starring" role as an English gossip columnist, and that it would have to be expanded if he were going to meet his contractual obligation to them. Ironically, while most movie actors fight venomously for more lines and more scenes, Hoffman was perfectly willing to take a backseat to Redgrave for the good of the project as a whole. But hastily, Hoffman, director Michael Apted, screenwriter Kathleen Tynan and other writers quickly rushed in to iron out the plot problems; all attempted to make the script acceptable to First Artists without ruining its original conception.

Tynan's notion had been to tell a story about the eerie relationship Agatha Christie establishes with her husband's mistress, and essentially it was a vehicle for two women; in the rewriting, it was turned instead into a love story between a man and a woman, Agatha and a journalist observing her. Screenwriter Tynan complained: "When I wrote the part of the jour-

nalist, he was a tall blond Englishman with a supporting, small minor role. Now, he's a small, dark American with one of the leads."

At any rate, they were halfway through the new script when the first day of scheduled shooting arrived. Hoffman frantically phoned First Artists, asking for an additional three weeks to iron out the script problems in a manner that would satisfy everybody, but was told instead to start shooting without a finalized script—as he had been instructed to do in the case of *Straight Time*. "I literally got on my knees and begged them not to start the film," Hoffman later explained. "Once you go on that floor to make a movie, it's crazy time. It's painting a picture on railroad tracks, with the train getting closer. *Agatha* was every actor's nightmare. The script was literally being rewritten every day. It was a rainbow of green, yellow, pink revision pages." Executive producer David Puttnam at this time wrote back to the States, saying, in part: "The production is out of control."

All the same, shooting did commence. And when the cast and crew, after working hard for several weeks of shooting by day and rewriting by night, finally took a Christmas break, Dustin's colleagues enjoyed their vacation while he jetted back to L. A., where he worked around the clock trying to assemble the final cut of *Straight Time* before his time limit ran out, getting the first quarter of the film completed, then hurriedly jetting back to Britain to fulfill his acting commitment on *Agatha*. First Artists sent a film editor to England with the *Straight Time* footage so Dustin could work on it while he was completing *Agatha*, which he would have done were he not still rewriting *Agatha* whenever they weren't actually in the process of shooting it. Then, First Artists announced he had to finish *Agatha* by the following Friday, when shooting would stop even if all the scenes were not completed.

All but one scene of *Agatha* was shot—a key one for his character, revealing the motivation for his obsession with Agatha. When the film was released and people asked Dustin why he should be so deeply affected by her, he insisted it would have been made clear in a scene which suddenly revealed that his newspaperman was in fact a failed novelist, "whose own failure causes him to be obsessed by Agatha and her success." In the meantime, though, trembling at the thought of how close he had come to making the film he wanted this to be, and terrified it would ring all wrong without that scene, Dustin ran to a phone booth where he called First Artists in America, offering to pay for the extra day's work on *Agatha* out of his own pocket, just to get it right. They flatly refused to let him do it.

Visibly shaken, Dustin wandered away from the phone, at least hoping to forget his heart-break by finding that film editor and putting all his energy into *Straight Time* instead. Abruptly, he was approached by a First Artists spokesman who informed him that *Straight Time* had been taken away from him and he would not be allowed to have anything further to do with its editing. Overcome with a feeling of powerless-ness, he at first threatened to refuse to do the looping on *Agatha's* sound—the post-dubbing of his voice into certain scenes. He did hold the final release of the film up, though in time he did do the looping—not out of fear of the legal power that First Artists tried to bring to bear, but voluntarily, because the voices of two other actors would have been looped into the film instead. No matter how terrible his relationship with First Artists had become by this time, he did want to protect his own reputation as an actor, and completed the film out of a sense of

A study in contrasts—Vanessa Redgrave and Dustin Hoffman.

The classic billiards sequence that cements the relationship between Agatha and Wally.

responsibility to the public that would come to see one of his pictures, expecting a certain level of professionalism from it. Even at this point, the film was still under siege—from relatives of Agatha Christie, who claimed the film represented an invasion of privacy.

Apparently, absolutely nothing worked out right. Except, amazingly enough, for the film itself—a near perfect picture which reveals no trace of the numerous difficulties encountered. The film opens with a disclaimer explaining that in December, 1926, Agatha Christie disappeared completely for eleven days. "What follows," we read, "is an imaginary solution to an actual mystery." What Tynan and Arthur Hopcraft did was lock themselves into a fascinating kind of writer's game: they could not tamper with the facts, but did leave themselves open to freely, imaginatively invent anything they wished in those areas that still remain blank spots in the factual accounts. As for the facts of the case, they are aptly dramatized here: Mrs. Christie (Vanessa Redgrave) becomes aware of her husband's love affair with his secretary, Nancy Neele (Celia Gregory), as well as that he—Col. Archibald Christie (Timothy Dalton)—plans to divorce her, then marry the pretty girl. Distraught, Mrs. Christie goes out driving recklessly in the night, cracks up her car, then boards a train and journeys to the Harrogate Health Spa, where Miss Neele is vacationing. Mrs. Christie registers at one of the resort hotels under the name of Theresa Neele, then proceeds to observe, from a distance, the young woman her husband has become infatuated with.

That much is true. Invented for the purpose of the picture is Wally Stanton (Hoffman), an American journalist who follows Agatha to Harrogate where he too registers under a false name and observes her, even as she observes Miss Neele, all the while striking up a friendship—and, ultimately, an unconsummated love affair—with the woman. The film is a fascinating study of role-playing—of a relationship between two characters who themselves create characters which then fall in love. In a sense, it was, up until *Tootsie*, the only movie Hoffman made *about* the art of acting; for in it, his character develops a character of his own. There is a notable chemis-

The cautious kiss.

try at work between Hoffman and Redgrave, growing out of their opposing but complementary styles—she from the English "old school," he an American method upstart—and from the fascinating fact that we get to see them not only performing but also analyzing, within the film's context, their vastly different but equally valid approaches to acting.

At the same time, it always remains a film about Agatha Christie, and on two levels at that. On the surface, it is a film about Mrs. Christie because Vanessa Redgrave plays that lady. Beyond that, it is a film about Agatha because Ms. Tynan designed the film in the style of an Agatha Christie thriller—that is, telling an imaginary story about the lady in the way in which she herself told stories. As Mrs. Christie questions the spa workers about the lethal possibilities of the electric chair used for some treatments, her eyes light up as she learns Miss Neele takes just that treatment, and we assume (as one would assume while watching a Christie thriller) that we know precisely what is happening: Mrs. Christie is planning a fitting revenge, devising an elaborate scheme to lure the girl into the chair and then turn on the switch. Indeed, the film encourages us, manipulates us even, into making just this assumption—without ever quite coming out and telling us this is the case. The suspense derives from watching Wally Stanton

Timothy Dalton as Archie Christie, at one of his more frantic moments.

The legendary *Daily Mirror* front page announcing Agatha's disappearance.

Truth is stranger than fiction: police drag a marsh for the missing Agatha's body, with the two stars in insets.

move toward a discovery of this plot, and finally rushing to prevent it. But as he arrives on the scene in the nick of time, we suddenly realize—along with him—that everything we have assumed is wrong, just as it would be in a top-form Christie thriller.

The trick to the ending is that Agatha's planned revenge is more bizarre than we suspected: she has herself slipped into the electric chair, and has induced the unsuspecting Miss Neele to pull the switch. A strange but sweet revenge, to be sure, and one that has been carefully prepared for from the very beginning, when Archibald insisted to his wife that under no circumstances did he want his future wife's name paraded in the newspapers, voicing a fear that such a scandal might tarnish his great love. Mrs. Christie's plot was to put herself out of her own misery without quite commiting the controversial, perhaps sinful, act of suicide, and at the same time incriminating her husband's lover in the act and thereby destroying their chances for happiness.

Vanessa Redgrave's Agatha is a marvelous assemblage of nervous mannerisms and awkward grimaces: no current actress is better equipped to play characters who walk the thinnest of lines between an outer normalcy and inner neurosis. Hoffman provides the perfect foil for her: his character is as typically American as she is traditionally English; as much a populist, self-made writer/celebrity as she is a born aristocrat; as short but stylish as she is tall and gawky; and as glibly comfortable with himself as she is self-consciously reticent.

Understandably, many viewers simply assumed that, like Agatha Christie, Wally Stanton was also a real-life character, so cleverly are his past history and present lifestyle sketched in by Kathleen Tynan and fleshed out by Hoffman. In fact, in his review for *The Nation*, Robert Hatch went so far as to spend considerable time pondering and interpreting Stanton's possible background: "Stanton, I would guess, is not the name he was born with, nor is his precise American diction what he heard at home. By industry, quick wits and boldness of address, he has risen far. . . . Hoffman gives much thought to his impersonations, and the results are gratifying." Likewise, most critics tended to be mildly ap-

Vanessa Redgrave as Agatha Christie.

preciative of the film and even more so of the Hoffman performance. In *Saturday Review*, Arthur Schlesinger, Jr. wrote that "Dustin Hoffman . . . conveys a marvelous sensitivity beneath an air of acquired confidence." Stanley Kauffman, who in his *New Republic* review found the film too precious, did admit that "Hoffman plays with point and swagger and complete clarity." David Ansen of *Newsweek* added to the compliments: "With his slicked-back hair and impeccable tailoring Hoffman paints a droll portrait of the studiously debonair American abroad." Only Pauline Kael took Hoffman to task, arguing that "Wally Stanton is just a concoction of a role . . . you feel that in *Agatha* he has an image of the character in his mind and he's impersonating it. . . . He's furiously theatrical in the role. . . ." On closer inspection, though, her criticism does not hold water. In *Papillon*, Hoffman played his role in a distressingly mannered style; here, he plays in a most natural style a man who is himself distressingly mannered.

Which is why, even though Hoffman never got the chance to film what seemed to him the "key"

Celia Gregory as "the other woman" in Archie Christie's life.

scene, the movie works beautifully. In fact, any further explanation of Stanton's motives might have made overly obvious what is better left only implied. On the level of personal expression, Wally Stanton displays more of Hoffman's own characteristics than any other single film role of his. First and foremost, Wally is short, and *Agatha* is the only film of Hoffman's that directly addresses his lifelong obsession with his own diminutive size. In one unforgettable scene, the two leads at last kiss, and—in a striking reversal of the usual stereotype situation—Agatha must lean down while Stanton stands on his tip toes so their lips can meet. The initial audience reaction is, naturally, light laughter, but halfway through the kiss, the audience changes its mind—or, rather, has its mind changed by the movie—as we come to realize there is nothing at all funny going on here. It is as touchingly human and subtly sexy a kiss as has ever appeared onscreen.

Like Hoffman, Wally is made to feel that he is the center of the universe, since he is as much a writer/celebrity as Hoffman is an actor/celebrity. But Stanton, like Dustin, is essentially a loner—

A nervous Agatha reads about her own disappearance.

and an observer. Like Hoffman, the character is supremely successful in his field but denigrates himself as a hack: he would rather have been a novelist than a newspaperman, just as Hoffman complains he should have remained a stage actor rather than a film star. And, mirroring Hoffman's own feelings of rejection, Stanton is at the end left standing alone. Hoffman's strong sense of rejection at various points in his youth must have surely had something to do with the poignantly painful expression on his face at the final fadeout.

Most importantly, though, *Agatha* expresses Hoffman's attitudes about the press in a dramatized context. Initially, his character plans on writing a story about Mrs. Christie's disappearance, and goes along with her ruse in order to keep the story completely to himself. However, at the film's end—after thwarting her suicide/vengeance plot—he hands her his manuscript, allowing her secret to remain private, having been emotionally moved by the experience with her and now understanding there are some stories which shouldn't be published. Wally Stanton serves as Hoffman's statement to journalists, a fantasy projection of the way in which he feels they ought to behave with nonpolitical stories involving the private lives of celebrities as compared to the way they (in his experience, at least) do. It's worth noting that the relationship is reciprocal: just as Stanton is touched and even changed by his near-miss relationship with Christie, so too does he move her; at the end, she rejoins her husband only in order to initiate divorce proceedings against him, so completely has Stanton instilled in her a sense of self-worth. In addition to this notion of a properly balanced male-female relationship, there is also an implied statement about the public, and the "fan" mentality: Mrs. Christie's disappearance sparks a grotesque fascination on the part of the public who avidly read her books; she is as much at the mercy of their whims as Hoffman has come to feel he is at the hands of his fans.

Director Michael Apted paced his film in a slow but never tedious fashion, while Vittorio Storaro shot everything as through both a gauze and a prism, in order to recreate the world of Agatha Christie's England: a world between wars, a world of sleek cars and tailored tweeds, a

world in transition from the old order to the modern mentality. Naturally, the spa itself comes to symbolize this passing order, with numerous shots of crumbling decadence. In one particularly telling scene, the dance floor is filled with people gliding through the motions of a slow, ordered tango, as Mrs. Christie watches them with comfort; but when they break into a Charleston, it is Wally Stanton who suddenly feels at home. In that moment, the different worlds they hail from and still belong to are wordlessly communicated, as is the vast difference between them that will, without undue explanation, cause their parting at the conclusion. Ultimately, *Agatha* turned out to be every bit as civilized as the intense but unconsummated love affair it chronicles, and no one should take that for anything but a compliment.

Agatha makes a frantic phone call as the adventure reaches fever pitch.

Kramer vs. Kramer

A Columbia Pictures Release   1979

Dustin Hoffman as the divorced father of young
Justin Henry.

CAST:

Dustin Hoffman (*Ted Kramer*); Meryl Streep (*Joanna Kramer*); Jane Alexander (*Margaret Phelps*); Justin Henry (*Billy Kramer*); Howard Duff (*John Shaunessy*); George Coe (*Jim O'Connor*); Jobeth Williams (*Phyllis Bernard*); Bill Moor (*Gressen*); Howland Chamberlain (*Judge Atkins*); Jack Ramage (*Spencer*); Jess Osuna (*Ackerman*); Nicholas Hormann (*Interviewer*); Ellen Parker (*Teacher*).

CREDITS:

Director-writer, Robert Benton; producer, Stanley R. Jaffe; adapted from the novel by Avery Corman; director of photography, Nestor Almendros; edited by Jerry Greenberg; associate producer, Richard C. Fischoff; music editor, Erma E. Levin; music by Henry Purcell adapted by John Kander and conducted by Paul Gemignani, music by Antonio Vivaldi adapted and conducted by Herb Harris; rating, PG.

When Dustin first read Avery Corman's novel on the suggestion it might make a good vehicle for him, he found the story too contrived and turned it down. Later, when Robert Benton (who had been picked by producer Stanley Jaffe to helm the project after Francois Truffaut proved unavailable) wrote the first draft of the script and hopefully submitted it to Hoffman, Dustin found it boring and again rejected it. But following several more drafts, the character of Ted Kramer and the story itself began to take on what Hoffman likes to call an "arc"—which interested him enough to want to do it. Significantly, Dustin got what he had been battling for for a full twelve years: a guarantee of collaboration.

He spent eight months working with writer-director Benton and producer Jaffe before shooting began, meeting every day with them in a hotel room where they could temporarily shut out the rest of the world and go over the script—scene by scene, word by word—analyzing each line of dialogue, questioning the validity of every sequence, going over it all over and over again. When they were finished for the day, Benton would take his notes home and rewrite the script to the specifics of the day's discussion, then bring it back the following day to go over it again.

Benton found that, because Ted Kramer did resemble Dustin Hoffman in certain key respects, it was best to write dialogue with Dustin's style of delivery in mind. In the golden days of Hollywood, screenwriters had often fashioned dialogue with a specific actor's screen image as the basis, whereas Benton was more interested in the way Dustin spoke in normal situations and so imitated the actor's unique phrasing in his script. That way, if Dustin decided to improvise some words—as his contract insisted he had the right to do—those moments would not stand out from the rest of the material. Hoffman had insisted on the right not only to improvise but also to demand extra "takes" if he felt them necessary, as well as the ability to enter the editing room after shooting was completed and supervise the cutting of the film up to—and including!—the final cut. "I've never let an actor in on the writing or editing of a film before *Kramer*," Benton later commented, adding: "I always thought the actors were hired to ruin the writer's lines. In all seriousness, though, Dustin helped

Dustin brings Justin to meet his mother again.

Meryl Streep as the mother finally seeing her son again.

the film immeasurably through his suggestions."

During the shooting, Dustin would often "see" a scene one way, Benton another. What made the filming so agreeable was they would film it both ways and, later, objectively compare the two, with Jaffe serving as the nearest possible thing to an impartial arbitrator. Importantly, Jaffe never complained that the extra takes cost plenty. Also important was that Benton shot in sequence, which is longer and harder than the usual moviemaking technique, and sometimes more expensive too, but allows the actors to mature in their roles, to develop as the characters themselves develop. Dustin's necessity of making a scene "feel right" affected various members of the crew. When shooting the scene in which Streep demands that her child be returned, the script called for her to ask for the boy as soon as she and Hoffman sat down in the restaurant. But Dustin felt uncomfortable with the scene as it played, and couldn't go through with the shooting.

The joys of fatherhood.

The cameras sat ready to roll, the lights were turned up, and everyone waited. Suddenly the script supervisor piped in, suggesting that some small talk, which was supposed to come later, might be transposed to the beginning of the scene. At once, Dustin sensed this was the way it would play best, and his "difficulty" disappeared; though he couldn't figure out a solution himself to the problem, he did inspire another collaborator to find a solution. But one touch in the scene that was his own is the smashing of the wine glass. Dustin improvised this as the cameras rolled because he sensed at scene's end that his character felt "bested" by Streep's, and without having further lines that would allow him to strike back at her verbally, he needed to spontaneously perform a bit of business that would amount to the same thing. The shocked look on Meryl Streep's face as she sits there, covered with broken glass, is not evidence of her acting talent, but an image of her actual shock—she didn't expect it.

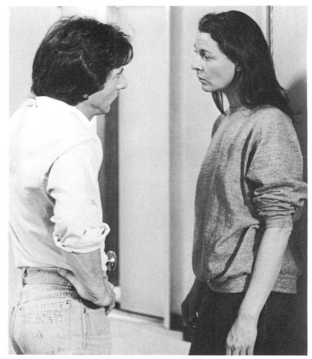

Dustin Hoffman and neighbor Jane Alexander argue during an emotional moment.

Kramer pleads with his wife not to leave him.

Kramer drops his son off at school before leaving for work.

Kramer tells his wife she can't have the child back.

Yet a reporter for the New York *Daily News* was told, while visiting the *Kramer* set, that Hoffman was acting more temperamental than ever, that "the cast and crew were bending over backwards to placate him . . . that he locks himself in his trailer at lunchtime and stares blankly out of the windows until he is awakened from his

trance" to shoot again. According to the same report, Hoffman had been very depressed after learning Jon Voight—his co-star from an early hit who had gone on to win an Oscar before Dustin—was actually the director's first choice for the role. Another rumor was that Dustin had taken the part mainly out of fear lookalike Al Pacino would get it if he didn't. As a gag, the crew members couldn't resist teasing Hoffman, and bought him a coffee mug inscribed "Pacino," which they presented to Hoffman one morning in mock solemnity. Dustin decided to joke back and, one morning, stopped in front of a crew member and said to the man what was so often said to Dustin: "You know, you look just like Al Pacino!" Without missing a beat, the crew member retorted: "*You*, or the *real* Pacino?" For once, words failed Dustin: he had no comeback.

All was not entirely calm during the shooting, and there were fights on this film, as there had been on earlier ones. But for the first time Dustin felt good about them, because he truly believed they were all fighting for the same thing—to get it done right, not just to get it done. There was an all-around commitment to quality, rather than the old situation of Dustin perceiving himself as the standard bearer, waving the flag of quality, while the rest of his army fought another war entirely. "Benton allowed me what no other director before had allowed me," he told reporters later. "He let me try to better it." As for Benton, he said of Dustin: "I found him a tireless worker, one who was constantly preparing, discussing, questioning scenes and situations. He was there every second I allowed him to be. His energy and intelligence sustained him when the rest of us were exhausted."

And the success of a film in which he was allowed full collaboration, as opposed to the commercial failure of those in which his collaborative input was cut short, certainly gave him a sensation of getting even. "Art is revenge," he grinningly told interviewer Wanda McDaniel. Still, he remained unsatisfied about his input. "I wish I could write myself," he later complained to reporters. "I've tried, and it bogs down. What I *can* do is help rewrite something, make it better, after someone else has first written it. Perhaps because I can't create something myself

I love the process of collaboration. Film is a collaborative medium—but, at the same time, a film is also one man's vision. I collaborated more on *Kramer* than any picture I've ever been associated with, but it is still Robert Benton's film."

Benton's film, then, opens as Ted Kramer (Hoffman) returns to his East Side high-rise apartment one evening to find his wife (Meryl Streep) in the process of walking out on him and their six-year-old child (Justin Henry). At first resentfully, then awkwardly, finally wholeheartedly, Kramer takes responsibility for the child's care, only to find—after establishing a touchingly close relationship with the little boy—that his ex-wife has returned to New York and plans on battling him in court for the custody of the child.

If the plot sounds thin, the impact is immense. Though the storyline would sound more suited to a sixty-minute television drama than a full-length film, the collaborators rounded it out rather than padding it out. As was the case with Hoffman's first starring role in *The Graduate*, *Kramer vs. Kramer* had been based on an engaging but inconsequential pop novel, and here too a gifted filmmaker managed to breathe significance and depth into the story, retaining the skeleton of the book but putting pounds of artistic meat onto it; once again a minor work of

Justin Henry as the anguished child.

207

literature was translated into a major work of cinema.

In a sense, then, Hoffman came full cycle. With *The Graduate*, he had been interpreted, whether he liked it or not, as a "generational hero," and that was the case with *Kramer*. The kids who had a dozen years previously seen in Hoffman a mirror-image of their own youthful frustration and defiance now were a part of the work force, and very often their once-hopeful plans for marriages more pure than their parents' had long since crumbled; once again, Hoffman appeared to speak not only to them but for them. If one substitutes Meryl Streep for Katharine Ross, it is not too difficult to perceive *Kramer* as a sequel of sorts to *The Graduate*, and one remembers with irony Mike Nichols' line that the seemingly special couple of that film would, in ten years or so, end up "just like their parents." As a work of personal expression for the star, *Kramer* allowed Dustin to play a character whose family difficulties almost directly paralleled his own. As he was playing Ted Kramer, his own marriage to Anne Byrne was in the final stages of dissolution.

No wonder, then, that Hoffman received some of his strongest reviews since *The Graduate*. Many critics who had once been enamored of him, then lost interest, came full cycle even as he did. "Dustin Hoffman . . . is back in form—a new and better form, in fact," Stanley Kauffmann wrote in *The New Republic*. "Hoffman burns through the givens into the unknowns even in this 'average' man. . . . Hoffman unites us with him and with one another, tacitly but well. And all of this is based on . . . what I'd call the drive of a talented small man. It's an energy that both James Cagney and Edward G. Robinson had in their own ways, an energy that probably has its source in psychic compensation but, in a gifted man, it quickly becomes authentic in itself." Writing in *America*, Richard A. Blake said: "Only artists as talented as Dustin Hoffman, Meryl Streep and Robert Benton could make us see and feel this modern perplexity in such a simple and straightforward story." In *New York*, David Denby wrote: "Dustin Hoffman gives the most detailed, the most affecting performance of his life. Hoffman's personality, his *soul*, has al-

ways been expressed in physical energy . . . you have to admire the fluency, the heat, of Hoffman's acting." As Frank Rich summed it all up in *Time:* "Hoffman gives a performance of nearly infinite shading."

The film certainly belongs to Dustin Hoffman: he is onscreen in almost every shot, while Streep is present for less than a third of the action. Amazingly enough, though, one never thinks of this as an "ego" movie, like so many of Al Pacino's pictures in which the camera is trained on him, in which he is the only character to be developed. There is a sense of *ensemble* to the way in which Hoffman, Streep, Henry, Jane Alexander (as a neighbor), Howard Duff (Hoffman's lawyer), and the others play together; Hoffman seems an equal with them (maybe a bit more equal than the others) and the beauty grows from the way in which the film refuses to take sides, to weight our reactions in favor of or against any character.

Kramer may be told from the male's point of view, yet it seems significant—and less than coincidental—that the film begins and ends with a focus on the tortured mien of the woman in question. For this is the most obvious departure writer-director Benton made from Corman's novel, told from an embittered narrative-voice and vitriolic in its anti-female bias. No such attitude exists in the film. Though Streep goes through the same motions as her counterpart in the book, she is never once characterized as the villain of the piece, but as an anguished, well-meaning character—imperfect but sympathetic. She has been both softened and rounded, in part by the filmmaker's insistence on a more complex approach toward her than was found in Corman's novel, in part because of Streep's delicate screen presence.

Just as important to this effect is that Hoffman is not playing the kind of wronged and wounded figure of masculine nobility that Burt Reynolds portrayed in *Starting Over*. Hoffman's insensitivity in the opening scene—his inability even to hear his wife's announcement she is leaving him owing to his own frantic rambling about his latest business deal—provide us not only with an essential key to the character's personality but, beyond that, an effective and complex tableau of a modern archetype. Later, his gradual and believable metamorphosis into a very different person (brilliantly carried out by Hoffman) made *Kramer* the perfect picture to close out the 1970's for without making any pretentious claims for itself, *Kramer* proved the ultimate film about what Tom Wolfe had labelled "The Me Decade."

At the outset, Hoffman's Kramer may concern himself with his own career over the other people who should matter to him, but without benefit of either est or consciousness-raising groups, we see him transformed into a character who conceives of the work he was once totally committed to as nothing more than a means of earning a living so that he may go on growing on his own, in the context of the separate peace he and his child have made with the world at large. And when that world—in the guise of his ex-wife—returns to take that away from him, the effect is more than melodramatic: in fact, it shapes up as something akin to full tragedy.

Tragedy that is not, unfortunately, supported by the film's last scene, in which without proper motivation, Streep allows the child to remain with Hoffman. When the film ends on this up note, we are at first relieved, then disappointed. Though the film's ending is true to the book's, the film itself veers so far away from the intents and purposes of the book that it certainly needn't have been anchored to such a contrived finale. Perhaps the wrongness of the ending keeps *Kramer* from ranking as one of the great films; perhaps not.

John Ford's *Grapes of Wrath,* Elia Kazan's *On The Waterfront,* and a score of other classic films suffer grievously from endings that come pretty close to defeating the purposes of the pictures that preceded them, yet what we remember of those films are the earlier portions—the honesty with which they lashed out at all that is wrong with the world they depicted. So let it be with *Kramer.* Surely, it is possible to accept the obvious flaw of the ending as a reminder that no film can (or should) be perfect—not even one that comes as close to perfection as *Kramer vs. Kramer* does, up to that last untenable and unsatisfying exchange.

Meryl Streep as the mother who rediscovers the joys of motherhood.

Tootsie

*A Columbia Pictures Release of a Mirage/Punch
Production   1982*

Dustin in the famous publicity shot for *Tootsie*.

CAST:

Dustin Hoffman *(Michael Dorsey/Dorothy Michaels)*; Jessica Lange *(Julie, the Soap Opera Star)*; Teri Garr *(Sandy, the Acting Student)*; Dabney Coleman *(Ron, the TV Producer)*; Charles Durning *(Les, Julie's Father)*; Bill Murray *(Jeff, Michael's Playwright Roommate)*; Sydney Pollack *(George Fields, Michael's Agent)*; George Gaynes *(John Van Horn)*; Geena Davis *(April)*; Doris Belack *(Rita)*; Ellen Foley *(Jacqui)*; Peter Gatto *(Rick)*; Lynne Thigpen *(Jo)*; Ronald L. Schwary *(Phil Weintraub)*; Debra Mooney *(Mrs. Mallory)*; Amy Lawrence *(Amy)*; Murray Schisgal *(Party Guest)*.

CREDITS:

Producers, Sydney Pollack and Dick Richards; director, Sydney Pollack; Assistant director, David McGiffert; story by, Don McGuire and Larry Gelbart; screenplay by, Larry Gelbart and Murray Schisgal; cinematographer, Owen Roizman, A.S.C.; production designer, Peter Larkin; executive producer, Charles Evans; editors, Fredric Steinkamp and William Steinkamp; music by, Dave Grusin; costumes designed by, Ruth Morley; Mr. Hoffman's make-up by, Allen Weisinger; running time, 100 minutes; rating, PG.

In his Academy Award acceptance speech for *Kramer*, Dustin mentioned many of his deeply felt objections to the Oscars. What he didn't speak of (and, perhaps, didn't consider) was a less philosophic, more practical problem. For reasons no one really comprehends, the Academy Award for Best Actor has in recent years become the kiss-of-death to a healthy career. The syndrome started back in 1967: Rod Steiger enjoyed much success in movies before winning for *In the Heat of the Night*, but was seen onscreen only intermittently, and in disappointing pictures, after that. In the 1970's, Jack Nicholson starred in a series of superhits *(Easy Rider, Five Easy Pieces, Carnal Knowledge, Chinatown)*, each of which won him an Oscar nomination and led to an even better part in an even bigger picture; but after finally receiving the award for *One Flew Over the Cuckoo's Nest*, he appeared in films of questionable quality and limited audience appeal. Dustin's onetime

Michael Dorsey (Dustin) and unemployed actress Sandy Lester (Teri Garr) encounter resistance when she auditions for a soap opera.

roommate Gene Hackman has had, since his Oscar for *The French Connection*, serious trouble finding scripts as solid as the ones he was offered earlier *(Bonnie and Clyde, I Never Sang For My Father)*, while Dustin's old *Midnight Cowboy* co-star Jon Voight has done nothing of merit since his powerhouse Oscar-winning performance in *Coming Home*.

Meanwhile, equally popular actors who did *not* win the Oscar (Clint Eastwood, Burt Reynolds, Warren Beatty, Al Pacino, Robert Redford and up until 1980 Dustin himself) continued to enjoy extremely successful careers. Dustin's fans were, understandably, filled with mixed emotions about his Oscar victory: on the one hand, heartened that he had finally received Hollywood's ultimate recognition as an actor, and, on the other, dismayed at the thought this might do to Dustin's career what it had already done to so many others.

Naturally, then, all eyes were leveled at his next project, and the press covered *Tootsie* with a scrutiny usually reserved for possible political conspiracies. Once again, Dustin had flatly refused to merely play a role in someone else's picture. In December, 1982, Dustin would look back on his three-year experience with *Tootsie* and try explaining it to me: "At the end of *Kramer*, I said to myself, 'I don't want to work

Disguised as Dorothy Michaels, Michael Dorsey (Dustin) wins the soap opera role but finds himself attracted to one of the show's stars, Julie Nichols (Jessica Lange).

Michael's attraction to Julie grows more complicated still when Julie's father, Les Nichols (Charles Durning) falls for Dorothy.

any other way from now on. I want to be like other artists—painters, writers—who get up in the morning and go to work. An actor interprets *other* people's things.' In *Kramer*, I'm playing a guy who gets divorced and has to worry about whether he's going to get to see his child. It was all happening in my own life. The director on that film told me to make it as *personal* as I possibly could. After it was all over, Murray

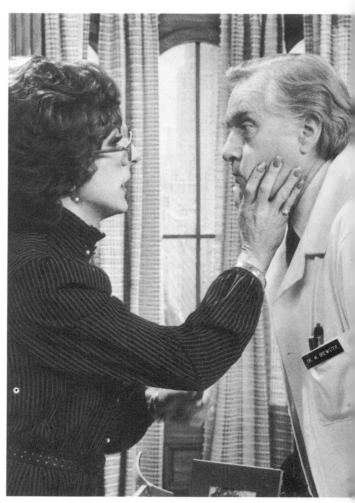

John Van Horn (George Gaynes), who plays the lecherous Dr. Medford Brewster in the soap opera, makes a pass at Dorothy/Michael (Dustin), allowing the hero to understand for the first time how a woman feels.

Schisgal asked me, 'What do you want to do next?' And I thought, in *Kramer* the guy was becoming a *mother* by the end, only they didn't let me take that element as far as I wanted. I was wondering if I could carry that business over to my next film. I was thinking, 'What is it really like to carry a baby? What is it like to go through the business of giving birth?' I've always wondered how many experiences we miss out on, being men. Is it a radically different experience going through life, depending on what sex you are? Let's see if I could play a man forced to impersonate a woman, then experiencing life from the other point of view.

"But we couldn't make that situation work on paper. And then Don McGuire sent me a script called *Why Would I Lie?* It was about an out-of-work actor, whose agent says, 'You want a part on a soap opera? Only problem is, the character's a woman.' I liked that, so I took the skeleton of the idea, and sent it to Schisgal to develop. And the acting part of it appealed to me, too, being that there are so few movies about acting. So we started to break down the idea of what it's like to be an actor. To want to create but to be unable to do it on your own, as a painter or a poet can. They can sit starving in their garrets but still *work*. To be an actor, you must find somebody *out there* who will give you a job. In the end, I did on this film what Woody Allen did on *Annie Hall*—I drew on my own life."

But from day one, the oddball quality of the storyline, coupled with Dustin's fabled "perfectionism" (a term he resents, insisting it's applied to him by people who don't care deeply about their work), soon turned this "little" movie into a monumental project. Word leaked out that Dustin was going to follow his incredible *Kramer* success with a disaster to end all disasters. "Hoffman's Gate," one wag labelled the still-in-production *Tootsie* shortly after Michael Cimino's $40 million monstrosity, *Heaven's Gate*, opened and closed in one week, practically taking United Artists down with it. The truth was, many industry insiders secretly feared *Tootsie* could do similar, if somewhat lesser, damage to Columbia Pictures.

Then on May 20, 1982, a bomb exploded. *The New York Times* published a story by Aljean Harmetz titled, "Is Columbia Facing End of a Long Line of Hits?" And while the title was guardedly phrased as a question, the intent of the article appeared less the objective coverage of an existing condition than an attempt to report certain isolated facts in such a way that, by virtue of the context which the writer assigned them, a situation would be manufactured. The journalist was acting as creator, rather than reporter, of the news.

First, the article mentioned the megahits *(Stir Crazy, Seems Like Old Times, Stripes)* Columbia had recently enjoyed, as well as their financial stability after being purchased by Coca-Cola for $750 million. Harmetz then went on to gloatingly report the company could nonetheless be in big trouble shortly, citing the disappointing early reactions to Ray Stark's $50 million musical *Annie* (receiving nationwide distribution that week), as well as the many troubles *Tootsie*, still shooting in New York, was experiencing. Though *Tootsie* began as the kind of personal little film Dustin and Schisgal had always looked forward to doing together, Murray had long since departed (citing "artistic differences" as his reason), while other writers who came and left included Robert Kaufman, Larry Gelbart, and finally Elaine May (who one unnamed insider insists was paid a phenomenal $450,000 for three weeks work as script doctor). Director Dick Richards gave way to Hal Ashby, who was eventually replaced by Sydney Pollack *(The Way We Were, Electric Horseman, Absence of Malice)*. He had never done a comedy before and was reportedly soon engaged in heated arguments with Hoffman.

Months later, on the eve of *Tootsie*'s release, Dustin would attempt to explain the difficulties to me. "Yes, we fought. But we didn't fight in public or in front of the crew. We always walked away first. We had one fight in the parking lot *after* the shoot was over. During the course of the filming, Pollack and I had a big problem. *I* had initiated the project, worked on it for years. We were getting ready to roll and we lost Hal Ashby, because long ago he had signed to do another project after ours, and then waited so long for us to start shooting that he was now on call for the other picture. Those people would

213

The pompous director, Ron Carlysle (Dabney Coleman) gives direction to John Van Horn (George Gaynes) as "Dorothy" (Dustin) looks on.

have injuncted him, because they had signed a contract. I walked into Columbia Pictures and said, 'What should we do now?' and someone suggested Sydney Pollack. I met him and talked about the project, and he said 'No.' He wanted final cut. I *pleaded* with him to let me have it. This was my *baby*. I wanted a say in everything. What does final cut mean? It means this: there were 500,000 feet of film shot, and 10,000 would end up in the movie. It could be a totally different movie based on final cut! You give that up, and you give up a lot. You give up a 'signature.' Finally, in desperation, I said: 'Look, let's compromise. I'll let you have final cut *if* you agree to let me show you the *alternatives* to what you do, and you must seriously consider them.' He agreed to that.

"Also, I wanted three weeks' rehearsal, and Pollack agreed. But then he got sick and couldn't rehearse, so we didn't have it. I kept saying, 'Let's rehearse, let's rehearse, because if we don't, we'll be having interpretive differences during the shoot.' And then you have a couple of hundred people sitting around, waiting while we argue about his concept as compared to mine. I've been through *that* before and I didn't want to go through it again. I've learned that the success or failure of a film is determined before the first day of principal photography. You have

it ready to go or you don't. If it's ready to go, I won't have to 'act' at all. And that's what I want most: I want it to appear *effortless*. If you're 'working,' it'll show onscreen. That's no good."

Enough time was lost so that the picture, scheduled to finish its shoot by July 1, could not possibly "wrap" before August 1, which meant it might prove impossible to have the final print edited and assembled for its planned Christmas 1982 release. Chief among the problems was the budgetary concern: this story, so small in scope, had ended up costing more than the marathon superproduction *Gandhi*, a 3½-hour epic of the Mahatma's life in India that Sir Richard Attenborough spent twenty years making. Partly to blame was Dustin's own $4½-million fee. Also a key factor in holding up production was the make-up problem. It took three and one-half hours to turn Dustin's character, Michael Dorsey, into his female alter-ego, Dorothy Michaels. But by the time this daily work was completed, Dustin's thick beard had already begun to show through as "shadow," making it obvious this was a man in woman's garb. Because of an inability to solve that situation, compounded by Dustin's perfectionist/professional refusal to work if his charade as a woman would not be completely convincing onscreen, costly days passed during which not a single shot was put on film.

So press people hovered around the *Tootsie* set, many hoping to turn this into a flop of the same magnitude as the success they had helped hype *Kramer* into three years earlier. Indeed, few films in recent history have enjoyed as much coverage during the shoot. When not referring to the film as "the troubled *Tootsie*," Manhattan gossip columnists enjoyed reporting that, disguised as Dorothy, Dustin had lunched in the Russian Tea Room, carrying on conversations with personal acquaintances, though no one had guessed his true identity. Janet Maslin reported in the July 13 *Times* that Dustin's 15-month-old son (by his second wife) enjoyed seeing his father in the costume. "Luckily, we can afford therapy for him later," Dustin quipped. "I've been doing this since he was eight weeks old. He thinks going to work means putting on a dress." But everyone connected with the project remained painfully aware that by the time *Tootsie* reached theater screens, it would be preceeded by Blake Edwards's acclaimed *Victor/Victoria,* in which Julie Andrews portrayed a female performer who masquerades as a man masquerading as a woman in order to secure work. After all the energy and effort, would *Tootsie* only prove anticlimactic?

In fact, the opposite proved to be the case. *Tootsie* turned out to be the necessary complement to *Victor/Victoria*. In the early 1980s, filmmakers had taken a cue from their audience's emerging sensibility and begun to examine male-female sex roles with more sensitivity than had ever been shown in commercial American movies before. What *Victor/Victoria* and *Tootsie* offered was a more enlightened view than Hollywood had previously been prepared to present of "normal" men and woman coming to grips with the potential within themselves to empathize with the opposite sex. In *Victor/Victoria,* the male role played by Julie Andrews's female character allows her to understand for the first time the powers and priorities enjoyed by the male of the species; in *Tootsie,* the female role created by Dustin's male character allows him to fully comprehend the problems and limitations imposed on a woman by a male society. It is the element of enlightenment—both for the character in the picture and, in a non-didactic way, for

the audience watching the film—that keeps *Tootsie* from turning into a modernized drag farce.

As director Sydney Pollack confided to me during an interview: "I like to think the theme was due to *my* influence. The first thing I said, in that first meeting I had with Dustin, was, 'If this is going to be a story of watching you in drag for two hours, I'm not interested.' Because if a man puts on a dress today, something better change. He'd better become a better man, come up with new insights, otherwise it's just an empty-headed comedy, and I don't have the skills necessary to pull that off. Comedy of that sort is not my strength. I had to make this into something that was within the realm of reality, but still funny, which meant structuring it very carefully so we avoided the kind of banana peel humor and pratfalls and sightgags. Yes, there are a few in the film, but a minimum of them."

When I spoke with Hoffman, however, he claimed that this was his intention all along. "I always react negatively when I hear the word 'drag' because, in my mind, it means you flaunt sexuality, in an almost caricaturish way, for an easy laugh. It was *always* my intent to create a character who was a woman, and, in fact, her sex is secondary from an actor's point of view. If an

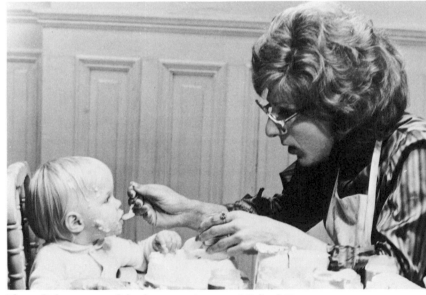

The enlightenment of the hero continues as Michael Dorsey/Dorothy Michaels cares for Julie's child, and at last learns what it means to be a mother.

Dorothy/Dorsey (Dustin) enjoys a relaxing holiday season at the upstate New York farm owned by Les (Charles Durning).

After his cover has been blown, Michael (Dustin) finally confronts Julie (Jessica Lange) in the streets of New York.

actor gets the part of playing Private Slovik, he's not portraying a soldier but a person who happens to be a soldier and also happens to be a male. So my approach to this was no different from, let's say, the actors in Shakespeare's day, who had to play all the female roles because women weren't allowed on the stage. So if you had a part of Lady Macbeth or Juliet or Desde-

mona, the sex was secondary. You were only aware of having a job to try and create a three-dimensional human being."

Tootsie proved an immediate hit with the press and public alike, making all those earlier stories about a disaster-prone project seem insignificant. In the December 20, 1982, issue of *Time,* Richard Schickel spoke for most of the nation's film critics when he announced: "Any movie's largest potential is for disaster. . . . Most movies, as everyones knows, end up in the ravine, bottoms up among the broken and rusty remnants of last year's improbable dreams. . . . Then, every once in a rare while, one arrives in style—these are the miracles of the industry, the stuff of Hollywood legends. This year's miracle is called *Tootsie.* It is not just the best comedy of the year; it is popular art on the way to becoming cultural artifact."

There was no question that *Tootsie* stood proudly in that special tradition of movies from *Gone With the Wind* to *Apocalypse, Now,* and including both *Casablanca* and *Jaws,* that survived their troubled histories and proved better films than anyone might have guessed possible from all the horror stories that surrounded the production. Indeed, many people believed that in the case of *Tootsie,* the problems may well have added to the quality of the film. In the Sunday, December 19, edition of *The New York Times,* Stephen Farber argued this very notion. In an article called "How Conflict Gave Shape to *Tootsie,*" Farber insisted that when Pollack joined the production, he immediately removed most of the anatomical jokes and bathroom humor that would have made for an outrageous comedy on the order of *La Cage Aux Folles,* and instead pushed for an emphasis on the "gentle love story" side of the project in which Michael Dorsey falls for his co-star on a soap opera (Jessica Lange) but, since he is known to her only as Dorothy Michaels, must become a friend instead of a lover. Certainly, the most marvelous element of the movie's chemistry is the way in which it treads a delicate balance between the two possible extremes, finding a middle route between the romantic and the outrageous that lends this film its unique combination of comedy and warmth.

To a degree, then, *Tootsie* reaffirms the notion of film as a *collaborative* art form; that is, each movie has a life of its own, based on the unique combination of collective talents who come together, while remaining independent of any one artist's attitudes. Yet paradoxically enough, it is also the ultimate justification of what Hoffman had been moving toward all along: the example *par excellence* of the actor as *auteur*. Indeed, he goes beyond the "personal" quality of *Kramer* and becomes almost autobiographical in the scenes that depict Dustin and his playwright roommate (Bill Murray) wandering the streets of New York together: the roommate character combines elements of Hoffman's playwright pal Murray Schisgal (can the casting of Murray as Murray be completely coincidental?) with Hoffman's reminiscences of wandering the New York streets with friends Gene Hackman and Robert Duvall in their early, struggling days.

True, the film would probably not work nearly so well without the romantic temperament Pollack brought to it. Yet it was Dustin who stayed with the film from its inception to its completion; Dustin who weeded out writers and directors (including close friends) until he came upon Gelbart and Pollack, both of whom he occasionally disagreed with but both of whom he sensed were right for the project. As Teri Garr, who plays one of his drama students in the film, told me in New York the day after *Tootsie* previewed for the nation's film critics: "Frankly, I think he should be a director. He really does get into the whole idea of a film, and he sees what a director should see in a movie—which is the thread running through it, the element that will tie it all together. He also draws from his own experiences. And that's what makes great art so wonderful—when someone's *guts* are there, and Dusty knows you have to do that. Even in a supposed 'light comedy,' Dustin knew he had to do it from the inside out."

Actually, though, Dustin has been smart to refrain from directing his own pictures. After all, it was the assumption of the director's role that has severly hurt Clint Eastwood's recent films; while we can understand his desire to want to control his projects and become master of his own fate, he has eliminated the kind of collabora-

tor who can draw the most disciplined and effective performances from him. Wisely, then, Dustin has managed to become the auteur of his films by being involved in the early writing, overall production, and final editing while still bringing in a gifted director like Pollack to provide a much needed balance to his own views, as well as the kind of "conflict-that-leads-to-quality" Farber spoke of.

Though he is not credited with directing this film, no one can argue that two of Dustin's most personal concerns are at the heart of what makes *Tootsie* click: for surely, if there is anything that has obsessed him more than his attempts to understand women, it is the emotional crisis of the out-of-work-actor. In the Michael Dorsey/ Dorothy Michaels role, Dustin devised a means of dealing with the two simultaneously. More impressive still, he managed the remarkable feat of turning a movie expressing his own most basic personal concerns into a work of overwhelming mass-audience appeal, proving it *is* possible for a film to be both personal and commercial, a work of deeply felt personal expression and a salable commodity. Perhaps his ultimate reward for achieving all this was to escape the stigma that has hung over the Best Actor Oscar for more than fifteen years, proven by his being nominated again for *Tootsie*.

Michael's agent, George Fields (Sydney Pollack) studies his "client," Michael Dorsey/Dorothy Michaels (Dustin).

Epilogue:
The Oscar and After

Dustin Hoffman today.

There was no question about it. From the moment of *Kramer vs. Kramer*'s release in December of 1979, the film was heralded by critics and the public alike as the film of the year. Interestingly enough, the simple, sincere story of three people and their emotional entanglements overshadowed such multi-million dollar super-spectacles as *The Black Hole* and *Star Trek: The Movie*, encouraging many serious-minded moviegoers and movie reviewers to at least hope that the day of the "special effects" picture was over and that the movie which told a human story could possibly make a comeback. Central to the film's success was Hoffman's performance, and there seemed little doubt he would be nominated for an Academy Award. The bigger question was: would he accept if he won?

Hoffman had been nominated before, for *The Graduate*, for *Midnight Cowboy*, and for *Lenny*. But he had only attended the Academy Awards ceremony once, and that had been the first time he was nominated. Dustin had been uncomfortable about being nominated at all: "I hope to God I don't win an Oscar tomorrow night," he said in 1968. "It would depress me if I did. I really don't deserve it." The night of the ceremony he called his old friend, actor Stanley Beck, at one in the morning and asked if he would pick Dustin up, insisting he had no place to stay. Beck sleepily declined to do so, but told Hoffman that if he cared to take a cab over, Dustin could sleep in Beck's living room. "He came, slept, left without making the bed," Beck recalls, "and I never even saw him." Hoffman always claimed to have been happy he lost that night: "Thank God I didn't get the Oscar for *The Graduate*," he insisted later. "After I got the nomination, I thought, 'Okay, it's *enough* already for this one part.'"

But Dustin's decade and a half "feud" with Oscar (and awards in general) would grow not from his winning or losing but from social values and political sensibilities. Martin Luther King had been assassinated the week before the ceremony was to take place, but the Academy was going ahead with the awards anyway. Originally, the ceremony was to have taken place two days after the assassination, but a decision was made to postpone it for one week, due largely to complaints from Dustin and about a hundred other film people who were to be involved with the show. Many of these people—Dustin included—were hoping the ceremony might be cancelled altogether that year, and the money instead given to some fund Dr. King had supported. In the meantime, the country went into a mini-Civil War for several days, with the riots in Watts and Newark bringing the reality of the racial tension erupting in the country home to the hearts of millions watching their TV news shows.

Following all this, Dustin had found himself sitting at the Academy Awards presentation, and was shocked to hear Master of Ceremonies Bob Hope make off-the-cuff jokes about having been forced to pack his bags twice to attend the show. Dustin was stunned. He wrote a letter afterwards to the then-president of the Academy, Gregory Peck, and expressed his displeasure over certain aspects of the presentation he felt could be improved on. Among other things, he was upset that the cameras were trained on the nominees in the audience as their names were read off, with the possibility that when the winner's name was announced, the cameras might continue to study the facial reactions of those who had lost. Hoffman never received an answer from Peck, and a certain degree of bitterness set in. At any rate, he didn't attend the ceremony again.

He did continue to rack up nominations, and also to make off-the-cuff comments, which were picked up by news services, about the awards. One year later, when John Wayne won the Oscar for *True Grit* over Hoffman for *Midnight Cowboy*, Dustin explained that he himself had rooted for Wayne, because in Hoffman's mind the Oscar should always be a "life achievement award for

good, meritorious work—an honor, not a contest."

At any rate, when *Lenny* was released—but before that year's nominations were announced—Dustin was directing the play *All Over Town*, written by his friend, Murray Schisgal, when he received word that California-based critic David Sheehan had loved the film, and wanted to do an interview. Sheehan came to the Washington, D.C., theater where Dustin and his crew were desperately trying to salvage a show that appeared at the time to be sinking, and suddenly asked Dustin: "You didn't go to the Academy Awards on *Midnight Cowboy*. Will you come this year?" Dustin answered that he probably wouldn't, and explained some of his serious reservations about the Oscars. As far as Dustin knew, the interview would be aired very shortly, and if the members of the Academy wanted to let Dustin's attitudes influence whether or not they were going to even nominate him, that was their business. However, the interview didn't air, Dustin was nominated, and then, the very night of the Academy Awards, the interview was finally shown on Los Angeles TV—leaving viewers with the impression that Dustin had said some strong and negative things about the Oscars that very day.

One of the people who happened to see Sheehan's show was Frank Sinatra, who would be serving as one of the Oscar hosts that evening. When Sinatra came on TV that evening, he was still burning over the roasting he believed Hoffman had just given the Academy, and felt the need to answer Hoffman publicly—by using one of the highest-rated national TV shows to answer a comment which had appeared earlier that evening on a local show. "With all due respect to Dustin Hoffman," Sinatra told the nation (and the world), "this is *not* an 'obscene ceremony.' " To this day, Dustin swears he never said any such thing about the Oscars, and that while watching the show that night at home, he went into a state of shock after hearing himself so misquoted—although he did admit he had said the Oscars were "ugly and grotesque."

Understandably, after *Lenny*, Dustin didn't receive any more Oscar nominations—despite some fine performances. The myth that Sinatra had created around him that night became a reality for people both within the industry and outside of it. In the meantime, it was becoming very popular to knock the Oscars, as George C. Scott, Marlon Brando, and Vanessa Redgrave all either refused the award or used the winning of it as a chance to seize the platform for political purposes. Then *Kramer* was released and the Academy members found themselves in a difficult situation. How could they deny the award to Dustin when it so obviously belonged to him? But if they did indeed give him the award, would he merely be the latest "no-show," or would he show up and cause even a worse scene than Redgrave had done? Meanwhile, other awards were going Hoffman's way: he won both the New York and the Los Angeles Film Critics Association awards as Best Actor of 1979.

In January, 1980, when he received the Golden Globe Award as Best Actor, he did show up at the Beverly Hilton, and in his acceptance speech made some more negative comments about the notion of awards in general. "I think that awards are very silly," he said. "I think they pit very talented and good people against each other, and they hurt the hell out of the ones that lose." Though his comments were reported out of context by some trade papers, it is not really fair to interpret them in such a way. Dustin's young co-star from *Kramer*, Justin Henry, had just lost two awards in a row—Best Supporting Actor and New Star of the Year—and was in tears. Though Hoffman's statement was widely reprinted as a cynical statement of the award he had just accepted, he was in fact talking not to the crowd at large but to the child, attempting to help the boy deal with what for someone his age must have been a highly traumatic experience. Even under such circumstances, though, Dustin's mischievous sense of humor was in evidence. As he stepped up to receive the award, he began his comments with: "I'd like to thank divorce."

When I interviewed Hoffman and, with the myth of his "obscene ceremony" statement still ringing in my memory, asked him if he would even deign to attend the ceremony, he surprised me with the enthusiasm of his answer. "Personally," he said, "I would *love* an Academy Award.

Like anyone, right? We *all* want an Academy Award—we all want awards for *anything*. There is that part of us that loves to receive awards, especially if you feel you've done good work. When John Wayne got the Oscar and people said, 'Oh, you should have gotten it,' I said, 'No, you're wrong. John Wayne got it for a *bulk* of work. That's the way it should be.' " By the time of *Kramer*, Dustin felt that if he received the Oscar, he could positively accept it under the belief he was really receiving it not just for *Kramer* but for the "bulk of good work" he had done ever since *The Graduate*.

And get it he did. As *Kramer* swept the awards, the TV cameras trained more and more closely on Dustin. He looked exasperated, but as the world was to learn later, it had nothing to do with himself or his own picture, which was doing terrifically, sweeping most of the awards. Earlier, Ira Wohl, a young documentary filmmaker whose movie *Best Boy* had been about family members since deceased, accepted his Oscar by tearfully recalling those relatives. In one of the least sensitive gestures in television history, William Shatner had scoffingly swept the man off-stage with the comment, "Thank heavens he doesn't have a larger family."

When Dustin ascended the platform to receive his award, he began with a typical Hoffman off-color comic comment; observing the statue carefully, he said, "He has no genitalia and he's holding a sword." Then his parents had to be thanked, but again, in a comical way: "I'd like to thank my parents for not practicing birth control." It would have been impossible to pretend that his longtime feud with the Oscars did not exist, and he didn't pretend that. "I'm up here with mixed feelings," he admitted. "I've been critical of the Academy—and for reason." Without mentioning Shatner by name, he paid his respects to the insensitive treatment the young artist behind *Best Boy* had received: "We are *laughed* at when we are up here!" He attempted to play down the competitive concept of the award: "I refuse to believe that I beat Jack Lemmon and Peter Sellers." He recalled his tough early experiences, and the fact that most performers never make it: "Most actors don't work and a few of us are so lucky!" He insisted on accepting the Oscar as a symbol of appreciation for all the moviemaking people who never receive their due recognition: "None of you have ever lost—I'm proud to share this with you." It was Hoffman's greatest moment—and Oscar's.

But with Hoffman, nothing is ever easy. When he posed backstage for the usual post-Oscar publicity pictures, he managed to get into a fight with several of the reporters and photographers. And the following day, the papers carried a story that Dustin was about to be sued by a writer who had earlier submitted a script very similar to *Kramer* and had had it rejected on the grounds that Dustin was not interested in doing such a story.

Since winning the Oscar, Dustin has slipped into his private life once more, though he has shown up at several award ceremonies to dish out statuettes to other winners. He has been working with old friend Murray Schisgal on a screenplay about out-of-work actors, and now has such complete collaborative input that he can insist on six months' time to research the material before they put a word of *Tootsie* down on paper. In the meantime, Jerzy Kosinski (*Being There*) has been fashioning a script especially for Hoffman. Whether one of those projects, or a possible sequel to *Kramer,* will lure Dustin back onto movie screens again, one can be sure that he will, for the time being, be able to pick the colors, mix the hues, and even apply some of the paint onto the cinematic canvas himself. That, of course, is what he's been after all along.

Afterword:
Our Last Interview

Douglas Brode interviewing Dustin Hoffman for a television special.

In preparation for this book, I interviewed Dustin Hoffman twice. The first time was the day following the New York press screening for *Kramer vs. Kramer,* when it was very clear that following some middling movies and unspectacular years, Hoffman would soon be re-catapulted into the first rank of stardom, would undoubtedly receive an Academy Award, and was now at that point in his career when such a retrospec-

tive of his work would be appropriate. The second time was three years later, when Columbia Pictures once again brought the nation's film critics to New York for a screening of *Tootsie.* During those intervening years, the body of this book was written, and though I would have preferred to converse with Hoffman during that time, he is—when not actively involved in the promotion of a film—reclusive almost to the point of rudeness, not merely refusing interview requests but ignoring them. Thus, unable to speak with him personally, I instead interviewed everyone I could reach who ever knew him or worked with him; read every article ever written about him in American publications; and screened his films over and over again.

"Talk to every one who ever loved him or hated his guts. . . ." That's the advice the editor in *Citizen Kane* gives to his reporter Thompson. And in time, I came to feel a little like Thompson, rummaging through yellowing newspaper stories in mausoleum-like buildings, picking up leads from sources who often times directly contradicted one another. But there was one major difference; in *Kane,* the subject of the reporter's story is deceased. In the process of researching such a book on a living man, a bizarre feeling overtakes an author. In time, the business of filing away facts and cross-referencing quotes finally leaves you with the impression you know more about that man than anyone in the world.

Indeed, you probably spend more time thinking about him and what makes him tick than he spends thinking about himself. This sense is actually heightened if he is not cooperating on the creation of the book, for you walk through your daily life with a conscious awareness of a close one-to-one relationship with someone you do not see or speak to but with whom you have become forever bound. You know that in time, he will walk by a Manhattan bookstore, stop and see in the window his name on the cover of a book that also carries your own name just beneath his. There is a growing, gnawing sense of responsibility as you come to realize the public may in time come to know him as you choose to report him: the way in which you present the facts of his life (and which of those facts you decide to include) will eventually form an image of him, an interpretation that, by virtue of being preserved between two covers, could conceivably survive some of his films as the means by which he is perceived and, in time, remembered.

On the one hand, the author feels uncomfortable about the voyeuristic tinge to his job, even if he has made a conscious decision to avoid the man's personal life and analyze only his professional career; on the other, he is awed by the power that's been put in his trust, and strives to create an objective vision that incorporates both the positive and negative that can be said about any human being. In the end, he feels confused by the one-sided sense of closeness: the author may know far more about this man than even his closest acquaintances do, yet he might not recognize the author if they were to pass on the street.

Dustin and I nodded and smiled but didn't speak when we both attended a screening of *Absence of Malice* in New York in December, 1981. I was there to interview the director, Sydney Pollack, for a magazine story; Dustin had come to view the then-current film by the man who would shortly be taking over *Tootsie*. A year later, Dustin and I talked at length during the two days that followed the *Tootsie* screening. And while he may be extraordinarily guarded about his right to privacy from the press during the time between promotable pictures, he is remarkably frank and open and honest whenever he does agree to do an interview. Most of his comments have been included in appropriate sections of the body of this book, but I've saved a few of his choice comments for the conclusion.

How would you feel if you won the Best Actor Oscar again?

There is no such thing as the "Best Actor."

Take that kind of thinking to the highest level, and you've got the question of who's number one: Jesus or Buddha?

At the beginning of Kramer, *you were telling your boss about a funny experience you once had buying a Burberry coat. I know that experience really did happen to you in your own life. But the best part of the story is the punch line about the New York blackout, and for some reason, that line is cut out in* Kramer. *Why?*

In the original cut of the film, I told the *entire* story, punch line and all. I wanted it in. It made the film more personal, made the character that much closer to me. But the people involved in assembling the final cut felt the scene went on too long, that it was necessary to quicken the pace of the film by putting Meryl Streep and myself into conflict a little bit faster. So they cut the line you refer to. I did have some input into the final cut and I *was* a collaborator, but I didn't win every battle. That's one I compromised on. That's part of why I fought even harder for more collaborative input on *Tootsie*.

How did you get your reputation for being a perfectionist, and why do you resent it so?

I got it from film people who don't want to work hard. I don't understand that. Sydney Pollack and I may have fought, but he's a hard worker, and I respect him and everything he had to say, even the stuff I didn't agree with. It's the ones who aren't hard workers I can't understand. They use that word "perfectionist" to describe me. It's the most ludicrous word! This is the only art form where you aren't allowed to make a mistake and then go back and get it right, because it's too costly, without someone complaining about you.

How do you view the state of the acting art today?

I remember when Brando came on the scene. People said he was terrible at first, because it didn't look like what they *expected* "acting" to be. It was a revolution. Now, acting has been revolutionized by television. On the news and the other non-fiction shows that are so popular in the last several years, you are continually seeing these little vignettes with real people. You're

The author meets with Dustin Hoffman during the 1982 press preview of *Tootsie*.

getting the best drama in the world, because it's *real*. And now, actors have to duplicate that! The public has seen it all. They know the reality of war and cancer patients and refugees and street people. So it can't be phony when you act it, or the public will know. You can't do it today if you're just reading dialogue. You must take it and "invent the moment" so it doesn't look like plastic drama. It can't be improvised, though, because that looks sloppy. One of the great movies of the year is *My Dinner With Andre*, which looks like ninety minutes of two men sitting in a restaurant improvising a conversation as they go along. But none of it was improvised. It looks like reality caught on the fly, but it was all planned out in advance, down to the last shot, to the last word. That's what acting has to be today.

You've been remarkably successful for the last fifteen years but, before that, you struggled. Did you ever go so far as to do what Michael Dorsey does in Tootsie?

No, that idea came in the first draft of the script that I read. It didn't occur to me to dress up like a woman, or I would have done it in a

minute. I'd have done *anything* to get a job. I used to go up to Equity, which is the actor's union, and look on the board. One time there was a newspaper strike and they needed someone to dress like a New England town crier and read the news off mimeo sheets while ringing a bell. I jumped at the chance and did it in Times Square. They needed somebody to play a dragon on a local TV show, and I did it, and I got sick from it because inside the costume, I had to squeeze Talcum out of my dragon mouth for smoke, and I inhaled the talcum in my lungs. There was no role I felt to be too demeaning, and I think I'm prototypical of most actors in that respect.

I taught acting in New Jersey and in Harlem. I would hear there was a job opening to direct and I'd be on the next plane to Fargo, North Dakota, directing community theatre. In *Tootsie*, I wanted to show that if you've been working at learning your craft, and are totally committed to it, you must face the fact that 90 percent of all actors are going to be unemployed. Especially in New York. In *Tootsie*, we go up to Syracuse to do our show, because thanks to Murray Schisgal—who had one of his shows premiere there when he met resistance in New York—I know there is important theatre being down there. I think there is important theatre being done today just about everywhere but in New York City. Broadway may still be the nationwide symbol of professional theatre, but it's the one place that's deteriorated. There are a lot of salable theatre pieces on Broadway today, but I don't think there's a place for serious theatre on Broadway at this moment. The shows now playing are, in the worst sense of the word, tourist attractions. And for a serious actor, who wants to do something in New York but understands the odds against him, something has to happen to that human being—that person who is good at something he or she can't do because no one will let them do it. So you either put on a dress to get a part or you jump off the bridge.

One last question. A year from now, when you walk past a bookstore and see The Films of Dustin Hoffman *in the window, how will you feel?*

(after a lengthy pause) Embalmed.